CHARLES I's
IN AMEI

MATTHEW JENKINSON

CHARLES I's KILLERS IN AMERICA

THE LIVES & AFTERLIVES OF EDWARD WHALLEY & WILLIAM GOFFE

OXFORD
UNIVERSITY PRESS

OXFORD
UNIVERSITY PRESS

Great Clarendon Street, Oxford, OX2 6DP,
United Kingdom

Oxford University Press is a department of the University of Oxford.
It furthers the University's objective of excellence in research, scholarship,
and education by publishing worldwide. Oxford is a registered trade mark of
Oxford University Press in the UK and in certain other countries

© Matthew Jenkinson 2019

The moral rights of the author have been asserted

First Edition published in 2019

Impression: 1

Published in the United States of America by Oxford University Press
198 Madison Avenue, New York, NY 10016, United States of America

British Library Cataloguing in Publication Data
Data available

Library of Congress Control Number: 2018956450

ISBN 978-0-19-882073-4

Printed and bound in Great Britain by
Clays Ltd, Elcograf S.p.A.

In memory of
B.E. Bevill
H.F.B. Bevill
E.J. Jenkinson
L.E.S. Jenkinson

Preface

If you drive about three miles north-west of Yale University, up the winding roads of New Haven's West Rock Park, you come to a collection of large boulders. These rocks or 'erratics' were deposited between ten and twenty thousand years ago, when a layer of glacial ice melted at the end of the last ice age, leaving a small network of narrow passages that are just large enough to conceal two adults from public view. A small plaque on one of the rocks notes that this hiding place was used, in the 1660s, by two men who had been complicit in the trial and execution of Charles I, the only king in British history to be tried and then put to death. Indeed, these men had signed the king's death warrant. On the run from agents sent to bring these regicides to justice, Edward Whalley and William Goffe concealed themselves in what is now called the 'Judges Cave' (the apostrophe has been removed). If we go forward three hundred and fifty years, the 'cave' is still there and is still being used for the purposes of concealment; though, in the early twenty-first century, this is the concealment of young couples anxious to keep their liaisons away from disapproving eyes. The rocks themselves are covered in graffiti (see Figure 1), some of which reflects the affection between various couples. The only inscription that appears to have any connection whatsoever to the devout Puritan regicides declares 'Dear God, thank you for this cave'. It is unclear whether the graffiti's author is thankful for its concealment of Whalley and Goffe, for its geological interest, or for the opportunity to pursue a relationship away from parental scrutiny.

This is not what one would imagine at a site that was for a long time revered as a symbol of America's liberty and the fight against British 'tyranny'. The cave was so symbolic of revolution, in fact, that

Figure 1. Photograph of the Judges Cave, New Haven, featuring twenty-first-century graffiti

the French revolutionary Charles Maurice de Talleyrand-Périgord, who contributed to the writing of *The Declaration of the Rights of Man* (1789), visited it in 1794 and 'made a very animated and impassioned address in French in relation to [Whalley and Goffe], their *amor patriae*, and their love of freedom'.[1] For centuries the cave has been visited by those interested in the story of the regicides and the myths and legends that have sprung up around them. This story of concealment would have been known, especially in the nineteenth century, by a large number of Americans. There was a time, as one journalist from the 1890s put it, when the story of Whalley and Goffe was 'related in every school history'.[2] Goffe went from being apprenticed to a London grocer in 1634 to being one of the most familiar characters in nineteenth-century American literature: a proto-American revolutionary. The regicides became the subject of fascination in many cultural forms, thousands of miles away from, and centuries after, their births. Now comparatively little attention is paid to the regicides in America or to the inscription on the cave in New Haven.

This book plots the rise and decline of the regicides in America—
how and why they were celebrated (or, sometimes, criticized), and how
and why their story was manipulated, twisted, and distorted to suit
different political sympathies and cultural tastes, across three and a half
centuries. *Charles I's Killers in America* is not simply the story of the
regicides on the run, as exciting as their flight may have seemed. Their
story carries with it intriguing historical and ideological baggage that
continued to be unpacked and repackaged in various cultural forms
on both sides of the Atlantic, but especially in America, into the
twenty-first century. So this book plots the lives and afterlives of
Edward Whalley and William Goffe—and, to a lesser extent, John
Dixwell, a third regicide in America—from their role in the English
civil wars to the point at which the 'Judges Cave' turned from historical monument to make-out point. By investigating these 'micro-
historical' figures over a long period of cataclysmic change it is
possible to inform a number of wider issues: the relationship between
crown and colonies in the late seventeenth century; the presence of
the English regicide in debates surrounding the American Revolution;
and the persistence of the regicides in America's founding narratives
and the forging of a distinct American national identity. We can
see how one of the most dramatic moments in British history—the
execution of Charles I—was remembered and represented across the
Atlantic over subsequent centuries.

Acknowledgements

I am grateful to the Huntington Library for awarding me Mayers Research Fellowships in 2011 and 2014. The Eatons and Juan Gomez were generous hosts and convivial companions while I researched and wrote in California, while Cory Way, Gay and Alison Amherst, and Tom Vignieri kindly provided accommodation while I worked in Cambridge, Mass., and Boston. I would like to thank Will Capel, Robert Gullifer, William Lawrence, Matthew Neufeld, David Smith, George Southcombe, and William Whyte, and the anonymous readers for Oxford University Press, who read early drafts and made several helpful suggestions to improve them. I also benefited from conversations with Jonathan Fitzgibbons, Tim Harris, and Steve Hindle. Thanks are also due to the staff at the following institutions who have been especially helpful: the Bodleian Library, Oxford; the British Library, London; the Houghton Library, Harvard; Merton College, Oxford; New College, Oxford; the Parliamentary Archives, London; the National Portrait Gallery, London; the New Haven Museum.

Susan Doran, Paulina Kewes, and Desmond King were supportive in helping to find the original manuscript a home. Luciana O'Flaherty, Martha Cunneen, and Solene van der Wielen at OUP have been very helpful in guiding the book to publication. Ideas and material from Chapters 4 and 5 were presented at Clive Holmes's retirement conference at Lady Margaret Hall, Oxford, in September 2011. I am grateful to the editors of the volume that arose from that conference, George Southcombe and Grant Tapsell, for allowing me to reuse some material here. It was while working on my DPhil under Clive Holmes's robust and good-humoured supervision that I came across the printed transcript of the trials of the regicides and Charles I's death warrant, in which I first noticed a regicide's disappearing act. Without the expert tutelage of Keith Baker, Adrian Green, and Toby Osborne I would not have been reading for a DPhil at all.

The warden and fellows of New College have helped to provide a stimulating and convivial setting for research, discussion, and writing. My colleagues and students have been supportive (and sometimes bemused) when I have turned my attention and energies towards some rather evasive regicides. Those regicides have also provided me with plenty of raw material when teaching the limitations and frustrations of historical sources, and why nonetheless we should keep striving to get as close as we can to the truth.

In addition to those listed above, several friends have retained an interest in the project and encouraged me to keep going with it, especially: Rupert Allen, Paul Baker, Mike Barker, Ben Baum, Anna Bayman, Oliver Brown, Michael Burden, Sandie Capel, Rosalind Carreck, Andrew Counter, Rosemary Cox, Cathleen and Tim Dawes, Mark Fenton, Richard Ferguson, Nick Fisher, Alex Gajda, Philippe Garnier, Tim Guard, Louise Gullifer, Edward and Elizabeth Hess, Rachel Hesse, Caroline and Edward Higginbottom, James Horton, Andy James, Matt Johnson, Simon Jones, Jemma Kilkenny, Jen and Walter Ladwig, Sophie Murray, David Parrott, Hugh and Liza Petter, James Phythian-Adams, Lianne and Richard Poyser, Robert Quinney, Melissa, Wade, and Winston Razzi, Andy and Caroline Showell-Rogers, Tracey Sowerby, Deborah and Michael Stitt, and Eleanor Thompson. All faults, naturally, remain my own.

My family has, as always, been unwavering in their support. In particular, this book is dedicated to the memory of my grandparents.

Oxford, 2018

Contents

List of illustrations

Abbreviations and conventions

Cal. S.P. Col.	*Calendar of State Papers Colonial, America and West Indies*
Cal. S.P. Dom.	*Calendar of State Papers Domestic*
CMHS	*Collections of the Massachusetts Historical Society*
CNYHS	*Collections of the New York Historical Society*
DRCHNY	*Documents Relative to the Colonial History of New York*
Jordan and Walsh, *King's Revenge*	Don Jordan and Michael Walsh, *The King's Revenge: Charles II and the Greatest Manhunt in British History* (London, 2012)
NEHGR	*New England Historical and Genealogical Register*
Pagliuco, *Great Escape*	Christopher Pagliuco, *The Great Escape of Edward Whalley and William Goffe* (Charleston, SC, 2012)
PMHS	*Proceedings of the Massachusetts Historical Society*
PNHCHS	*Papers of the New Haven Colony Historical Society*
Spencer, *Killers*	Charles Spencer, *Killers of the King: The Men Who Dared Execute Charles I* (London, 2014)
Stiles, *History*	Ezra Stiles, *A History of Three of the Judges of Charles I* (Hartford, CT, 1794)
Welles, *History*	Lemuel Aiken Welles, *The History of the Regicides in New England* (New York, 1927)
Welles, *Tercentenary*	Lemuel Aiken Welles, 'The Regicides in Connecticut', *Tercentenary Commission of the State of Connecticut* (New Haven, CT, 1935)

A study of the regicides in America brings with it some challenges with regard to sources. On a fundamental level, people who are on the run, attempting to disguise their identity and location, tend to leave behind few concrete clues. That is not to say that no correspondence by—or relating to—Whalley and Goffe survives. It does, and it tells us a good deal about their time in America. But there are still large gaps that need to be filled with speculation and supposition, or recourse to oral histories that themselves become corrupted as they are passed from generation to generation, embellished to enhance their drama or to promote the role of a particular individual or family in the regicides' tale.

All dates correspond to the Julian Calendar, not the Gregorian as introduced in 1752, but the new year is considered to start on 1 January, not 25 March as in contemporary practice. Spelling and punctuation have been modernized when appropriate.

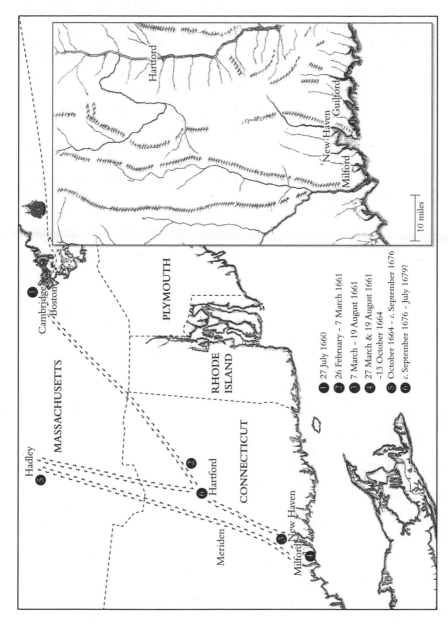

Figure 2. Map of New England showing Whalley and Goffe on the run

1 27 July 1660
2 26 February – 7 March 1661
3 7 March – 19 August 1661
4 27 March & 19 August 1661 –13 October 1664
5 October 1664 – c. September 1676
6 c. September 1676 – July 1679?

Here, take this gift,
I was reserving it for some hero, speaker, or general,
One who should serve the good old cause, the great idea, the
   progress and freedom of the race,
Some brave confronter of despots, some daring rebel;
But I see that what I was reserving belongs to you just as much
   as to any.

Walt Whitman, 'To a Certain Cantatrice', Leaves of Grass

PART
I

Lives

I

Introduction

God does seem evidently to be throwing down the glory of all
flesh. The greatest powers in the kingdom have been shaken.

William Goffe at the Putney Debates, 28 October 1647[1]

On 30 January 1649, King Charles I stepped onto a platform that
had been specially erected outside the Banqueting House at
Whitehall Palace in London. Wearing two shirts so he would not
shiver in the cold and be accused of trembling with fear, Charles
addressed the assembled crowd. He was, he claimed, about to die as
'the martyr of the people'. The king then turned to his executioner,
instructing him to wait until his final prayers had been said, at which
point Charles would stretch out his hands as a sign that he was ready
to die. William Juxon, the bishop of London, accompanied the king
on the scaffold and handed him a cap, under which Charles pushed
his hair to leave his neck bare for a clean cut. The king announced that
he was going 'from a corruptible to an incorruptible crown; where no
disturbance can be'. Then, after removing his doublet and pendant of
the Order of the Garter—the item of jewellery that signified his
membership of the most august chivalric order in the land—Charles
prayed for the last time and stooped to place his head on the block.
He thrust out his hands. The executioner's blade, in one blow, severed
the king's head from his body.[2]

Charles had lost the English civil war, a devastating conflict that divided the nation during the 1640s, and that had been precipitated by the king's economic and religious policies as well as the increasing intransigence between king and Parliament. This was underlined by Charles's principled, or stubborn, adherence to the divine right of kings: the theory that God put Charles on the throne, so Charles answered only to God, not to his subjects or Members of Parliament. Charles had continued this intransigence in the wake of his military defeat, refusing to lower the authority and dignity of his kingly office as the nation searched for a post-war settlement. When Charles restarted the civil war in 1648, shedding further blood, it became clear to many of his enemies that a settlement would not be reached while the king remained alive. Charles was, they argued, guilty of treason. Following his trial, during which Charles refused to go along with the proceedings of a court whose authority he would not recognize, the king's death warrant was signed. There were fifty-nine signatories. The third was Oliver Cromwell, who would later become lord protector. This book is about the fourth and fourteenth: Cromwell's cousin Edward Whalley and Whalley's son-in-law William Goffe. Just over a decade after they signed the king's death warrant, Whalley and Goffe found themselves on the run to America. The thirty-eighth signatory, John Dixwell, would join them a little later.

The monarchy was restored in 1660, following a series of constitutional experiments in the Commonwealth and Protectorate of the 1650s. Many of those who had been prominent in those experiments— and the regicide that augured them—feared for their lives. In reality, the early Restoration settlement had a conciliatory tone: Charles II simply had to forgive many of those who had been active in the civil wars, Commonwealth, and Protectorate if he were to achieve a peaceful return to England. There was a grey area between those who definitely were going to be forgiven and those who definitely were not, and speculation continued right up to the trials of the regicides about whose crimes against the Stuarts had been so heinous that they would not be granted indemnity against prosecution. But some key figures were always going to be excluded from the forgiving and forgetting—what was called in a law of 1660 the 'indemnity' and 'oblivion'. Among those who most definitely were not to be forgiven were the almost forty signatories of Charles I's death warrant who were still alive at the Restoration.

Civil war

A report written to the lord chancellor at the Restoration of the monarchy highlighted Edward Whalley as 'a great stickler against the king and Goffe another'.[3] For a full understanding of why Whalley and Goffe had achieved this reputation, we need to explore their prominent roles in the twenty years prior to that Restoration. William Goffe (see Figure 3) came from a family divided over the issues of religious faith and loyalty to Stuart monarchs. On the one hand, the Goffes had a history of opposing the policies of the Stuart monarchy and dedicating their lives to the Puritan cause. William's father, Stephen, had been active in delivering Puritan petitions to Charles I's father, James I. (One such petition of 1603, for example, called for the abolition of bishops in church governance; the king later famously declared, 'No bishop, no king!') On the other hand, William's elder brother (also called Stephen) supported the Royalist cause in the civil war and negotiated on the continent for troops on Charles I's behalf. He was also chaplain to the Puritans' *bête noire*, Archbishop William Laud, as well as to Charles I, Queen Henrietta Maria, and Charles II's illegitimate son, James Scott, later duke of Monmouth. One account even suggests that it was this Stephen Goffe who passed on to Charles I's sons the news of their father's execution in 1649—an execution that Stephen's own brother had been instrumental in orchestrating.[4]

William Goffe's first significant act of opposition to Charles I was in 1642 when he contributed to a petition to the king insisting that Parliament should control the city militia in London. This was an important moment on the road to civil war, one point among many

Figure 3. Early nineteenth-century stipple-engraved portrait of William Goffe by Robert Cooper

at which control over the nation's military forces was under debate. Charles I, in the eyes of many Members of Parliament, had demonstrated consistently that he could not be trusted with such control—or at the very least Parliament should have sufficient military capacity to defend itself against any sinister encroachments by the king. In January 1642, indeed, Charles I had entered the Commons with his soldiers, attempting to arrest five MPs whom he considered to be particularly troublesome. The fact that, in Charles's own words, these 'birds' had 'flown', pre-warned about the king's arrival in Parliament, was a humiliating moment for the king. The Speaker of the House of Commons refused to tell the king where the five MPs had gone, while Charles had demonstrated that he could not be trusted to preserve the rights of Parliament to sit unimpeded by the will of the monarch. Riots broke out in London and Charles I was forced to flee.

The king had lost his capital and a few months later Royalist troops faced Parliament's soldiers at the first battle of the English civil war.

The king's attempted arrest of the five MPs was the culmination of a decade and a half of tension between Charles I and many of his subjects. Charles's elder brother and James I's original heir to the throne, Henry, had been popular and charismatic, balancing martial prowess with interest in the arts. He was the consummate seventeenth-century prince. Charles, in contrast, was short and suffered from a stammer and in his younger years did not cultivate the charisma, political awareness, and contacts necessary for an effective future king. When Henry died unexpectedly in 1612, Charles was not fully prepared. Furthermore, he was exceptionally principled—a devout believer in the divine right of kings, that he was answerable only to God from whom his power and authority were derived. This could be lauded as a positive quality, had Charles not lived and reigned at a time when effective statecraft necessitated some degree of flexibility and cynicism. Charles was attempting to govern three kingdoms that had been religiously fractured since the previous century, and with an increasingly assertive Parliament whose frustration grew as their grievances were not redressed: an eleven-year period between 1629 and 1640. In such a sensitive and increasingly tense political and religious landscape, some tact or Machiavellian guile may have been more successful than excessive adherence to a principle.

Charles was especially forthright when it came to matters of religion. His emphasis on the 'beauty of holiness', administered by his equally obdurate archbishop of Canterbury, William Laud, to many smacked of a return to the Roman Catholic faith. Since the break from Rome in the 1530s, Catholicism had been frequently tainted with images of immoral popes and priests who broke their vows and focused on secular and financial advancement instead of spiritual purity. In the British context, this was augmented by memories of the brutal execution of Protestants by Queen Mary—300 in three years—during the brief return to Catholic rule in the 1550s. Later, when the Gunpowder Plot of 1605 was discovered and the spectacular immolation of James I and Parliament thwarted—Guy Fawkes and his co-conspirators had packed with explosives a cellar under the king's opening of Parliament on 5 November—the Catholic faith was further associated with terror and assassination. In the eyes of many Protestants, not least those on the extreme Puritan wing, for Charles I to look and sound like a Catholic, or even sympathetic to Catholicism, was to threaten the Protestantism of his nation and to put its salvation in jeopardy. Being fed up about taxation is one thing—and can indeed lead to open rebellion—but the prospect of eternity in Heaven or Hell was a matter more likely to cause subjects to take up arms.

Charles found this in 1637 when he tried to introduce Laud's new Prayer Book into Scotland. The Presbyterian Scots rebelled against the imposition. They were much more sympathetic to John Knox's anti-bishop, austere, and scripture-based Calvinism than William Laud's episcopal, ornate, and ceremony-heavy High Churchmanship. Charles I attempted to impose the Prayer Book by force and he faced down the Scots in the First Bishops' War of 1639: the twenty thousand crown-raised forces were deemed so unimpressive that the Scots were left alone at the Pacification of Berwick. The conflict reignited the following year, even though Parliament had refused the king's request for funds for a larger army. The Scots invaded the north of England and Charles was forced to sign the Treaty of Ripon, under whose terms the king had to pay £850 a day to ensure that the Scottish army remained in Newcastle, Northumberland, and County Durham without marching further south. At this critical point the king could no longer dissolve Parliament as he needed it to raise the money, through taxation, required to pay the Scots.

In 1641, therefore, Parliament took advantage of the fact that it could not be closed down and issued further complaints to the king, as well as putting Charles's friend and chief minister, Thomas Wentworth, earl of Strafford, on trial for treason. Parliament called for the abolition of monopolies and Ship Money, a levy traditionally raised on the coasts to strengthen the navy but which Charles had extended to inland counties, as well as the suspension of the prerogative courts (such as the Star Chamber and the Ecclesiastical Court of High Commission, which had previously punished Puritans). Members of Parliament also called for the right to vote against the king's desire to dissolve Parliament, for Parliament to be summoned at least every three years (a challenge to a system that had allowed Charles to rule without Parliament for eleven years), and for Parliament to be able to choose the king's ministers. Whereas Charles previously had been able to dissolve Parliament in the face of such temerity, now he had no choice but to live with MPs' grievances and increasingly confident, indeed strident, demands.

A further crisis point was reached in October 1641. There was a rebellion in Ireland, during which thousands of Protestants were massacred in Ulster. Charles I and Parliament were united over the necessity of quelling the rebellion but were divided over who should have command of the army doing that quelling. The king automatically assumed that he would have overall command. Yet MPs, suspicious of a king who had ruled without them for eleven years and increasingly confident about shaving away his powers, feared Charles would use the army against them. John Pym, one of the most assertive MPs, demanded that Charles sacrifice one of his prerogative powers and allow Parliament to decide who would control the army. 'By God, not for an hour', came Charles's reply. The following month, Parliament presented even more grievances to Charles in the 'Grand Remonstrance' and, once again, demanded that it should choose the king's advisers. In essence, the two sides were becoming further and further entrenched, with demands being made by one side to which the other would never agree.

It was at this point in January 1642 that the king arrived in Parliament to arrest five of the more recalcitrant MPs. In June 1642, Parliament issued yet more demands to the king who by now had fled his capital: the church was to be reformed, as Parliament—not Charles or Laud—wished; the king's ministers and all affairs of state were to be approved by Parliament; Parliament was to control the army. The king, however, was never going to concede these fundamental monarchical rights. In June 1642 he issued the Commission of Array, calling on those subjects loyal to him to fight against the rebellious Parliament. Then in August he rode to Nottingham and raised the royal standard, the king's flag and a rallying point for Charles's loyal soldiers. Parliament, in turn, issued the Militia Ordinance, meaning that lord lieutenants were appointed by Parliament and hence those militias stationed in counties—the only readily available land forces in peace-time in a country without a standing army—were under Parliament's control. Each side was preparing the military forces necessary for a civil war and the Battle of Edgehill followed in October 1642.

Both Edward Whalley and William Goffe fought with distinction in the English civil war and progressed rapidly through the military ranks. Goffe quickly become a captain, then colonel. Whalley, simi-larly, was a cornet (the lowest grade of commissioned officer in a cavalry troop) in Parliament's sixtieth regiment of horse in August 1642, before becoming captain by March 1643, then a major in Oliver Cromwell's own regiment of horse. Whalley was a first cousin of Cromwell—his mother, Frances, was daughter of Sir Henry Cromwell of Huntingdonshire. After fighting at the Battle of Gainsborough in 1643, Whalley served as lieutenant colonel at Marston Moor. Then, following the formation of the New Model Army, a force more pro-fessional than the previous Parliamentary army and one devoted to an offensive war against Charles I, Whalley fought at the decisive Battle of Naseby in 1645. He was in the front line of the Parliamentary army's right wing, tucked just inside the outermost Parliamentary forces that struggled through the warren to the east of Turnmoore Field.[5] Whalley was responsible for two divisions that defeated two Royalist divisions of horse, for which he was given a commission as colonel of horse. Whalley also fought at Langport the following month and, the following year, proved himself adept at siege warfare. He helped besiege Bridgwater (July 1645), Sherborne Castle (August 1645), Bristol (August–September 1645), Exeter (February 1646), Oxford (March 1646), and Banbury (May 1646). Whalley was also active at the siege of Worcester in July 1646, though he departed before the city surrendered.

Even though the king surrendered to the Scots at Newark in 1646 and even though Parliament won the civil war, Charles I was still the king and was still determined not to concede his power and authority. During the following two years the army and Parliament tried to reach a settlement with Charles, just as MPs had tried to wrestle away some powers from a king they could not trust in the two years before the civil war. Just as the proposals in 1646–8 echoed those of 1640–2, so too was Charles I's response characteristically stubborn.

Prisoner and guard

For two and a half months of this period, from 24 August until 11 November 1647, Charles I was held prisoner at Hampton Court. Edward Whalley guarded him. But the man who had been so prominent in helping defeat Charles in war was not totally enthusiastic about his new role as the king's gaoler. This was, in large part, because the king was not really a prisoner. Whalley wrote to John Lenthall on 15 November 1647 lamenting that he was 'not to restrain [Charles] from his liberty of walking: so that he might have gone whither he had pleased' or 'to hinder [Charles] from his privacy in his chamber, or any other part of the house: which gave him absolute freedom to go away at pleasure'. Whalley complained that Hampton Court contained one and a half thousand rooms and he simply did not have sufficient forces to guard the king properly. All he could do, therefore, was to keep as close an eye on Charles as he could during the day and then place sentinels outside the king's chamber once he had gone to bed.

Whalley identified another problem that was impeding his duty: Charles was allowed in his presence too many gentlemen of his bed-chamber who were loyal to him. These were men like Captain Legge, former governor of Oxford, or John Frecheville, whom Whalley referred to as an 'active enemy' and who played tennis with the king at Hampton Court.[6] If there were plans afoot for Charles to escape, Whalley complained, these gentlemen were unlikely to divulge them to the king's captor. Whalley's final concern was that of his own reputation. If Charles did 'escape'—a term Whalley was reluctant to use because the king was not properly a 'prisoner'—then Whalley would be considered at best incompetent and at worst a traitor to the Parliamentary cause.

Whalley's concerns were written four days after Charles I actually did 'escape'—or 'leave' in Whalley's terms—his custody at Hampton Court. He was writing to defend himself against any accusations that he had been complicit in the king's departure and to explain why Charles had left so effortlessly. The day of the king's escape had been one set aside for Charles to write letters in his bedchamber, which he would normally do until five or six o'clock in the evening. At around five o'clock, Whalley arrived at the room next to the king's bedchamber, where the king's gentlemen informed Whalley that Charles was still writing letters. Whalley waited until six o'clock; still the king did not appear. Whalley was assured that the king had a particularly long and important letter to write to the Princess of Orange. By seven o'clock, Charles still had not appeared. Whalley suggested that the king might be ill but was informed that Charles had given strict orders that he not be disturbed. Whalley looked through the keyhole to see if he could see the king but could not do so. By eight o'clock, Whalley went to the keeper of the privy lodgings to accompany him to the king's bedchamber by another route. When they arrived at a room next to the king's bedchamber, they discovered Charles's cloak lying on the floor. Whalley took the cloak back to the king's gentlemen and, at this point, insisted that he be granted access to the bedchamber, 'in the name of Parliament'. Whalley agreed, however, that he would stand at the door instead of entering the bedchamber. But this was sufficient to determine that Charles had gone. Whalley instituted a search of nearby grounds and houses but his men found nothing.

Charles had travelled to the Isle of Wight, apparently fearing for his personal safety, and worried that there was a plot to assassinate him at Hampton Court. This plot allegedly was being laid by the more radical elements of the New Model Army and was communicated to the king by a letter secretly sent to Hampton Court and read to the king by Whalley himself.[7] Whalley protested that he had no part to play in any such plot: 'I was much astonished, abhorring that such a thing should be done, or so much as thought of, by any that bear the name of Christians...I was sent to safeguard, and not to murder him...I would first die at his foot in defence'.[8] The irony of these words would become clear over the next year or so.

'A man of blood'

One of the men most significant in hardening attitudes towards Charles I, and expediting his trial and execution, was William Goffe, the husband of Whalley's daughter, Frances. Goffe was prominent at the Putney Debates that began in October 1647, while the king was still at Hampton Court. These debates took place between so-called 'Leveller' agitators from the regiments of the New Model Army and the 'grandees' in command of that army. While the agitators were concerned mainly with the drafting of a new political constitution, legal reforms, and some extension of the right to vote, they could not avoid the issue of how Charles I should be treated. There were complaints that the 'grandees' had been too lenient and servile in their dealings with the king. Goffe called for a prayer meeting before the debates began—a common feature of Puritan worship wherein the godly would seek divine guidance in making decisions or healing divisions—and found that his antagonism towards the king deepened through prayer and his contemplation of scripture.

Goffe firmly believed that he was living through the End of Days. Fuelled by his passionate millenarianism—the belief that Christ was about to return to earth and rule as king alongside the saints, with the just recalled to life—Goffe was determined not to deal with Charles the Antichrist. Instead negotiations should cease and a solution be found that would save the souls of true believers, before Christ's Second Coming. 'God does seem evidently to be throwing down the glory of all flesh', Goffe insisted at Putney; 'it seems to me evident and clear that this hath been a voice from heaven to us, that we have sinned against the Lord in tampering with his enemies'.[9] He was not without his sympathizers: Henry Ireton, Cromwell's son-in-law, remarked that Goffe 'hath never spoke but he hath touched my heart'. Cromwell himself told Goffe that 'I am one of those whose heart God hath drawn out to wait for some extraordinary dispensations, according to those promises that he held forth of things to be accomplished in the former time'.[10]

Goffe's millenarian principles remained just as strong the following April at the Windsor Prayer Meeting, a two-day gathering of the New Model Army's Council of War, during which its Puritan leaders were to interrogate their consciences and ask for divine guidance in ascertaining the root of, and solution to, the nation's plight. Once again Goffe relied on scripture for his reasoning, especially the 'Warning against the invitation of sinful men' in the Book of Proverbs: 'Do not go along with them, do not set foot on their paths; for their feet rush into evil, they are swift to shed blood' (Proverbs, I, 15–16). The implication was that negotiating a settlement with the monarch was akin to dealing with those who 'lie in wait for innocent blood . . . ambush some harmless soul . . . [and] swallow them alive, like the grave' (Proverbs, I, 11–12). William Allen, former adjutant-general of the army in Ireland, was present at the meeting and noted that those in attendance were convinced that they had 'departed from the Lord' by negotiating with Charles. Goffe used Wisdom's Rebuke in verse 23 of the First Book of Proverbs, in particular, to cement the conviction of those present that dealing with the king had not just been a mistake, it had been sinful: 'Repent at my rebuke! Then I will pour out my thoughts to you, I will make known to you my teachings'. If those present at Windsor did not repent and did not mend their ways, 'calamity' would overtake them 'like a storm'; 'disaster' would sweep over them 'like a whirlwind' (I, 27). The results of Goffe's intervention were dramatic:

> ...it had a kindly effect...upon most of our hearts that were then present; which begot in us great sense, shame, and loathing ourselves for our iniquities, and justifying the Lord as righteous in his proceedings against us: and in this path the Lord led us not only to see our sin, but also our duty; and this so unanimously set with weight upon each heart, that none was able to speak a word to each other for bitter weeping, partly in the sense and shame of our iniquities of unbelief, base fear of men, and carnal consultations (as the fruit thereof) with our own wisdoms, and not with the word of the Lord, which only is a way of wisdom, strength and safety, and all besides it ways of snares: and yet were also helped with fear and trembling, to rejoice in the Lord...[11]

It was a short step then to cast Charles Stuart as a 'man of blood', the implications of which were rhetorically to strip Charles of his crown— he was a 'man', not a 'king'—and through providence and scripture (Numbers, XXXV, 33) to seek revenge appropriate for a man who had shed the blood of his own subjects: the desire of blood for blood would bring the king to trial, and ultimately to his execution.[12]

It was abhorrent enough that Charles had fought against his own people in the first civil war, but even worse when, having escaped from Hampton Court, he signed a military Engagement with the Scots in 1647 (securing their military support in exchange for some proposed religious concessions) and caused even more deaths by starting the second civil war in 1648. Charles garnered support, especially in south Wales, Kent, and Essex, from former Royalists and new Royalists frustrated with the lack of pay for soldiers from Parliament and the increasing prominence of the New Model Army in Parliament's decision making. The bloody battles and sieges that ensued further hardened opinion against the king. Whalley himself fought in the summer of 1648 at the Battle of Maidstone and at the siege of Colchester, commanding the cavalry that chased the earl of Norwich into Essex. It was now very clear that Charles I could not be trusted to accept that defeat in war meant concessions in power and authority. Attempts at reaching a settlement had failed. In the view of the

Puritans, with the End Times fast approaching and with the man of blood causing the spillage of even more blood, it seemed that the only option was to put Charles Stuart on trial.

To ensure that Parliament would be packed full of MPs who would vote to try the king, it was necessary to 'purge' it of those reluctant to follow such a path. Colonel Thomas Pride stood at the doors of Parliament in December 1648, turning away those MPs who would not vote to put the king on trial. One account has suggested that Whalley stood by Pride's side as the purge took place.[13] This is perhaps a metaphorical reference, as Whalley did sit subsequently on a committee justifying Pride's, and the army's, actions.[14] The House of Commons passed an Act appointing a High Court of Justice on 6 January 1649, though the court did not meet formally until 20 January. Whalley sat as a commissioner, attending all but one day (12 January) of this process. Goffe, too, was a commissioner. Charles was accused of high treason, of shedding the blood of innocent subjects, and found guilty. On 27 January the court's decision was made public: Charles was to suffer the death penalty. Edward Whalley and William Goffe were two of the fifty-nine men who put their signatures to the king's death warrant (see Figure 4).

Figure 4. The death warrant of King Charles I, 26 January 1649

Interregnum and Restoration

The judicial execution of Charles I on 30 January 1649, the only time in British history that a king had been put on trial and then put to death, left a blank canvas on which new political arrangements could be drawn. Whalley and Goffe were present and prominent throughout these constitutional experiments, while at the same time retaining their military roles. Goffe commanded a regiment against the Scots at the Battle of Dunbar in September 1650, when Cromwell noted that 'at the push of pike' Goffe 'did repel the stoutest regiment the enemy had there',[15] and resisted attempts to put Charles II on the throne by fighting at the Battle of Worcester in September 1651. By 1650 Whalley was commissary general and commanded four regiments of horse. He, too, distinguished himself at Dunbar and Worcester. At the former he was wounded in the hand and wrist and his horse was killed but, undaunted, Whalley found another horse and resumed fighting.

Both Whalley and Goffe were also active in non-military affairs in the 1650s. For example, they backed John Owen's proposal to the Rump Parliament—a derogatory term for the 'backside' of the Parliament left after Pride's Purge—to create a state church characterized by wide, if not total, toleration.[16] Following the revolutionary promise of the regicide, Whalley, like Oliver Cromwell, grew impatient with the Rump's apparent self-serving tardiness when it came to constitutional reform. So he presented a petition from the army to encourage major changes and, when the Rump's reforms were not deemed sufficiently extensive, Whalley backed its dissolution in the spring of 1653. Goffe was also present at the dissolution of the next ill-fated assembly, the Barebones Parliament, in 1653. Bussy Mansell, who represented Wales in the assembly, reported that Goffe was one of those who forced out, with 'two files of musketeers', those MPs who refused to leave.[17] Whalley represented the county of Nottinghamshire in the Protectorate Parliaments; Goffe sat for Great Yarmouth, in addition to being a 'trier'; that is, someone screening

potential churchmen for their adherence to the principles of the new
Puritan regime. Goffe also remained concerned with military matters.
In March 1655, he assisted the crushing of the Royalist insurrection,
Penruddock's Rising. Later, in July 1655, there were suggestions that
the regular army be cut substantially in size, which Goffe opposed.[18]

Whalley and Goffe reached the summit of their political careers in
1655: each was appointed a major general in Cromwell's constitutional
experiment, the 'Rule of the Major Generals'. Cromwell's aim was to
establish godly rule at gunpoint, with the country divided into dis-
tricts, each ruled by one of the militant godly. Goffe was put in charge
of the counties of Sussex, Hampshire, and Berkshire. Whalley was
given Derbyshire, Leicestershire, Lincolnshire, Nottinghamshire, and
Warwickshire. They distinguished themselves as two of the most
earnest major generals in an ultimately ill-fated project. It was ill-fated
for a number of reasons. First, local populations were inimical to having authority foisted on them from London even if, like Goffe, the
major general had family connections to the area. Second, patrons of
alehouses and theatres did not take kindly to their entertainments
being curtailed by the righteous. Third, an unpopular Decimation Tax
was earmarked to fund the major generals scheme but proved difficult
to collect. Goffe himself found the whole project exhausting. He
reported that he was 'discouraged' and 'so much tired that I can scarce
give an account of my doings'.[19] Whalley was keen on moral reform,
though he was hampered in his efforts by local magistrates. He had
some successes, for example, in arresting vagrants and closing down
unlicensed alehouses, but the 'Rule of the Major Generals' ended in
January 1657—another unsuccessful attempt in the search for a constitutional settlement in the 1650s.

A new constitutional proposal was tabled in 1657: the Humble
Petition and Advice. Once again, Whalley and Goffe were present.
Part of this proposal was an offer of the crown to Cromwell. Whalley
and Goffe both initially rejected the idea, though we should not over-
estimate the vehemence of their resistance. While Whalley was a
teller of the 'noes' when it came to a vote on the offer of the crown,

John Reynolds, an Irish MP, reported in March 1657 that 'honest Whalley and Goffe were moderate opposers [to kingship], almost indifferent'.[20] Cromwell himself refused to lift up the crown that, as he put it, 'God had lain in the dust'. By April 1657, however, it appeared that Whalley and Goffe were becoming less averse to the idea of kingship, in name at least. Whalley declared that he could 'swallow' the idea of the 'title' of king, if it meant that the best parts of the Humble Petition and Advice were kept.[21] In the event, the following month Cromwell once again refused the crown.

One of the features of the Cromwellian regime most common in the popular imagination is the 'abolition' of Christmas. Again, Whalley and Goffe were active in the regulation of a festival considered to be both extravagant and redolent of the survival of a Catholic ceremony that had no basis in scripture. On 25 December 1657, the diarist John Evelyn was celebrating Christmas in the chapel of Exeter House on the Strand in London when, during Communion, the chapel was surrounded by Cromwell's soldiers. The congregation was kept imprisoned, albeit fairly comfortably in Evelyn's case: he was detained in a house where he was able to dine with the countess of Dorset. In the afternoon, both Whalley and Goffe arrived to examine the congregation and to imprison some of them. Evelyn was asked 'why contrary to an ordinance made that none should any longer observe the superstitious time of the Nativity (so esteemed by them) I durst offend, and particularly be at common prayers'. They were particularly irked that the congregation was praying for Charles Stuart, when there was no basis for this in scripture. Evelyn's response was that they were praying not for Charles Stuart but for 'all Christian kings, princes and governors'. This did not placate Whalley and Goffe, however, as they claimed Evelyn and the congregation were therefore praying, in effect, for the Catholic king of Spain, 'who was their enemy, and a Papist'. Evelyn was set free but not before Whalley and Goffe had spoken 'spiteful things of our blessed Lord's nativity'—presumably about Evelyn's interpretation of the Christmas celebration rather than the birth itself.[22]

Between the dissolution of the Second Protectorate Parliament in February 1658 and Cromwell's death seven months later, one observer suggested that Goffe was in such 'great esteem and favour at court, as he is judged the only fit man to have Major General Lambert's place and command, as major general of the army'. (John Lambert had been a leading figure in Cromwell's Council of State earlier in the 1650s, as well as a popular military leader, but by 1658 he had fallen out of favour with the lord protector.) While this observer was critical of Goffe's 'evil tincture of that spirit that loved and sought after the favour and praise of man more than that of God', he went so far as to suggest that Goffe's personal trajectory one day might take him to the protectorship itself.[23] In the event, just before Cromwell died on 3 September 1658, he named his son, Richard, as his successor.[24] Whalley and Goffe were reported to be in attendance at Cromwell's deathbed; Goffe was one of the chief mourners at his funeral.[25]

Whalley and Goffe were both supporters of Richard Cromwell's protectorship: Whalley sat in Richard's 'other house'—Parliament's upper chamber that had replaced the House of Lords—during the Third Protectorate Parliament of 27 January to 22 April 1659. But Richard's was a short-lived rule. A country gentleman with little support in the army, he soon found himself facing an army mutiny led by General Charles Fleetwood. The army began to demand a return to republican rule, for the payment of arrears, and a promise of indemnity for any actions they had carried out. The Third Protectorate Parliament lasted only three months: Parliamentary republicans, supported by the army, forced Richard to dissolve it. Lambert, the man to whom Goffe had been mooted as a potential successor, requested the return of the Rump Parliament—that is, those members of the Parliament of December 1648 which had put Charles I on trial. Lambert further called for the establishment of a commonwealth, 'without a King, single person, or House of Lords'. On 7 May 1659 Richard acquiesced to demands from the Council of Officers and reinstated the Rump. Twelve days later, Parliament elected a new Council of State. Within days Richard Cromwell resigned.

Different civilian and military forces now competed to fill the power-vacuum that had been created. Having called for its reinstatement, Lambert and his fellow soldiers grew impatient with the Rump, with disputes arising over the granting of indemnity and the appointment of army officers. Lambert expelled the Rump on 13 October and began a period of martial rule. Two months later the navy mutinied, Lambert's support collapsed, and the Rump returned. Amidst this chaos, the figure of George Monck appeared to establish some kind of political and social order. Commander of the army in Scotland, Monck had refused to meet with Whalley and Goffe who had themselves attempted to rally support for Lambert's expulsion of the Rump in October. On 21 February the moderate Monck reinstated those MPs who had been purged in December 1648. The Long Parliament was back.

With the restored MPs outnumbering those of the Rump, various measures were passed to begin settling the nation: a new moderate Council of State was elected; figures associated with the army, like Whalley, had their commissions removed; Monck was made commander-in-chief of the army; and, most importantly, the Long Parliament dissolved itself as Monck began negotiating with Charles I's son to return to England as King Charles II. New elections were called to allow MPs to assemble and ascertain the terms of this Restoration. On 4 April 1660 Charles made a series of promises that would smooth his return: soldiers' arrears would be paid; a general pardon, with some key exceptions, would be proclaimed; and *some* religious toleration would be allowed. On 8 May 1660 Charles II was proclaimed king—the monarchy was restored.

2

Regicides on the run I

Gravesend to Milford

I am banished from my own house; but feasted in the house of God.

William Goffe, *Diary*[1]

On the evening of 26 August 1765, a rebellious mob gathered on King Street in Boston. Incensed by legislation passed by the British government—especially revenue-yielding laws like the Stamp Act that required the American colonies' official printed and legal matter to have Parliament's stamps affixed—the mob was planning its next move. Fuelled by a potent mixture of anger and alcohol, they broke into the house of William Story, register of the Court of Admiralty, then that of Benjamin Hallowell, comptroller of the customs for Boston. Destroying property and dispersing papers as they went, the mob was warming up for an assault on one of the finest houses in Boston, that of Lieutenant Governor Thomas Hutchinson. Pre-warned of an attack, Hutchinson had barred his windows and doors, but his defences provided little resistance to the axe that was thrust through his front door. Before long, Hutchinson's house was swarming with rebels, and for over two hours they broke down its interior walls, threw down slate from its roof, laid waste to its garden, and ransacked its contents. These contents included cash, furniture, hangings, and paintings, but also hundreds—if not thousands—of documents.

By 4 a.m. the house was but a shell, and blowing through the streets were sheets of paper, many torn from books, that had hitherto been stored safely in Hutchinson's study and library.[2]

One such document was the diary of the regicide William Goffe, which he had kept during his first seven years in America in the 1660s. The diary had later been passed to the Puritan minister John Russell in Hadley, Massachusetts, before being passed to Russell's son in 1692. Russell's son then moved to Barnstaple, before handing on the diary to his own son in 1711. John Russell's grandson then kept hold of the diary until his death in 1758, at which point it was passed on to the Mather library, a depository of documents relating to colonial America derived largely from the respective collections of Richard, Increase, and Cotton Mather. Cotton Mather's son, Samuel, kept the library together and married Thomas Hutchinson's sister, which meant that Hutchinson had access to the library including, fatefully, Goffe's diary.[3] Had Hutchinson not removed the diary to the governor's house, it would not have been destroyed when the house was attacked that summer evening in 1765.

Fortuitously, some early entries were transcribed and stored elsewhere before the diary disappeared,[4] and they offer a tantalizing glimpse into the movements and psychological state of the regicides in their early days after the Restoration of the monarchy in 1660. It is from these entries that we know of Goffe's reaction to Charles II's return to England. Mid-May, Charles was proclaimed King at Gravesend; on 25 May he arrived in person at Dover. To those who had fought against the Stuarts in the civil wars, and who remained loyal to the Good Old Cause, the plight of Parliament, and the New Model Army, few things could have been more disastrous. There may have been 'much rejoicing among the people', Goffe noted, 'but God's people lamented over the great profaneness with which that joy was expressed'. Inauspiciously, 'many dogs did that day run mad; and died suddenly in the town'.[5] Considering that Whalley and Goffe had signed Charles I's death warrant, and had been so prominent in the politics of the 1650s, they were sure that they would not be exempt from prosecution and execution. Assuming the aliases William Stephenson and Edward Richardson—they were, indeed, the sons of Stephen Goffe and Richard Whalley—they wasted no time in racing to Gravesend on the south bank of the River Thames. Waiting for them there was *The Prudent Mary*.

At seventy-six feet long and twenty-seven feet wide, *The Prudent Mary* could hold over one hundred people. Acquired by the British Navy in 1652, it had seen action against the Dutch at the Battle of Kentish Knock in 1652 and at the Battle of the Gabbard the following year, before being returned to its owners. Mid-May 1660 it sat in harbour ready to sail for the New World; *The Prudent Mary* was to be the regicides' method of escape to a place, they hoped, more accommodating to them than Charles II's England. Also on board were various individuals who would become people of note in the American colonies, some through their protection of Whalley and Goffe and others through their own achievements. Marmaduke Johnson would go on to print John Eliot's 'Indian Bible', a translation of the Geneva Bible and the first Bible printed in British North America. Major Daniel Gookin would become selectman (a town official) for Cambridge and attend meetings of the governor and Council of Massachusetts, as well as sessions of the general court. William Jones would become deputy governor of Connecticut.

On 14 May 1660, eleven days before Charles II himself landed at Dover as the restored king, *The Prudent Mary* left Gravesend with Whalley and Goffe on board. Just four days after that departure, the House of Lords decreed that members of the regicide court were to be seized, pending trial and, most likely, execution. Charles II backed this decree by issuing a proclamation on 6 June that gave the regicides two weeks to appear before him. If they failed to do so, they would forfeit any chance of a royal pardon. Even if Whalley and Goffe had received this news, it is very unlikely they would have returned to London. Two men who had been so enthusiastic about and publicly complicit in the execution of Charles I, and who had been so prominent in the civil wars, Commonwealth, and Protectorate, were not going to be pardoned. The opportunity of becoming martyrs and dying for the Good Old Cause might have been attractive. But more appealing was the chance of remaining loyal to that cause and staying alive, while promulgating their principles and faith in the New World.

Cambridge and Boston

Whalley and Goffe could have gone into exile much closer to home, like several of their co-regicides. They could have joined John Lisle and Cornelius Holland in Switzerland, William Say and Andrew Broughton in the Netherlands, Hardress Waller in France, or John Barkstead and John Hewson in Germany.[6] But there were several reasons why New England was an attractive location for two old Roundheads. Influential members of the New England administration, past and present, had been on their side against Charles I. Matthew Cradock, governor of the Massachusetts Bay Company in the late 1620s, had worked against the king in the Long Parliament; Edward Winslow of Plymouth County had returned to England to fight for Cromwell; Edward Hopkins, a founder of the New Haven and Connecticut colonies, had served under Cromwell in England in the 1650s; and John Leverett was active in the Massachusetts Bay general court in the 1650s and 1660s, having fought for Parliament in Thomas Rainsborough's cavalry in the 1640s.[7] There was also significant sympathy and correspondence between Puritan ministers on both sides of the Atlantic. New England ministers like John Wheelwright and John Cotton had been friends and correspondents of Cromwell. Goffe may have been able to use the colonial contacts of John Allin, a former New England Puritan minister, whom the regicide would have met during his time as major general of Berkshire, Hampshire, and Sussex; based in Rye, Sussex, Allin was founding a 'city on a hill' which looked forward intensely to the imminent Second Coming of Christ.[8] Also, having signed the death warrant of a king and taken part in the English Republic, Whalley and Goffe would have been attracted by the 'godly republicanism' of the Massachusetts Bay colony: a 'free state' that was almost independent from England, whose laity had significant power in the running of their virtually independent churches, and whose civic leaders—terrified of the potential of tyrannical and arbitrary power in the hands of rulers—worked to make themselves accountable to the people.[9]

On 27 July 1660 Whalley and Goffe arrived in America mid-way between Boston and Charlestown. They had survived the 3,000-mile journey, spiritually and providentially emboldened by the belief that God had chosen not to abandon them on such a perilous voyage. While most who crossed the Atlantic in the mid-seventeenth century survived, and many may have enjoyed the exhilarating adventure, the regicides' ten weeks at sea would have tested their physical and psychological endurance. The claustrophobia and discomfort of being penned in a seventy-six-foot wooden vessel would have been compounded by stories of shipwrecks, pirates, and sea-monsters and the realities of tumbling waves, driving rain, pervasive illness, and rancid odours. This turbulent vulnerability placed the Puritan passengers face-to-face with their God's wrath and compassion, bonding them in a way that would later aid Whalley and Goffe in their journey through New England.[10]

From Charlestown it was a short journey to Boston itself, with a ferry connecting the two settlements. Well-established roads through North End would have taken the regicides south towards Boston's dock and cove, near to which the main civic institutions were situated. To the south was Boston's fort, to the south-west the common, and to the west the road to Cambridge and Harvard College. To the east were the cold and choppy Atlantic waters, which brought tall ships into Boston's natural harbour. A burgeoning shipbuilding, fishing, and trading port, in the late seventeenth century Boston's population grew between twenty and forty per cent each decade; when the regicides arrived there were approximately 3,000 inhabitants (a population nearby Cambridge would not reach until the early nineteenth century). Though they had travelled as Richardson and Stephenson, the regicides did not hide their true identity from the eminent Bostonians who greeted them. On the contrary, they presented themselves openly and were received warmly. One of the first individuals to greet them was Governor John Endecott, Massachusetts Bay's chief magistrate, who governed and administered the colony alongside the deputies (representatives from outlying areas) and assistants (a coterie of prominent colonists) of its general court.[11]

Whalley and Goffe had arrived in American colonies facing both opportunities and challenges. The low temperatures that characterized the 'little ice age' of the time made the north-eastern colonies less susceptible to the diseases that ravaged the more southern and swampy English colonies of Maryland and Virginia, but they brought with them piercing cold, storms, and blizzards. The acquisition of land for settlement and farming inevitably led to conflict with the indigenous populations from whom that land was being appropriated, including: the Pennacook and Massachusetts to the north of Boston, the Nipmuck to the west, and Pokanoket to the south; the Wampanoag in Plymouth Colony; and the Mohegan, Pequot, and Narragansett around Rhode Island and Connecticut. The English colonists also faced competition for trade and territory from other European nations keen to expand their overseas empires: the French colonized the area around the Great Lakes, up the Lawrence River and east towards Newfoundland and Nova Scotia; the Spanish had been in Florida since the early 1500s; while the Dutch colony of New Netherland sat ominously close to the west of Connecticut and New Haven.

Though the Puritan settlers of North America had fled the religious divisions and persecution of early Stuart Britain, the colonies themselves soon became factionalized. In a colony like Massachusetts Bay, Anglican intolerance of Puritans was replaced with Puritan intolerance of Anglicans, Catholics, or Quakers; Whalley and Goffe arrived in Boston just weeks after the execution there of the Quaker Mary Dyer, who repeatedly disobeyed the law banning those of her faith from the Massachusetts Bay colony. Puritans further split over key points of church organization: the relationship between church and state, and the relative power between minister and congregation. Whalley and Goffe's moderate Puritanism had much in common with the colonists they first met. The two regicides disputed the claims of their more radical sectarian fellows that the civil magistrate should have no say in religious affairs. Goffe and Whalley, who has been described as 'argu-ably the most eirenic and moderate of the major generals',[12] therefore fitted in comfortably with the style of Massachusetts Puritanism advocated by the likes of John Cotton, the foremost minister of that colony.[13] Indeed, two days after arriving in America, Whalley and Goffe felt sufficiently content to take part in public worship with the Massachusetts Bay Puritans.[14]

In 1660 John Crowne, who later became a playwright for Charles II,[15] was a Harvard College undergraduate observing Cambridge's recent arrivals. He noted how Whalley and Goffe 'held meetings in their house, where they preached and prayed and gained...applause'; they showed no 'penitence for the horrid murder for which they fled', to the extent that Whalley 'did frequently and openly' claim 'that if what he had done [against] the king were to be done he [would] do it again'.[16] The residents of Cambridge and Boston knew that there were regicides in their community. On 11 August John Davenport wrote to the governor of Connecticut, John Winthrop Jr, that he knew the identity of the recently arrived gentlemen and hoped to meet them.[17] It was not quite so well known how dangerous such an association might prove.

A month after the regicides' arrival in America, Parliament passed the Act of Indemnity and Oblivion specifying those men whose crimes against the Stuarts would be forgiven and forgotten. Whalley and Goffe were not on the list. In the space of those four weeks, the two regicides fraternized with some of the colony's most significant dignitaries and they stayed initially with Daniel Gookin, with whom they had crossed the Atlantic. They met the president of Harvard, Reverend Charles Chauncey. They heard the scholar and divine John Norton (in whose house Crowne was residing) lecture on Hebrews II, xvi, before being 'lovingly entertained, with many ministers' at his house.[18] On the night of Norton's lecture, Whalley and Goffe saw for the first time the published proclamation from the House of Lords calling for those who had sat in judgement of Charles I to be arrested and their estates secured. Goffe chose to meditate on Hebrews XIII, v–vi, with its striking final verse: 'Let your conversation be without covetousness; and be content with such things as ye have: for he hath said, I will never leave thee, nor forsake thee. So that we may boldly say, The Lord is my helper, and I will not fear what man shall do unto me'. To Goffe's mind, human punishment remained a very real possibility; he could have chosen few verses more appropriate to soothe his state of mind.

The colonial hosts continued to support and welcome their guests. They were asserting their autonomy from Charles II's England and maintaining connections with individuals representative of the Good Old Cause with whom they had significant sympathy. Yet they also knew that they relied on trade with England for the strength of their precarious economy and benefited from the protection of English ships against colonial encroachments by the French and Dutch.[19] For the moment, however, they chose to prioritize their sympathy for the Good Old Cause. Crowne noted that the king's commands for the regicides' apprehension, issued by printed proclamation, were not carried out, to the 'best of [his] remembrance'. He even went so far as to suggest that the Boston authorities did not issue this proclamation; 'otherwise it would have been impossible for the murderers to escape'.[20] Chauncey showed 'much affection', insistent that 'the Lord had brought' the regicides to America 'for good both to them and ourselves'. The Cambridge farmer and religious leader Edmund 'Elder' Frost received them 'with great kindness and love'. Many others visited them.[21]

Despite this support, Goffe's state of mind remained troubled. The last surviving entry in his diary, dated 6 September 1660, tantalizingly describes him waking with his 'heart being oppressed with much deadness'; his 'spirit was confused'. The anxiety Goffe exhibited in his diary, in his early days in America, was consistent with the worries he had previously expressed in England. He seemed to have an apprehensive temperament. When he was appointed major general in 1655, Goffe worried about his 'great inability to manage this great trust, as I ought'. He conceded that he had been 'a little discouraged, because things were so exceeding long in settling'.[22] Moreover, his millenarian enthusiasm and self-doubting caused an anxiety which would plague him for the rest of his time in America.

Trials and executions

Just over a month after the last surviving entry in Goffe's diary, those regicides who had not fled England began to face their punishments for bringing Charles I to trial and for being complicit in his execution (see Figure 5). Charles II appreciated that a peaceful and successful restoration of the monarchy would be compromised if retribution

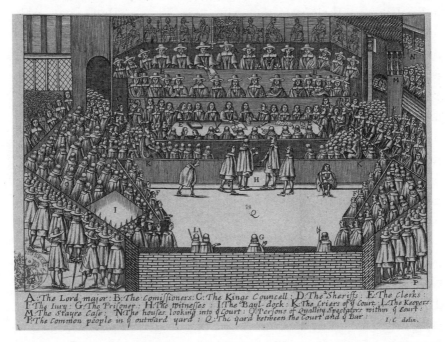

Figure 5. View of a regicide trial from *A Looking Glass for Traytors* (1660)

were widespread and if there were bloodshed on a grand scale.
Nonetheless, there was no way that indemnity and oblivion, forgiving
and forgetting, would include the most prominent and unrepentant
architects of the regicide. Oliver Cromwell was not allowed to rest in
peace: his body was exhumed and displayed as that of a traitor in 1661.
So were the corpses of Henry Ireton, Cromwell's son-in-law and
general in the Parliamentary army, and John Bradshaw, president of
the High Court of Justice for Charles I's trial.

Before these exhumations, the trials of the regicides had begun on
11 October 1660.[23] Twenty-nine of those regicides who were still
alive were brought to trial and found guilty of 'imagining and compassing the king's death'—that is, treason. The first regicide to be
executed, Thomas Harrison, was hauled to the gallows two days later.
Harrison was quick to take advantage of the public exposure afforded
him by his trial and his speech on the scaffold to defend the Good
Old Cause and to lay claim to martyrdom. Indeed, Harrison was at
the vanguard of those regicides who disrupted the proceedings of the
judicial theatre. Various tactics were adopted, some humorous and
some more serious. The defendants challenged and rejected potential
members of the jury until the legal limit of such challenges was
reached. They accused the court of denying them their right to legal
counsel. They refused to plead according to English legal custom and
insisted that God would judge them, not a court whose authority
they refused to recognize. They pointed out that this assembly included
turncoats who had fought against Charles II and supported Cromwell
but had now changed sides to save their own skins. These turncoats,
however, now sat in judgement on crimes in which they themselves
had been implicated.[24]

Executions in the seventeenth century were popular and public
events. In front of an assembled crowd, the criminals on the scaffold
were meant to repent their sins in their last speeches and prayers.
There was a discrepancy between theory and practice, however,
especially when those individuals on the scaffold were being executed
for crimes of conscience. The regicides in 1660 could look back to a

number of 'model' deaths including martyrdoms and the crucifixion of Christ himself and, more recently, those of the Protestant martyrs in the reign of Queen Mary (1553–8). With some irony, too, they could have contemplated how well Charles I himself had died on 30 January 1649. The dying regicides followed the traditional formula: highlighting how godly their lives had been even up to the moment of their deaths; forgiving those who had sent them to the scaffold and the executioner who would end their lives; and dying without fear in the conviction and belief that their actions would secure them a place in Heaven. Harrison and his co-regicides did all of these things and their dying words—or alleged dying words—were distributed by their sympathizers in print. Thus Charles II's opponents hoped that the king and his courtiers would not be able to manipulate the theatre of the regicides' trials and executions simply to glorify the Stuart monarchy and erase the memory of the civil wars and republic. On the contrary, the spirit and principles of that cause were revisited, revocalized, and reprinted.[25]

Those who were hanged, drawn, and quartered included Hugh Peters, a figure closely associated with New England.[26] Peters had arrived in Boston in 1635 and spent the years preceding the English civil war in Salem where he administered the church and took a close interest in the foundation of the Connecticut colony. Peters returned to England in 1641 and, following the outbreak of war, became closely involved in the Parliamentary army as an inspirational and provocative preacher. In 1648 he openly supported and encouraged Pride's Purge, which resulted in the expulsion from Parliament of those MPs who would not put Charles I on trial. Peters was not exempt from punishment in 1660: he was executed on 16 October. Peters and the regicides who died alongside him exploited the public nature of their executions to insist that God had ordained the execution of Charles I. They were doing God's work and would not shy away from that godly and honourable cause. News of their fate reached Whalley and Goffe: in Boston they discussed Peters's execution, and they were among those 'that durst not condemn what ... Peters had done'.[27]

John Jones was the eighth person to be put to death for involvement in the regicide. Born to humble parents in Wales, Jones had gained repute in the 1640s fighting for Parliament in the civil wars, first as a captain of foot and later as governor of Anglesey.[28] Most notably, Jones was the forty-second signatory of Charles I's death warrant. In chains in Newgate gaol during September and October 1660, Jones pondered his imminent death. He spoke with some optimism about his fate and the impending martyrdom of the regicides. They were going to 'reign with the King of Kings in everlasting glory'. Jones recognized, however, that there were some regicides who would not. Not because their cause was unworthy of martyrdom or because they had abandoned it, but because they had run away from the 'justice' that the Restoration authorities were now meting out. By avoiding the scaffold, these regicides were denying themselves the opportunity to declare publicly, one last time, in their dying speeches and prayers, their commitment to the Good Old Cause. More importantly, by remaining alive and not dying for that cause, they were not fulfilling the formula for martyrdom laid down by Christ. The regicides on the run were not dying for their cause, and they could not contemplate with unbridled enthusiasm the place in Heaven that such a death would earn them. Instead, Jones lamented, 'in what sad condition are our dear friends beyond the sea, where they may be hunted from place to place, and never be in safety ... how much have we gotten the start of them, for we are at a point, and are now going to Heaven?'[29] Whalley and Goffe must have been two of the men that Jones had in mind.

One observer noted there was some hope that those regicides who had been found guilty of treason, but not yet executed, would be kept alive. 'God seems a little to balance things', he said, 'that we have yet some competent liberty'.[30] The House of Commons had passed the bill to have them executed, but it did not get through the House of Lords. Indeed, some thought the best course was to let the bill 'sleep' in the Lords without a definitive vote either passing it or rejecting it. In July 1661 Charles II told Lord Chancellor Clarendon that he was 'weary of hanging except upon new offences', though 'I cannot pardon [the regicides]'. Clarendon's solution was that 'the bill should sleep in the Houses [of Parliament], and not be brought' to the king.[31] That way, Charles had not pardoned the regicides for their role in the trial and execution of his father, and Parliament had not overtly endorsed keeping the remaining regicides away from the gallows. Instead, the issue would be left gradually to seep from people's minds in the same way that the regicides would be left gradually to rot away in prison. They would not receive a pardon or have the opportunity to garner public sympathy, and the streets of London would not reek of bloodied corpses.

Quite predictably, Whalley and Goffe and their protectors in America were very interested in the fate of the regicides in England. News and newsbooks arrived from England; information, not all of it accurate, circulated around the colonies, sometimes reaching the ears of Whalley and Goffe. It was reported in New England, for example, that three other regicides—Lord Monson, Sir James Harrington, and Sir Henry Mildmay—would lose their titles and honours and suffer the annual indignity of being pulled to the Tyburn gallows from the Tower of London, with ropes around their necks, before being taken back to the Tower where they would remain as prisoners. They would not die as martyrs but would understand the fate that the state could inflict on them, if it so chose. News also came through Boston that Presbyterians, Independents, Anabaptists, and Quakers were all 'declared enemies of the state', alongside an exaggerated account of the fate of those regicides in the Tower who had been found guilty of treason but were not going to be executed. Instead, like Monson, Harrington, and Mildmay, they were to be dragged to Tyburn each year where they would stand for six hours with their faces and hands covered in blood. Another letter confirmed that the Lords had not passed the bill for the execution of the remaining regicides.[32] Whalley and Goffe could not have expected similar treatment, should they be caught and transported back to England. Their signatures on the king's death warrant, initial flight, refusal to be brought to 'justice', and continued espousal of the republican cause would have secured their execution.

Massachusetts Bay

Whalley and Goffe were in a curious situation, which might explain why Goffe's 'spirit was confused': it might have been more dignified to remain in England, to face their ideological foes, and to die proudly alongside those who remained committed to the fight against the Stuarts. Whalley and Goffe might have interpreted their flight to New England as a cowardly act that might deny them their privileged position in Heaven. Alternatively, they might have revelled in outwitting the Restoration authorities by remaining loyal to their cause in life rather than in death, no matter how much sympathy the dying words of their co-regicides may have inspired. Perhaps their exile was to be temporary. Perhaps the Restoration of the monarchy would be another short-lived constitutional experiment in the long line of attempts at governmental stability that had characterized the 1650s. In the early 1660s the regicides in America could hope, but they could not know for certain.

In February 1661 there was speculation that no more of Charles I's judges were going to be put to death.[33] Yet Whalley and Goffe could not feel safe: a £100 bounty had been put on each head by the king in September 1660;[34] at the end of November news of their exclusion from the Act of Indemnity reached New England. Their hosts, once so welcoming, started to wonder about the wisdom of offering the regicides protection, or at least of allowing them to remain in Boston without risk of prosecution. Though hardly a secret that Whalley and Goffe were among them, certain influential figures realized that this was potentially provocative to Charles II and the Restoration authorities. Samuel Maverick told the lord chancellor, the earl of Clarendon, that the colonists' loyalty could be gauged by their 'courteous entertainment' of Whalley and Goffe.[35] News of the regicides' presence in Boston would soon be relayed in London, as Captain Thomas Bredon, a Bostonian and a Royalist, had recently sailed for England where he was unlikely to keep this inflammatory information to himself.[36] Bredon, moreover, had been openly abused by the marshall general who taunted the captain, 'speak against Whalley and Goffe if you dare, if you dare, if you dare'. Governor Endecott himself had told Bredon that nothing would happen to the regicides, so long as there was no commission, no formal royal investigation (perhaps backed up by the king's representatives in person), forthcoming from England.[37]

Endecott and the colonists might have wondered whether such a commission would appear as, for the most part, they were used to being left alone. The board of governors of the Massachusetts Bay colony historically had escaped the direct oversight of king and ministers. Its local rights were shielded by a charter granted by Charles I on 4 March 1629, the legal protection of which enabled a not insignificant degree of independence.[38] There had since been flashpoints when that charter may have been threatened, and the Navigation Act of 1651 did challenge the colonies' control of their own trade: it prohibited foreign ships (principally Dutch ones) from carrying goods from outside Europe to England and its colonies. But agents had rarely been required to travel from the colonies to London to defend those colonies' interests. Technically, the colonies were not permitted to pass legislation that contradicted English law, but equally they did not have to send that legislation to England for scrutiny. Massachusetts Bay had also been judicious in preserving its independence in the civil war years. While sympathetic to the Parliamentary cause, it had not overtly come out on Parliament's side, and it had ducked away from Parliamentary supremacy over colonial affairs. Massachusetts Bay had also left aside the question of whether Parliament would recognize its charter; it issued writs in its own name; and its general court re-passed any legislation emanating from Parliament that would be to their advantage.[39]

Charles II in 1661 was concerned that his newly recovered empire was to be economically advantageous to him. Threats to Massachusetts Bay's proud self-governance and sovereignty would have imperilled that by disturbing the colony's existing political and economic systems, while causing unnecessary tension with a potentially lucrative trading post.[40] Even the furious deposition from Bredon about the disloyalty of Massachusetts Bay, and the colony's protection of the regicides, elicited a careful and moderate response. Bredon reported to the Council for Foreign Plantations, a body of forty-nine commissioners appointed by Charles II in 1660 to advise on colonial matters and oversee foreign trade, in London on 11 March. He informed it that in Massachusetts Bay the Act of Parliament and the king's proclamation against the regicides were 'vilified' and described as 'malignant pamphlets'. He reported that 'if any speak for the king's interest, they are esteemed as against their frame of policy or government and as mutineers', while the regicides kept uttering inflammatory statements about an impending 'change of government in England'.[41]

The Council for Foreign Plantations professed to be keen that the colonists of Massachusetts Bay should be brought 'to such a compliance as must be necessary, as they are an English colony, which ought not and cannot subsist but by a submission to and protection from his Majesty's crown and government'. But the Council passed the matter over to Charles II and his privy council, preparing a letter to Massachusetts Bay that communicated 'all possible tenderness, avoiding all matters which might set the people at a greater distance or stir them to any fears or distrust that it is not safe for them to submit cheerfully and wholly to the King's authority and protection, taking no notice of their adherence to Goffe and Whalley'.[42]

Before Bredon's deposition, the colonists of Massachusetts Bay had begun to hedge their bets in case Charles II was not going to be quite so moderate and was indeed going to pursue the regicides abroad: there had been movements in Boston to consider the arrest of Whalley and Goffe. Governor Endecott had summoned the court of assistants on 22 February 1661, for a meeting in which the apprehension of the regicides was raised. If the colonists arrested Whalley and Goffe, relations with Charles II might be improved. The king, in return, might be less inclined to undermine the autonomy of the colony, while encouraging more trade between England and New England.

Ultimately, though, the court would not ratify the arrest: the Massachusetts Bay authorities were not willing to sacrifice the independence of their commonwealth. Nonetheless, Whalley and Goffe realized that a safer haven was required. Within four days they were on the move. It is probable that their host had tipped them off: Daniel Gookin took part in the court's discussions about the regicides' future and would have informed his guests of their potentially precarious and dangerous situation. The royal declaration of 22 September 1660 remained in force with £100 resting on each regicide head, with the clear implication that aiding and abetting the regicides in America was a criminal act. Aside from the financial incentive provided for capturing Whalley and Goffe, some colonists might also have feared for the autonomy or very existence of their colonies if they provoked Charles II by sheltering the men who had signed his father's death warrant.

New Haven

The regicides' next residence was New Haven, the core of which was approximately one hundred households in a grid formation around a green. It took the two men nine days to complete this journey of approximately 150 miles, which passed through Springfield and Hartford. They were hosted in Hartford and given a guide, Simon Lobdell, by Governor John Winthrop. Whalley and Goffe would have been travelling through dense forest in the midst of a New England winter, but they would have realized the advantages of their new location. First, New Haven was the Puritan colony furthest from Boston, one of the first places to be searched should the Restoration authorities cross the Atlantic. Second, New Haven had proved to be the colony most resistant to the Restoration of Charles II: news of the king's return to England had arrived there on 27 July 1660 and its open rejection of a Stuart monarchy was considered a real possibility. Third, because of its open hostility, and perhaps because it was operating independently of an English proprietor—there was no individual ruling the colony answerable only to the king—New Haven harboured little hope of Charles II issuing them a charter guaranteeing legal recognition and protection. It was therefore barely worth cooperating with Charles against Whalley and Goffe.[43] Fourth, one of the leading figures in New Haven was William Jones, son-in-law of Governor Theophilus Eaton, with whom the regicides had crossed the Atlantic and become friendly on *The Prudent Mary*. Fifth, New Haven was the home of John Davenport, a preacher who delivered a sermon encouraging his congregation to 'hide the out-casts'.[44] Davenport was a friend and correspondent of Whalley's brother-in-law, William Hooke, who had spent time in New Haven during the 1640s.

A fuller exploration of Davenport's 'out-casts' sermon suggests just how appropriate it was to the situation in New Haven in the late winter and spring of 1661. 'Withhold not countenance, entertainment, and protection from such, if they come to us from other countries, as from France or England or any other place', Davenport preached, before quoting Hebrews XIII, 2–3: 'Be not forgetful to entertain strangers; for thereby some have entertained angels unawares. Remember them that are in bonds, as bound with them; and them which suffer adversity, as being yourselves also in the body'. Davenport went on to be even more specific, invoking God's injunctions to Moab: 'provide safe and comfortable shelter and refreshment for my people in the heat of persecution and opposition raised against them...While we are attending to our duty in owning and harbouring Christ's witnesses, God will be providing for their and our safety, by destroying those that would destroy his people'.[45]

Just one day before the authorities of the Massachusetts Bay colony issued a warrant for the regicides' arrest, Whalley and Goffe arrived at Davenport's house. However, the arrest warrant was a half-hearted attempt to catch them: Governor Endecott would have known that Whalley and Goffe had left his jurisdiction and that few, if any, Bostonians would be inclined to chase them through the New England woods in inclement weather. By issuing the warrant, Endecott could give the impression that he was following orders from England and attempting to arrest the regicides. Yet by delaying the warrant until the regicides were safely out of his colony, he could be sure for the time being that this warrant would have no practical effect.

Whalley and Goffe stayed with Davenport until the end of April with only one diversion. They visited Milford on 27 March, perhaps to give the impression that they were travelling south to join the Dutch colony of New Amsterdam, which was just over seventy miles away. Very soon another mandate for the apprehension of the regicides arrived in Boston. It was dated 5 March and signed by Edward Nicholas, Charles II's secretary of state:

CHARLES R.

Trusty and well-beloved,—We greet you well. We being given to understand that Colonel Whalley and Colonel Goffe, who stand here convicted for the execrable murder of our royal father, of glorious memory, are lately arrived at New England, where they hope to shroud themselves securely from the justice of our laws;—our will and pleasure is, and we do hereby expressly require and command you forthwith upon the receipt of these our letters, to cause both the said persons to be apprehended, and with the first opportunity sent over hither under a strict care... We are confident of your readiness and diligence to perform your duty; and so bid you farewell.

Given at our court at Whitehall, the fifth day of March, 1660–1.

By his Majesty's command,

Edw. Nicholas.[46]

This mandate was addressed 'To our trusty and well-beloved the present governor, or other magistrate or magistrates of our plantation of New England'. The colonial authorities may have been mistaken or mischievous in their interpretation of the wording but were aided by Edward Nicholas's questionable syntax. The colonial authorities read the address as if it included an extra comma: 'to ... the present governor, or other magistrate or magistrates[,] of our plantation of New England'.

This way, the mandate could be read as if it were addressed to 'the present governor...of New England'. Nicholas, however, may have intended the address to refer to a 'governor' of any colony in which the mandate was read, while only the 'magistrate or magistrates' had to pertain to New England. Whatever Nicholas's intentions, once it arrived in America, the mandate was read as if it were addressed to 'the present governor...of New England', leading to anxiety, consternation, and delay.

This anxiety did not come from nowhere: there was a history of fears that the American colonies were to come under the control of a general governor (or governor general). The company that had founded New Haven, including John Davenport, had passed through Boston during the 1630s, when the Massachusetts Bay charter was under threat from Charles I's government and the arrival of a governor general, endangering the colony's self-governance, looked ominous.[47] The September before Nicholas's mandate, there had already been fears that a royal governor was going to be sent from England to deal with complaints levelled against Massachusetts.[48] The March mandate, following on from this, was perceived as a threat to the autonomy of the individual colony—was there going to be an overall governor of New England?

As such a figure as the 'governor...of New England' did not exist, the ensuing deferral of the 5 March mandate's execution could be disguised under the cloak of bureaucratic confusion and hesitation. Governor Endecott of Massachusetts Bay dithered for over a week, long enough for news of the regicides' renewed danger to reach them and for preparations for the journey towards another safe haven to be made. Whalley and Goffe left Davenport's house on 30 April, two days after the Massachusetts arrest warrant arrived in New Haven. They moved to the safer residence of William Jones, their companion during the Atlantic crossing, whose father was the regicide executed six months previously. William Jones's attitude towards Charles II and the Stuart monarchy can be gleaned from the oath of fidelity he swore to the king when he was chosen magistrate for New Haven the following year. He took the oath 'with subordination' to the king but hoped that Charles would 'confirm the government for the advancement of Christ's gospel, kingdom and ends in this colony, upon the foundations already laid'. His oath, however, included a more controversial addition that 'in case of alteration of the government in the fundamentals thereof' he would be free from 'the said oath'.[49] Jones was willing to go through the motions of declaring loyalty to the king—the king who, through Parliament, had ordered the execution of his father—but demonstrated clearly that his primary loyalty was to the godly government and community of New Haven. If Charles encroached on that government, then Jones would free himself from his bonds of fidelity to the king. His loyalty to Charles II was conditional and limited: so limited, in fact, that he enthusiastically protected those who had signed Charles I's death warrant.

Governor Endecott's commission

Governor Endecott signed the 5 March mandate on 6 May. He appointed two English Royalists resident in Boston, a merchant named Thomas Kellond and a sea captain named Thomas Kirke, to search for Whalley and Goffe and to carry letters, dated 7 May, to the deputy governor of New Haven, the governor of Connecticut, and the governor of 'Manhatoes' or New Netherland, to aid in that project.[50] This was not a wholly popular move: some magistrates thought that Endecott had assumed too much authority for himself in ordering the arrest and appointing Kellond and Kirke. John Hull noted that 'Many very honestly minded of the deputies, and some among the magistrates, could not consent to own the governor's acting without the Council in executing the King's Majesty's warrant for apprehending Colonels Whalley and Goffe. Though they own it a duty to be done, yet his acting without the major part of the Council assembled made them loath to own the act at all'.[51]

Popular or not, Endecott made the right noises to suggest that he was keen to apprehend the regicides. Whalley and Goffe, he wrote, were 'guilty of so execrable a murder'; the Boston officials had 'not been wanting' in their efforts to capture the regicides; and he was confident that his fellow governors (or deputy governors) would carry out their duty to Charles II in a 'faithful', 'effectual', and 'speedy' manner.[52] Endecott acted, though, as if Whalley and Goffe had fled to the Dutch jurisdiction of New Netherland under Governor Peter Stuyvesant. On paper, at least, Endecott gave the impression that the regicides had fled from justice by hiding in the 'remote parts' of the Dutch colony far to the west of where they actually were. Endecott asked, therefore, that Stuyvesant apprehend Whalley and Goffe and return them to an area of English jurisdiction so that they could be returned to Boston.[53] Endecott was playing the old game of appearing diligent in the pursuit of the regicides, while expending his energies in a direction that he knew would come to nothing. Perhaps that is an uncharitable assessment. Perhaps Endecott genuinely thought that Whalley and Goffe had decided they would be safer in a colony outside English jurisdiction. Perhaps he had heard about their trip to Milford in the direction of New Netherland.

Kellond and Kirke began to travel westwards, seemingly following Endecott's tip-off, but new intelligence soon determined their route. Accompanied by a guide called John Chapin, they left Boston on the evening of 7 May and arrived on 10 May in Hartford, through which Whalley and Goffe themselves had travelled, where they met Governor Winthrop. The following day, the search in Hartford began, though Winthrop assured Kellond and Kirke that the regicides had already left in the direction of New Haven.[54] With Winthrop's assurance that a thorough search of Hartford would still be made, Kellond and Kirke wasted no time in travelling to Guilford where they met Deputy Governor William Leete on 11 May. Because Governor Francis Newman of New Haven had died on 18 November the previous year, Leete was the present chief magistrate of New Haven. Alongside him was New Haven's general court, which had begun in 1639 as seven 'pillars' of the church community (its numbers later grew), who elected a magistrate and four deputies largely responsible for judicial issues in the colony.[55]

Leete claimed to Kellond and Kirke that he had not seen Whalley and Goffe for nine weeks, around the time they had first arrived in New Haven. It is quite possible that Leete had not seen them in person, but this did not mean that the regicides had already moved on. Kellond and Kirke believed reports that Whalley and Goffe had been seen in New Haven more recently. Kellond and Kirke then met a man named Dennis Crampton, who openly told them that John Davenport was housing the regicides and that Deputy Governor Leete was aware of the secret. Davenport allegedly had recently acquired a suspiciously large quantity of provisions—enough, perhaps, to provide for two extra grown men. Other rumours suggested that the regicides had been spotted travelling between Davenport's and William Jones's respective residences and that they had been seen recently in nearby Milford (where they had been in March), inflammatorily suggesting that 'if they had but two hundred friends to stand by them, they would not care for Old or New England'.[56]

As it would be on other occasions, Kellond and Kirke's pursuit was hampered. They requested horses to transport them from Guilford to New Haven to assist the search. The horses duly arrived, but not until the colonial authorities had stalled for a little more time.[57] 11 May 1661 was a Saturday. The evening was drawing in. Deputy Governor Leete could not countenance, he claimed, anyone travelling within his jurisdiction during the approaching Sabbath. Furthermore, the government in London and its Royalist agents had undermined their cause through a mistaken use of language. Their commission was addressed to the 'governor of New England'. New Haven Colony usually had a governor; Connecticut Colony had a governor; Plymouth Colony had a governor; but New England as a whole had no such individual as the governor of New England. So Leete insisted—and we can see him stalling for time here—that he would have to consult his fellow magistrates before recognizing Kellond and Kirke's commission and assembling a search party. Leete, however, would give the commissioners a letter to hand to the magistrate in New Haven, their next destination.[58]

But this next destination would have to wait for another thirty-six hours or so—the time between Kellond and Kirke's meeting with Leete and sunrise on the following Monday, after their enforced Sabbath day in Guilford. This delay, of course, allowed plenty of time for the regicides to hear of their impending danger and make preparations to leave William Jones's house. And word would certainly spread because Leete had been careful to read Kellond and Kirke's letter out loud, so anyone present in the room would know the exact nature of their business and could forewarn the fugitives. There were reports that a local Native American had left the town in the direction of New Haven; a John Meigs was accused of preparing to leave for New Haven. But Leete refused a request from Kellond and Kirke that Meigs be brought in and interrogated. Never again would the regicides be pursued so closely by men who wished to play their part in avenging the execution of Charles I. Kellond and Kirke's intelligence was good but almost useless if they could not intercept their prey. Hearing of the Royalists' impending arrival, Whalley and Goffe set off for Westville about two miles outside New Haven, while Kellond and Kirke spent the same Saturday night frustrated in their Guilford inn.

The delay in Guilford over the weekend of 11–12 May 1661 allowed news about Kellond and Kirke to reach others as well as the regicides. Leete may have given the commissioners a letter to hand to a New Haven magistrate on their arrival but, apparently, he also sent a note to another New Haven magistrate, Matthew Gilbert, to make sure he would not be present when Kellond and Kirke arrived, and therefore the process would be hindered even further while Gilbert was looked for. Also, Leete assured Kellond and Kirke that he would follow them from Guilford to New Haven, but he managed to contrive a couple of hours' delay to frustrate Kellond and Kirke even more. Then, to add

to the farce, when Leete appeared in the court chamber, he notified
Kellond and Kirke that he did not think Whalley and Goffe were in
New Haven after all. Leete told them he would arrange a search of
Davenport's and Jones's respective houses—but only once the local
freemen had assembled. Kellond and Kirke told Leete that the king's
honour was being 'despised and trampled upon' and they believed
Leete was 'willing' that Whalley and Goffe should abscond. We can
imagine the commissioners' blood pressure rising as Leete met the
New Haven deputies and magistrates for almost six hours until he
emerged to make the same statement he had made before the meeting began. Again, Kellond and Kirke told Leete that Charles II 'would
resent such horrid and detestable concealments and abettings of such
traitors' and insisted that Leete honour the warrants they presented
from Governors Endecott and Winthrop.[59]

The tense and comical proceedings in New Haven suggest that a
wider issue was at stake: not only did the colonial authorities resent
the commissioners' attempts to arrest Whalley and Goffe, but the
colonists also disliked the royal commissioners and the government
they represented, as the discussion on Monday 13 May 1661 in the
New Haven court chamber indicates. The 'governor of New England'
ambiguity was a useful excuse to delay their proceedings with Kellond
and Kirke. On that edgy May evening, Kellond and Kirke asked the
New Haven magistrates 'whether they would own his Majesty or
no'—that is, would they respect his authority and yield by giving up
the regicides? This depended, the colonial authorities replied, on
'whether his Majesty would own them'—in short, would Charles
respect their independence and refrain from introducing a sinister
overbearing figure like a 'governor of New England'?

The New Haven magistrates, however, did convene the general
court four days later and issued warrants to search for Whalley and
Goffe in each plantation. Yet, once again, this action paid mere lip-
service to the royal commissioners: the magistrates knew the regicides
were only two miles away; so a search of a region like Virginia was
not going to reap many rewards. Perhaps they had a genuine interest

in finding the regicides once they had lodged their protest about a 'governor of New England'. On 14 May Kellond and Kirke had abandoned their dealings with the New Haven authorities who had displayed such determined and comical recalcitrance. They had carried out a cursory search of New Haven and offered a financial reward to find Whalley and Goffe. But they returned to Boston via New Netherland where Stuyvesant commanded a search of private boats, found nothing, and refused any more assistance. The commissioners had got within two miles of the two men they were after, but the colonists of New Haven had ensured they would not get any closer.[60] Kellond and Kirke retired to their new 250-acre estates outside Boston: a sizeable reward from the Massachusetts Bay general court for an ineffectual mission. Perhaps such a generous pay-off was designed to deter Kellond and Kirke from pursuing their search any further.

Surrender?

Whalley and Goffe were not yet to know that their pursuers had retreated with their tails firmly put between their legs by the authorities of New Haven. While Leete played for time, it is generally thought that the regicides were spirited away to a mill, two miles north-west of New Haven, where they remained for forty-eight hours before being taken to 'Hatchet Harbour' a further three miles away from New Haven.[61] On 15 May they began their stay at the site that has become legendary and synonymous with the regicides on the run: the Judges Cave at West Rock, just north-west of New Haven. Two days later, probably to divert attention from the regicides' real whereabouts, Leete issued a warrant for the search of Milford.[62] On the surface, the search of Milford was presented as an earnest affair: Thomas Sanford, Nicholas Campe, James Tapping, and Lawrence Ward investigated all 'dwelling houses, barns or other buildings'.[63] But quite predictably they yielded no results. Whalley and Goffe's cave, meanwhile, stood on a peak overlooking land owned by a farmer, Richard Sperry. While the regicides were lucky to avoid the cave during the bitter winter months, New Haven summers could be rainy with gusts of wind exceeding fifty kilometres per hour; so, in particularly bad weather, Whalley and Goffe retired to Sperry's house.[64] The New Haven wildlife, too, could pose a problem: one night Whalley and Goffe awoke to the sight of a mountain lion that, like the bad weather, precipitated a speedy retreat to Sperry.

At this point it seems that the regicides may have been prepared to surrender themselves. Word had reached them that Davenport was still under suspicion of protecting the fugitives. Leete had offered, after all, to arrange a search of Davenport's house exactly a month earlier. Although Leete knew that nothing would be found, he had put Davenport firmly in the frame for providing sanctuary to the regicides. Whalley and Goffe would not have wished to endanger anyone, least of all Davenport. Presumably they had heard from Sperry or Jones that Kellond and Kirke had long gone from New Haven, but they may have been concerned that further instructions or individuals would appear from London, urging their capture and the punishment of anyone who offered them protection. Whalley and Goffe also might have anticipated the actions of those in New Haven who, fearing for their colony's autonomy, might have been preparing a rapprochement with Charles II, which would have involved surrendering the regicides to the king. We should consider, in addition, the psychological state of two individuals who had been on the run and in hiding for almost four months. The last of those months had been spent, for the most part, in the open air, at the mercy of the elements, bereft of the conviviality and fraternity they had enjoyed when they first arrived in America. They had had a good run but perhaps this run was coming to an end. Perhaps the prospect of surrender and a glorious martyrdom was now preferable to the undignified, uncertain, and interminable existence in a cave.

So after a brief sojourn in a neighbouring colony to give the impression they had not been just outside New Haven the whole time, Whalley and Goffe appeared publicly in New Haven on 22 June, making their whereabouts known to the newly appointed Deputy Governor Gilbert. Davenport could not be accused now of clandestinely hiding them—they had appeared openly, had they not? But just as the New Haven authorities had little interest in catching the regicides at the start of May, they made no moves to capture them now. In the event, Whalley and Goffe did not actually give themselves up. There is a suggestion that the two men requested a short period of time to themselves, perhaps to make their peace with God before submitting themselves to the authorities, but they used that time to evade their captors and escape through a cornfield to their cave.[65] It is hard to believe that Leete and Gilbert did not choose to look the other way. Davenport later corroborated the story that Whalley and Goffe actually intended to give themselves up during their time in New Haven. He claimed that Leete, aware of the regicides' intentions, waited two days until other New Haven magistrates were present before making any moves to apprehend the fugitives. Two days were more than sufficient, however, for them to move on again, and though 'diligent search was renewed' with many 'sent forth on foot and horseback', the search was in vain.[66] Of course it was, and the New Haven authorities intended it to be so: they had given the impression that they were engaged in serious attempts to arrest the regicides but they had been sufficiently shrewd in their delay to ensure that Whalley and Goffe were long gone before their half-hearted and fruitless search began.

Observers were not fooled by the colonial authorities' apparent inability to capture Whalley and Goffe. Too many chances were being missed, too many feet were being dragged, for the government in England not to think that there was wilful protection of the regicides taking place. Even before the inflammatory behaviour of Leete and Gilbert, the Massachusetts Bay authorities' London agent had written to inform them that the Council for Foreign Plantations in London had noticed the tardiness in capturing the regicides. It seemed that Charles II's government was happy to interpret the colonists' behaviour as deliberate obstruction rather than innate incompetence. It did not help that the New England colonists seemed reluctant to proclaim Charles II as king: Connecticut did so in March 1661, New Haven in June, and Massachusetts Bay in August—about fifteen months after Charles's return to England. Indeed the Restoration government passed on to the Massachusetts Bay authorities its displeasure at rumours, circulated by Thomas Bredon, that there was 'much opposition to the agreeing' of the Bay's proclamation of the king. The Council for Foreign Plantations was already predisposed to interpret the colonists' actions as disloyal.[67]

The fear that Charles II's government seemed unhappy with the colonial authorities' attempts to capture the regicides was seemingly sufficient to spur Massachusetts Bay into further action. On 10 June its general court received a report from one of its committees, which it swiftly ratified, insisting that 'the apprehending of Colonel Whalley and Colonel Goffe ought to be diligently and faithfully executed'. The general court also declared that 'in case (for the future) any legally obnoxious and flying from the civil justice of the state of England, shall come over to these parts, they may not here expect shelter'. On 19 June the general court made a further declaration that if 'any opportunity present to write for England, the governor is desired by the first conveyance to certify his Majesty or the secretaries of state, what himself and the Council have acted touching searching for [Whalley and Goffe], in the prosecution of his Majesty's warrant'.[68] Massachusetts may not yet have officially proclaimed Charles II as its king, but it was attempting to make some loyal noises.

In July 1661, Leete—by this time governor of New Haven—received a missive from the general court in Boston. The letter demanded that Leete arrest Whalley and Goffe, without any more of his characteristic dithering. Leete was warned that his behaviour threatened 'the present state of these colonies and your own particularly'. And there was to be no more pretence that the regicides had fled, because they had been spotted in New Haven within the last fortnight. News had reached Massachusetts that Whalley and Goffe had been willing to surrender towards the end of June but that Gilbert had been remiss in not guarding or arresting them. 'How this will be taken is not difficult to imagine', Leete was told, 'to be sure not well'.[69] Though these threats were vague, they should have been intimidating to a colony as fragile as New Haven.

Should Charles II decide to swipe away the New Haven colonists' territory, they would have had no legal defence. John Davenport and his company had founded the colony through the purchase of land from indigenous tribes, not through a royal patent or warrant. In the mid-1640s there had been unsuccessful attempts to gain a patent, first (rather ambitiously) through using the Massachusetts Bay charter as evidence for New Haven's own right to settle, and then through a proposed joint patent with Connecticut. Then, in 1651, New Haven petitioned the Council of State in London, which passed on the petition to the Council of Trade and then the Committee for Foreign Affairs, before the project failed.[70] New Haven was essentially, then, a 'squatter' colony.[71] To compound this lack of legal protection, New Haven was economically precarious: immigration was falling, a costly effort to set up a trading post on the Delaware had failed in 1641, attempts at direct trading with England had foundered in 1646, and there remained commercial or military threats from Native Americans and the Dutch. Furthermore, the rigid godly system of government set up by Davenport and the colony's other founders had its detractors, while New Haven now found itself squabbling with Massachusetts Bay, its bigger, more powerful, and more successful colonial neighbour.[72]

Despite—perhaps because of—this fragility, the New Haven general court came out on the offensive. On 1 August its answer to the general court in Boston was prepared. Aware that New Haven's standing with Charles II would be 'worse...than the other colonies',[73] the officials conceded their 'not so diligent attendance' to the warrant to capture the regicides. But they maintained that this was 'not done out of any mind to slight or disown his majesty's authority' or 'out of favour' to Whalley and Goffe.[74] They stood by their treatment of Kellond and Kirke three months previously.

The commissioners might have had more success, the court suggested, if they had brought the correct commission and not one addressed to a 'general governor' of New England, the spectre of whom was sinister and threatening. And as for Whalley and Goffe's second escape, in June, the New Haven authorities maintained that the fault lay with Deputy Governor Gilbert's ignorance or incompetence and a sincere belief that Whalley and Goffe were intending to give themselves up.[75] Furthermore, the court was not going to stomach the somewhat hypocritical rebuke from Massachusetts Bay: Boston and Cambridge, as well as other places, had entertained and protected the regicides. To add to its injured pride, the court insisted that Whalley and Goffe were not 'hid any where in this colony'.[76] This statement, however, was disingenuous: the regicides were only three miles away from the man committing these words to paper.

Three weeks later Colonel Thomas Temple sent some intelligence about the regicides to William Morrice, Charles II's secretary of state. In a letter dated 20 August 1661, Temple told Charles's court about the attempts by Kellond and Kirke to find the regicides. He underlined his insistence that Whalley and Goffe were still in America, 'concealed in some of the southern parts until they may find a better opportunity to make their escape'. Temple clearly did not believe Davenport's claim that the regicides were willing to surrender: two individuals whom he described as 'two of the most considerable persons' in the colonies had convinced him otherwise. One, named as 'Pinchin', was perhaps John Pinchon, deputy to the Massachusetts general court; the other, Captain Richard Lord, was one of the original proprietors of Hartford. They had apparently combined in a 'secret design', known only to them, 'to apprehend and secure' Whalley and Goffe. Whatever this plan was, it did not work. Perhaps 'Pinchin' and Lord, too, were engaged in a ruse to fool the Restoration authorities—pretending they and the Massachusetts general court were loyal to Charles II by talking up their 'plan' to capture the regicides, while actually doing nothing about it.[77] Even if their plan were genuine, it would have been short-lived as Captain Lord died in May 1662. Whatever was the case, the regicides remained at large.

Following their appearance in New Haven in June, Whalley and Goffe had returned to their cave to the north-west of the town. They remained there until 19 August 1661 before travelling to nearby Milford where for at least two years they lodged at the house of a Micah or Michael Tomkins. Whalley and Goffe remained in hiding for some considerable time and in Milford depended on friends who would turn a blind eye or keep their mouths closed. Tomkins's house was in the centre of the town—would no one have noticed the extra supplies arriving there? Did Whalley and Goffe really never venture outside for two years? John Davenport, their old friend and protector, visited them regularly while prominent members of the Milford com munity probably shared private prayer meetings with them: Robert Treat, future governor of Connecticut and great-grandfather of a sig-natory of the Declaration of Independence; Roger Newton, Harvard graduate and second pastor of Milford Church; and Benjamin Fenn, magistrate and commissioner of the United Colonies of New England for New Haven along with, of all people, William Leete.

Guilt and repentance?

Once Whalley and Goffe had avoided the clutches of those who wished to capture them, their New England protectors began to express concern and contrition. Just how genuine this penitence was is questionable. Leete, for one, attempted to rewrite history. He claimed that, upon meeting Kellond and Kirke in Guilford on 11–12 May, he had given them a letter to deliver to Matthew Gilbert in New Haven that instructed the magistrate to begin an immediate search of the town. Yet Kellond and Kirke could not find Gilbert so the search was never carried out. Leete further claimed that, once he had arrived in New Haven on 13 May, he had begun writing out a search warrant himself but had been prevented by Gilbert and another magistrate, Robert Treat of Milford. Gilbert and Treat persuaded Leete, he claimed, that such a warrant could not be issued until the general court had been convened.[78] Leete wrote to John Norton, who had entertained Whalley and Goffe, about the regicides' situation and even travelled to Boston to 'disburden his heart' to Norton. Norton, in turn, wrote on Leete's behalf to Richard Baxter, the Presbyterian minister who briefly had been appointed chaplain in ordinary to Charles II, but who previously had served as a chaplain in Whalley's regiment during the civil war. Baxter held Whalley in such esteem that he dedicated to the regicide his *Apology Against the Modest Exceptions of Mr T. Blake* (1654). This dedication had a prescient epistle: 'think not your greatest trials are all over . . . The tempter, who hath had you on the waves, will now assault you in the calm; and hath his last game to play on the mountain, till nature cause you to descend'.[79]

Norton told Baxter that Leete was allegedly 'depressed in his spirit' because of his inept attempts to capture Whalley and Goffe. But, if we are to believe this claim at all, was Leete 'depressed' and concerned because he had not done that which he ought to have done, or because he was afraid that his protection of the regicides would incur anger and punishment from London? Norton suggested that Leete was 'not without fear of some displeasure that may follow': Leete had been warned that the neglect of the regicide warrants would 'prove uncomfortable' despite the rather desperate claim that 'his neighbours attest, they see not what he could have done more'.[80] There was plenty more that Leete could have done: he knew it and maybe feared that Charles II might know it too. But one observer noted that all Leete's 'pitiful letter' had done was to remind the English court of the New Haven magistrate's behaviour, when he might have been better off saying nothing and letting English minds remain preoccupied with domestic issues. Robert Newman, formerly of New Haven but resident in England in the early 1660s, noted that he had heard of no danger to the likes of Gilbert and thought the business 'would have died', had it not been for Leete's whimpering.[81]

Davenport also lied about his involvement in protecting the regicides. He wrote from New Haven to the English court in August 1661 and reflected on the regicides' time in that colony. Davenport protested his 'innocence in reference to the two colonels' and claimed that his actions might be 'misrepresented'. He highlighted his age—he was in his early sixties—and stressed the 'weakness' of his 'body' to excuse his inability to travel to London. His letter, he hoped, would vindicate him against those individuals who 'railed' against him and implicated him in the protection of the regicides. He claimed that he had been industrious in attempting to catch Whalley and Goffe—as the governor and magistrates of New Haven had been—but pronounced with some audacity that God's 'overruling providence' had thwarted them. Davenport clearly was not content to join the English court in condemning the regicides. Thus, on the one hand, Davenport protested his innocence of shielding the regicides; on the other hand, he implied that such protection was not really a crime at all because it was part of God's plan.[82] Few would have been convinced by Davenport's pleas of innocence: it was an open secret that Davenport and his associates in New Haven had done their utmost to trick Kellond and Kirke and keep the regicides at liberty. As Whalley's brother-in-law wrote to Davenport himself in 1661, 'I am almost amazed sometimes to see what cross capers some of you do make. I should break my shins should I do the like'.[83]

3

Regicides on the run II

Milford to Hartford

You know my trials are considerable, and did you know my weakness, you would surely pity, and pray earnestly for me.
William Goffe to Increase Mather, 12 April 1677[1]

During the early days of their stay in Milford, Whalley and Goffe had good reason to fear being discovered because, on the surface at least, the search was being stepped up. On 5 September 1661, just over a fortnight after the regicides' arrival in Milford, commissioners from the colonies of Massachusetts Bay, Plymouth, Connecticut, and New Haven met at Plymouth. They recited Charles II's declaration that the regicides were to be arrested, made it public that it was 'probable' that Whalley and Goffe were still hiding in New England, and warned the colonies' inhabitants 'not to receive, harbour, conceal or succour' them. Anyone who had protected the regicides since the king's first command for their arrest would incur Charles's 'highest displeasure'; they would be considered 'enemies to the public peace and welfare of the united colonies'. As such, they would be 'proceeded with accordingly'.[2] The regicides' protectors were being cast not only as enemies of the king but also as enemies of these United Colonies. The now allegedly repentant Leete was one of the declaration's signatories.

Nonetheless, despite the strong terms of the declaration, one of the New Haven commissioners dissented. Benjamin Fenn, resident of Milford where the regicides were now hiding, refused to consent to the declaration. While Leete would now add his name to documents that might put the lives of Whalley and Goffe in greater danger, there remained significant New England figures who would maintain their protection. Furthermore, there were others who doubted the sincerity of those who did sign the declaration to renew the hunt for the regicides: they saw the September meeting as another chapter in the long story of New England magistrates pretending to assist Charles II in the apprehension of Whalley and Goffe, while actually doing little about it. One of Davenport's London correspondents wrote to him on 28 October 1661 that 'The Bay stirring so much' for the arrest of Whalley and Goffe signified very little to those in London, because the regicides had been in New England for so long already and the magistrates so far had done 'nothing'.[3] Reports circulated in New England at this time that it was 'frequently taught and preached as a duty to hide the fugitives', and that Charles II was 'spoken slightly of'. Rumours even spread that the restored monarchy would fall within a year—all, it seems, to maintain hope in the colonies that a return to the Good Old Cause was imminent in England.[4]

Three captured regicides

Aside from being a great friend and protector of the regicides, John Davenport was a key figure in the network that enabled Whalley and Goffe to receive news from across the Atlantic. Reverend William Hooke, who was married to Whalley's sister, wrote letters to Davenport that were also passed on to Goffe. Yet the passing of correspondence was potentially dangerous, even if the authors hid their letters inside books, relied on intermediaries they could trust, or used pseudonyms and ciphers to disguise their true identities and intentions.[5] Goffe's wife, Frances—who lived with William and Jane Hooke in London,

and frequently met up with Whalley's second wife, Mary—advised
her husband not to send letters too often, 'for fear of the worst; for
they are very vigilant here to find out persons'. Nonetheless, she
wished to encourage her husband, telling him that he had many
friends and supporters back home, but thought it prudent not to put
those friends' names in writing.[6] One letter was intercepted and came
to the attention of Charles II's secretary of state, William Morrice.
It was lucky for the regicides and their protectors that the author was
not detected, for it was apparently 'as pernicious a letter against the
government as had been written since his majesty came in'.[7] Or perhaps this was a sign that Frances Goffe had exaggerated the Restoration
authorities' vigilance and interest by this time, in intercepting the
regicides' letters.

It was through this correspondence that Whalley and Goffe learnt
of the fates of their co-regicides who had gone into hiding in continental Europe and whose relative proximity to the English court
made them more vulnerable. Increase Mather, the Massachusetts-
based Puritan, wrote to Davenport on 2 June 1662 informing him of
the arrests of the regicides John Okey, Miles Corbet, and John
Barkstead (though the letter was not received for another eighteen
days).[8] Whalley and Goffe had been lucky that the agents sent to
pursue them were men like Kellond and Kirke who were tricked so
easily and abandoned their pursuit after little more than a fortnight.
Those regicides who had fled to continental Europe, however, were
tracked by a more determined huntsman: Sir George Downing.
Downing was a Harvard-educated former Parliamentarian who turned
on his allies at the Restoration and became envoy extraordinary to
the Netherlands. It was in the Netherlands, in Delft, that he was
able to penetrate the organization of those individuals protecting the
regicides in Europe. He suborned Abraham Kicke, an English merchant, who had been acting as an intermediary in the regicides' postal
network. In exchange for £200 per head, Kicke betrayed the regicides
to Downing. Downing pounced in March 1662 and arrested Okey,
Corbet, and Barkstead as they were visiting Delft. To ensure that local

sympathizers could not subvert his plan to return the regicides to England, Downing smuggled them out of their prison cells in the middle of the night and delivered them by boat to a waiting English frigate. Okey, Corbet, and Barkstead were executed on 19 April 1662.[9]

There were essential differences in the situations of those regicides who had fled to Europe and those who took ship to America. Charles was able to pursue his foes in Europe with more tenacity because it was easier to send agents across the English Channel and he had a determined individual in Downing who was relentless in pursuing his quarry. Meanwhile, the king and his ministers either got on with the onerous task of governing a polity beset with internal traumas or distracted themselves with their mistresses. It was Downing's determination that ensured that the regicide John Lisle was pursued to a churchyard in Lausanne and shot in the back with a blunderbuss. In contrast, it was very difficult to reach the colonies that sheltered Whalley and Goffe; relations between Whitehall and New England had to be managed carefully; Kellond and Kirke were not as competent as Downing; and the terrain over which any pursuit would take place was unfamiliar to Charles II, his ministers, and his agents. And, most significantly, in relations with the American colonies, Whitehall was dealing with very able and very stubborn authorities that at times proved themselves willing to complicate and impede any search for the regicides.

Just a fortnight after the executions of Okey, Corbet, and Barkstead, Goffe received a letter with further portentous news about the religious changes afoot in England. In the summer of 1662 the Act of Uniformity was passed. Any hopes that the Restoration Church of England would embrace or tolerate non-Anglican Protestants were dashed. While Charles II's Declaration of Breda and the Worcester House and Savoy Conferences of 1660–1 may have raised hopes, for Presbyterians in particular, the great ejection of Nonconformist Protestant ministers from their livings made it clear that the Restoration church settlement would be a narrow one. Those excluded could fear prosecution and persecution. The impact on the English religious landscape, both physical and psychological, was immense. Some observers of the changes thought that they could perceive divine intervention on behalf of Nonconformist Protestants. Davenport wrote to Goffe that he had heard of nine Anglican ministers who had gone to their bishop to receive their new orders. Upon returning to their livings seven were 'immediately struck dead', the eighth was 'struck blind', and the ninth went 'mad'. This was, Davenport reported, 'a very remarkable hand of God'.[10]

While the deaths of Okey, Corbet, and Barkstead would have saddened Whalley and Goffe, erroneous reports that they, too, had perished in a similar way in Switzerland—or, indeed, that they were still alive, but in Brussels[11]—would have emboldened them. While there were more accurate counter-rumours in England towards the start of 1663 that Whalley and Goffe 'were in the head of an army in New England',[12] on the rare occasion that the regicides' names came up in domestic intelligence, that intelligence was hazy and unproductive. One informant told another of the king's secretaries of state, the earl of Arlington, that he had not seen Goffe for two years, that he was 'not intimate' with Whalley, and that the regicides' wives *might* know something of their whereabouts.[13]

Perhaps encouraged by the recent success of discovering and bringing to 'justice' Okey, Corbet, and Barkstead, but wary of their limited intelligence on Whalley and Goffe, Charles II's court once again turned its attention to New England and issued a toothless warning to the colonial magistrates. The king's letter reminded the Massachusetts Bay authorities that the Act of Indemnity and Oblivion had forgiven those who had rebelled against him and his father, 'excepting only such persons who stand attainted by our Parliament here of high treason'. Charles reminded them that if any such individuals had 'transplanted themselves' to New England, then the colonists from 'duty, affection and obedience' to the king should arrest the regicides and arrange their return to England.[14] But this paper threat was virtually useless. Almost two years passed and the colonial authorities did not feel sufficient duty, affection, or obedience to Charles to ensure the regicides' return across the Atlantic.

A royal commission

While the court in London did not completely forget Whalley and
Goffe, by 1664 there was little expectation they would be captured.
On 25 April of that year instructions were given to four royal
commissioners—Richard Nichols, Robert Carr, George Cartwright,
and Samuel Maverick—to travel to the New England colonies and to
New Amsterdam. This may sound like a major attempt to capture the
regicides but it was not. First, the wording of the commission sent
from London was, with regards to the regicides, intriguingly subtle.
Second, the commission had many other responsibilities; the regicides
were a minor concern. Third, like Kellond and Kirke, the quality of
the personnel put behind any 'search' was questionable.

Charles II presented a velvet fist in an iron glove: four warships
and 400 soldiers arrived in Boston and Portsmouth in July 1664.
New Netherland was the ostensible target of this show of strength,
but the New England colonies also felt under threat. Also, the commission was worded more diplomatically than the ships and soldiers
might have suggested, especially with reference to Whalley and Goffe.
The commission's four officials were to make 'due inquiry' whether
any regicides had travelled to, and resided in, these areas. If any such
individuals were discovered, they were to be returned to London
where due legal process would result no doubt in the regicides'
execution. It was unlikely that there was much hope behind these
instructions that Whalley and Goffe really would be captured: they had
not been caught so far and the longer the regicides remained in New
England, the wider their network and security, the greater their knowledge of the terrain, and the greater their awareness of hiding places
would become. Instead, almost half of the commissioners' instructions
concerned those who had offered sanctuary or might offer it in the
future to the regicides. Their mandate displayed a detachment and
only latent aggression: the commissioners were to identify by whom
the regicides had been 'received and entertained', but they were not

to arrest them since that would violate the Act of Indemnity and Oblivion, which forgave many of Charles II's political enemies, and hence those who had sheltered his enemies. Rather, these people received the message that they might 'be taken the more notice of, and may hold themselves to take the more care for their future behaviour'.[15] The threat of retribution lingered behind a carefully worded and judiciously friendly warning.

It is possible that the commission had instructions from the king to deal carefully with the Puritan Massachusetts authorities; perhaps Charles was trying to 'woo' them and coax their loyalty towards him after their lukewarm enthusiasm in recognizing him as their king.[16] Furthermore, Anglo-Dutch mercantile and military competition had intensified by 1664; English success would rely on the Restoration government maintaining existing trade routes and expanding territorial control, especially in the American colonies.[17] Since his exile in the 1650s, and after his return to England in 1660, Charles had been advised by Lord Chancellor Clarendon to engender 'a great esteem for the plantations and the improvement of them by all ways that could reasonably be proposed', and the king was indeed keen to 'increase the trade of the nation', especially with regard to the colonies, to counter his domestic financial problems.[18] If Charles and his courtiers had taken a tough line against those who had harboured the regicides, they would have further alienated many notable figures in colonial governance. Then any hopes of imposing a new charter on Massachusetts, or fully exploiting England's domination of trade in the area, would have been lost. There was also a growing sense that the chances of capturing Whalley and Goffe were diminishing; so another failed attempt at their capture would be less humiliating if it were subtle and measured, rather than overtly aggressive and intrusive.

In any case, the commissioners' visit had a number of purposes: to advance Charles II's claims over New Netherland; to ascertain whether the Acts of Trade, which reduced colonial reliance on imported goods from other nations and limited colonial trade to England, were being imposed; to investigate whether the king might be able to control the

colonies' militia and even appoint the governor; to determine the
state of the colonies' defences; in general, to gauge the colonies' economic, political, and religious state; and to express the king's unhappi-
ness at the reluctance of the Puritan authorities in Massachusetts to
allow the use of the Church of England's Book of Common Prayer
in their colony. The authorities feared that use of the Book of
Common Prayer would undermine Massachusetts's religious purity
and might foreshadow the kind of Anglican dominance and persecution which had precipitated the colonists' flight from England in the
early seventeenth century and the outbreak of civil war in the 1640s.
The commissioners also had instructions to hear and pass judgement
on territorial disputes in New England, for example concerning the
boundary between New York and Connecticut.

To begin with, and at least on paper, both king and colonists were
attempting a balancing act; both sides expressed gratitude at the
respect afforded one another but were suspicious of conceding jurisdiction to the other side. The king had guaranteed 'all the privileges
and liberties' of the Massachusetts charter but still insisted on sending
commissioners to investigate issues over which his government had
jurisdiction. The Massachusetts authorities were relieved and worried: relieved that their charter had been upheld, but worried that
sovereignty would be conceded if the king's commissioners were
allowed to investigate with unrestricted freedom.[19]

Yet two factors conspired to disrupt this initial equilibrium: the
Massachusetts officials' predisposition to view any such commission
with extreme scepticism and distrust, and the commissioners' lack of
subtlety in their dealings once they had arrived in Massachusetts. The
Massachusetts Bay general court responded to the commission in a
letter to Charles II in October 1664. They had many complaints,
one of the most essential being that 'instead of being governed by
rulers of our own choosing (which is the fundamental privilege of
our patent) and by laws of our own, we are like to be subjected to
the arbitrary power of strangers'. Between January and May 1665,
Cartwright, Maverick, and Carr resided in Boston, and had to

live among a suspicious population, who openly levelled scurrilous accusations against the commissioners.[20]

The commissioners, with the exception of Richard Nichols, had elements in common with Kellond and Kirke: they were partisan adventurers of underwhelming ability, who were easily given the run-around by colonial officials. Maverick loathed Massachusetts Puritans, and maintained correspondence with the earl of Clarendon in which he griped at their lack of loyalty or subjection to the Restoration government; Carr has been described as 'undistinguished by principle or ability'; Cartwright allegedly 'lacked qualifications in point of knowledge and tact'.[21] These were inauspicious appointments for a commission that would require some subtlety to deal with the New England magistrates. Indeed, the commissioners alienated the Massachusetts officials by asking them in May 1665 to assemble the colony's inhabitants, so that they could question them directly about colonial affairs, deliberately bypassing the magistrates. Those who did not attend, Cartwright claimed, would be cast as traitors. The commissioners issued a public statement against those colonists who had slandered the commission's behaviour and intentions, once again provoking their ire. The commission's ultimate failure came when they arranged a meeting at Thomas Bredon's house to hear a complaint of Thomas Deane against the Massachusetts government, only for that government to reject the legitimacy of such a hearing, before sending a herald to Bredon's house, trumpeting that the commissioners' meeting had been prohibited.[22] As with Kellond and Kirke before them, the commission led by Nichols, Carr, Cartwright, and Maverick was an unsuccessful one, and they were recalled after an ineffectual mission. When, in April 1666, Charles II summoned agents from Massachusetts to London to answer questions on these recent turbulent colonial affairs, the Massachusetts Bay colony's insubordination was further underlined when the agents simply refused to go.

Meanwhile, Whalley and Goffe had gone back to their cave above New Haven for a week and a half. Yet this was to be the regicides' final stay in those hills. It is possible that Charles II's most recent missive and the arrival of the commissioners had shaken them. Perhaps Whalley and Goffe thought that their past or future protectors would feel unduly threatened by the king's friendly warning. Perhaps they felt that their hosts had already endangered themselves enough. Indeed, the king's commissioners had already taken action against their friends: in Rhode Island they had seized cattle owned by Daniel Gookin, when they discovered that he had held and managed property for the regicides.[23] Gookin had sailed from Gravesend with Whalley and Goffe, had hosted them, had taken part in discussions about them in the Boston court of assistants, and most likely tipped them off in February 1661 that their position in Boston was becoming more dangerous. The commissioners had tracked down a figure who had been closely involved in receiving and entertaining the regicides, but Gookin did not assist them in getting any closer to their quarry.

It was reported that Gookin stood 'upon the privilege' of the colony's charter, 'refusing to answer before the commissioners', so 'there was no more done in it'. This report concerning Massachusetts made a telling point about the colony's perception of their relationship with the English crown. The magistrates argued that Charles I had granted the charter that allowed Gookin to remain silent and the colony 'to make laws, and to execute them'. This charter was, they suggested rather provocatively, 'a warrant against himself and his successors'. So long as they paid the king a fifth of all the gold and silver ore they acquired, they were not obliged to obey the king, 'but by civility'. Moreover, the Massachusetts Bay magistrates were content to use the distance between themselves and London and the slow nature of any correspondence between the two to 'spin' out any disputes, including those about the regicides. The colonists hoped that the regime in London might change by the time they had to resolve any disagreements caused by such delays. Some even dared to suggest that the Dutch might effect such regime change.[24] Charles II's restored monarchy was still relatively young. Some colonists still hoped that Charles's reign would be another unsuccessful venture lasting only until the Dutch invaded and ensured liberty of conscience in the mother country of the regicides. All the colonists had to do in the meantime was delay their dealings with the Restoration court so that the regicides remained free.

Free they may have been, but Whalley and Goffe would have been alarmed at the discovery and disturbance of their belongings in the cave above New Haven by Native Americans on a hunting expedition.[25] Surely news of such a curious discovery would circulate and spread through local towns. Whatever their motivation, Whalley and Goffe set off for a frontier town, Hadley, situated roughly a hundred miles to the north-east of Milford and New Haven. Even with modern facilities and connections, it is at least a day and a half's walk up the Connecticut Valley. A town so remote from major settlements and about ninety miles from Boston appealed to the regicides. As with their previous locations, Whalley and Goffe could depend on local residents for support, sympathy, and protection. John Davenport probably arranged that the regicides would lodge with Hadley's minister, Reverend John Russell. Four years previously, Davenport had been a supporter of Russell when the minister left the church in Wethersfield, Connecticut with a splinter group and settled on the frontier.[26] So, on 13 October 1664 Whalley and Goffe made their way from their cave to Hadley.

Hadley

Also living in Hadley was William Goodwin who, like Russell, had connections with Davenport. Goodwin lived across the main street and about six doors down from Russell's house where Whalley and Goffe resided.[27] Goodwin visited them often. Another of the regicides' visitors, on 10 February 1665, was a third regicide who had fled to America, via Hanau: John Dixwell (see Appendix IV). Little is known about this meeting. All three men signed Charles I's death warrant and evaded punishment, which would have cemented their solidarity and companionship. Furthermore, they would have had stories to swap about life on the run and how they had kept their liberty. There was little chance, though, that Dixwell was going to join Whalley and Goffe in Russell's house permanently: aside from the lack of space, Dixwell had been used to travelling alone. Moreover, beyond being regicides, they had little more in common. Dixwell had never risen to the rank of major general, nor did he have the familial ties or shared adventures that bonded Whalley and Goffe.

The regicides had been in Hadley barely six months before a fresh incentive for their protection emerged in the most disastrous form. From late April to June 1665 the bubonic plague made its way from the outer suburbs of London into the City. By November 1665, approximately 100,000 of London's inhabitants had perished.[28] In a letter to Goodwin in 1665 Davenport mentioned this 'sword of the angel, in the noisome pestilence', and he interpreted the disaster as divine punishment for the sins of the age and a sign that Christ's return to earth was imminent. These sins Davenport outlined as follows: 'scattering the churches gathered unto Christ, in silencing the faithful ministers, in imprisoning and banishing the innocent, in corrupting religion with Antichristian superstitions, in killing sundry that deserved better usage for their zeal for God, and faithfulness to the public good, and in adding to all these, manifest contempt of God, and of the covenant'. Davenport, however, was not just talking about the sins of Old England: New England, too, had 'cause to tremble'. Divine retribution would visit them also if colonists did not repent quickly and avoid the 'corruptions' of Old England.[29] There was one way that the likes of Goodwin and Russell could work to avoid these corruptions: by supporting faithful and 'innocent' individuals, like Whalley and Goffe, who expressed their godly zeal. They could protect themselves and their colonies by exercising their godliness and righteousness to save those who had signed the death warrant of an ungodly tyrant. Davenport's letter to Goodwin was priming Hadley's residents to shelter these godly fugitives, lest they provoke God's wrath and retribution with their own disastrous plague.

For some observers of the religious, political, and moral life of England in the mid-1660s, the plague of 1665 was a mere precursor to the divine events that were expected in 1666: the year marked by the number of the Beast. Puritans would have needed little encouragement to believe they were living in the End Times: their ministers in England had been expelled and they lived under the threat of prosecution; the libertine royal court appeared to provoke God's wrath with its licentiousness and blasphemy; and to add insult to injury, Charles II cavorted with Barbara Villiers, his mistress, in the Westminster house that formerly had been occupied by Edward Whalley.[30] One of the king's own chaplains told the congregation of St Martin-in-the-Fields that Charles and his courtiers should take the blame for the divine judgement expressed in the Great Fire of London.[31] Those with an apocalyptic turn of mind believed with mounting excitement that the natural disasters of the mid-1660s were presaging the Second Coming. For Whalley and Goffe, all the fear and hardship would have been worthwhile when their Saviour once again walked the earth. They must have been bitterly disappointed, then, when the year passed with no such development. The regicides remained concealed in Russell's house, at times suffering the cramped indignity of hiding behind a chimney stack. The fugitives probably had more to fear, however, from locals keen to profit from their exposure than direct intervention from Charles II's government. In 1667 the earl of Clarendon, the lord chancellor, fell from power and took with him, for a few years at least, any imperial policy that may have included determined pursuit of the regicides. By 1668, the activity of the Council for Foreign Plantations had ceased, and with it for the moment went one of the key mechanisms for oversight of the colonies.[32]

A decade into his time in New England, William Goffe still considered himself somewhat isolated from the American colonists. He referred to himself as a 'stranger' and thought that he must not be a 'needless meddler'. Nevertheless, he was still willing to offer his support to the 'ship' of New England, which was rightly sailing away from the Roman Catholic faith, but risked being 'tossed with tempest' and was in 'danger of being overwhelmed'. The ship was in danger, it seems, because the 'laborious mariners' were 'at some disagreement among themselves'. Goffe offered his love to those New Englanders

who had become embroiled in internecine squabbling and pointed
them to Psalm 133: 'Behold, how good and how pleasant it is for
brethren to dwell together in unity!'[33] Despite his concern for these
divisions, Goffe told his wife that he was thriving and she replied on
13 October 1671: she was pleased to hear that Goffe's latest home was
agreeing 'so well' with him, though she was concerned to learn of the
cold from which he was suffering and offered to send him a periwig.[34]

In the same letter of October 1671, Goffe's wife gave him news of
his fellow brethren in England: while they enjoyed relative peace in
the capital, they endured persecution in the country.[35] During the
latter part of 1671 and the early months of 1672, though, the fortunes
of Nonconformist Protestants seemed to be changing. The king, with
his 'Cabal' ministry, was inclining towards a Declaration of Indulgence
that would allow non-Anglicans to worship without the punishments
outlined in the 1660s. Goffe's wife wrote to her husband that Charles II
was 'very favourable to many of the fanatics, and to some of them
that he was highly displeased with'. Her optimism was tempered with
a note of warning: while the king may have shown indulgence to
some Nonconformist Protestants, 'Whalley and Goff[e] and Ludlow'
were to be summoned, presumably to be put on trial. Any new tenor
of forgiveness, which had even seen Colonel Thomas Blood pardoned
after trying to steal the crown jewels, should not lead to the regicides
being lulled into a false sense of security. 'It is to be feared', wrote
Goffe's wife, 'that after this sunshine there will be a thick darkness'.[36]
She was correct: the Declaration of Indulgence was rejected by
Parliament and within a decade the country was witnessing one of
the most repressive periods of its history.

Whalley and Goffe had the good sense to stay in New England
where they enjoyed a considerable degree of support. This support
was more than the mere provision of a place to stay or emotional
encouragement; it was also financial. Edward Collins, deacon of the
First Church in Cambridge, wrote to the regicides in June 1672
about a £50 donation given to them by Richard Saltonstall who had
just travelled to England. (Saltonstall's father, Sir Richard, had been
implicated in a plot to depose Charles II in 1660.) Goffe instructed

Collins that the money should be given to 'our dear and reverend friend' Russell, or anyone else whom Russell might appoint.[37] The fugitives were also able to engage in covert trade with Native Americans and, via their network of supporters in the colonies, received gifts from individuals in England, including Whalley's sister, Jane Hooke. In July 1672 Goffe noted that recently they had received forty shillings in silver and possessed jointly over £100. The regicides had also received six pairs of gloves, which would have been useful in the bitter winter climate: so 'exceeding piercing' that 'a sickly person must not dare to venture out of doors'.[38]

By August 1674 Edward Whalley was one of these 'sickly' people. Goffe and William Hooke's correspondence from that time underlines two points: the regicides' deep commitment to their faith and Whalley's deteriorating health. When Goffe asked Whalley whether he wished to add anything to his letter to Hooke, Whalley replied that he desired 'nothing but to acquaint myself with Jesus Christ and that fullness that is in him for those that believe and have interest in him'. Goffe noted, however, that Whalley uttered his words 'with some stops, yet with more freedom and clearness than usual'.[39] Whalley by now was in his seventies and had spent much of the last fourteen years in inhospitable nooks or caves. Furthermore, his state of mind may have become more fragile during these difficult years, anxious perhaps that Royalist agents might put an end to his freedom and concerned that he should have died a martyr, instead of suffering the indignity of constant subterfuge in his dotage. The precise details of Whalley's death remain unclear, but it certainly occurred in Hadley, and probably by 1675.

Rebunking myths: the Angel of Hadley

Although he was supported by individuals like John Russell, Peter Tilton, and William Goodwin, William Goffe was now without his companion of fifteen years. Little is known about Goffe's first months alone, but his reappearance was so dramatic that it would captivate audiences for centuries. Both Thomas Hutchinson and Ezra Stiles, two of the earliest historians of the regicides, were keen to include in their histories one very famous story about Goffe from the time of King Philip's War (King Philip being the English moniker of the Wampanoag chief Metacom), the devastating conflict between English colonists and the indigenous tribes of Wampanoags, Nipmucks, and Narragansetts that raged between 1675 and 1678. This war was the defining experience of the second generation of English colonists, and one that caused both psychological trauma and economic devastation. Native Americans besieged, raided, ransacked, and razed colonial houses and farmsteads, slaughtering livestock in their wake. They exploited their superior knowledge of the North American wilderness to lay in wait and launch surprise stealth attacks, terrifying colonists who lay tensely in wait, sometimes being picked off one by one, sometimes being maimed and killed in wholesale attacks on towns. The isolated and vulnerable colonists starved, and were tortured, raped, flayed, scalped, and beheaded. After a period of stunned equivocation they retaliated with brutal infantry-driven force, decimating the Narragansett and Wampanoags. By the end of the war some 2,000 New Englanders had perished; over fifty townships had been assaulted, of which twelve were totally destroyed. The war costs of a quarter of a million pounds set back the New England economy for decades.[40]

One town under attack was Hadley, the settlement on the Connecticut River where Whalley and Goffe had moved in October 1664. The family of John Leverett, governor of Massachusetts Bay during King Philip's War and a soldier under Whalley during the English civil war, handed down the anecdote of what became known as the 'Angel of Hadley'. This was the story as Hutchinson reported it some ninety years later:

> The town of Hadley was alarmed by the Indians in 1675, in the time of public worship, and the people were in the utmost confusion.— Suddenly, a grave elderly person appeared in the midst of them—In his

mien and dress he differed from the rest of the people.—He not only
encouraged them to defend themselves; but put himself at their head,
rallied, instructed, and led them on to encounter the enemy, who by
this means were repulsed.—As suddenly the deliverer of Hadley disappeared.—The people were left in consternation, utterly unable to
account for this strange phenomenon.[41]

At first sight, the Angel of Hadley story seems implausible: an
unknown ageing figure appears from nowhere and single-handedly
coordinates the defence of a town before disappearing into the ether.
The story combines key ingredients of action, drama, and mystery, but
it does not sound particularly likely. Nonetheless, the tale remained
unchallenged for almost 200 years until the appearance of an article
by local historian George Sheldon in 1874, and then the inclusion of
Sheldon's argument in the reprinting of Sylvester Judd's *History of
Hadley*, the 1905 edition of which had an introduction by Sheldon
which tore the myth, it was claimed, 'to tatters'. So important was the
'debunking' of this tale that it featured in *The New York Times*, which
reported Judd's republication and took delight in dispelling the myth
of the Angel of Hadley 'repeated a thousand times by historians, novelists and painters'. The debunking was simple: Hutchinson's *History of
the Colony of Massachusetts-Bay* (1764) dated the Hadley attack to 1
September 1675 but no such attack on Hadley between 24 August and
14 September 1675 was recorded in the contemporary and otherwise
exhaustive account of King Philip's War by the Congregationalist
pastor Solomon Stoddard.[42]

However, this is not to say that the Angel of Hadley episode never
happened; we might just need to re-date it. The debunking of the
debunking of the Hadley story resulted from the careful analysis of
Douglas C. Wilson in an award-winning article from 1987.[43] On 18
April 1677, John Russell wrote a letter to Increase Mather in which he
referred to Mather's recently published *A Brief History of the Warr with
the Indians in New-England* (1676). 'I find nothing considerable mistaken in your history', he said, but 'that which I most fear in the

matter is lest Mr B or some of Connecticut should clash with ours and contradict each other in the story as to matter of fact. Should that appear in print which I have often heard in words, I verily fear the event should be exceeding sad'. Wilson interpreted these rather cryptic words as being a reference to the section in Mather's book about an attack on Hadley on 12 June 1676:

> The enemy assaulted Hadley, in the morning, sun an hour high, three soldiers going out of the town without their arms, were dissuaded therefrom by a sergeant, who stood at the gate, but they alleging that they intended not to go far, were suffered to pass, within a while the sergeant apprehended, that he heard some men running; and looking over the fortification, he saw twenty Indians pursuing those three men, who were so terrified, that they could not cry out; two of them were at last killed, and the other so mortally wounded, as that he lived not above two or three days; wherefore the sergeant gave the alarm. God in great mercy to those western plantations had so ordered by his providence, as that Connecticut army was come thither before this onset from the enemy. Besides English, there were near upon two hundred Indians in Hadley, who came to fight with and for the English, against the common enemy, who was quickly driven off at the south end of the town; whilst our men were pursuing of them there, on a sudden a great swarm of Indians issued out of the bushes, and made their main assault at the north end of the town, they fired a barn which was without the fortifications, and went into a house, where the inhabitants discharged a great gun upon them, whereupon about fifty Indians were seen running out of the house in great haste, being terribly frighted with the report and slaughter made amongst them by the great gun. Ours followed the enemy (whom they judged to be about five hundred, and by Indian report since, it seems they were seven hundred) near upon two miles, and would fain have pursued them further, but they had no order so to do.[44]

Sheldon, who had 'debunked' the Hadley myth, had discounted the 12 June attack as being the occasion on which Goffe could have appeared as the town's 'Angel'. On that day, he observed from Mather, there were Connecticut men present in Hadley, commanded by Major John Talcott. The inhabitants would need no mystical saviour, therefore, because they had hundreds of soldiers who would protect them.

Wilson was not content with this explanation but pointed out that Mather's account of that attack, the only one extant, was ambiguous and might not have been completely reliable.

It seems that Mather's account of the Hadley attack of 12 June 1676 was erroneous. In April 1676 the eastern side of the colony was under threat, so Major Thomas Savage and his forces were stationed there. In May the colonists mounted an assault on Native Americans massed near Deerfield, less than twenty miles north of Hadley (see Figure 6). The Connecticut and Massachusetts colonies saw an opportunity to carry out a joint offensive and pincer movement: the Massachusetts forces would start from Hadley and march up the east side of the Connecticut River, while the Connecticut forces would start from Northampton and march up the west side. Connecticut soldiers arrived in Hadley on 8 June and soon crossed to Northampton before 12 June. Massachusetts soldiers did not arrive in Hadley until 14 June. So there were no soldiers in Hadley on 12 June since the 500 Connecticut soldiers had already moved on to Northampton. Wilson concluded, therefore, that Goffe could indeed have saved Hadley on 12 June 1676.

Russell's cryptic words may have been a coded reference to the people of Connecticut not to reveal that Goffe had indeed appeared in Hadley. He would have good cause to 'fear' this exposure and it would be 'exceeding sad' because it would have divulged Goffe's location and implicated various individuals in the sheltering of the regicide. Wilson also pointed out that Russell was the brother-in-law of the two men in command of the forces closest to Hadley on 12 June: Major John Talcott and Captain Benjamin Newbury. So if they had known about Goffe's appearance, they would not have implicated one of their own relatives, Russell, in the regicide's concealment and protection. There were two other men who would have kept quiet about any appearance by Goffe: William Leete, now governor of Connecticut, and Robert Treat, now deputy governor, who had done so much fifteen years previously to hide the whereabouts of the regicides.[45]

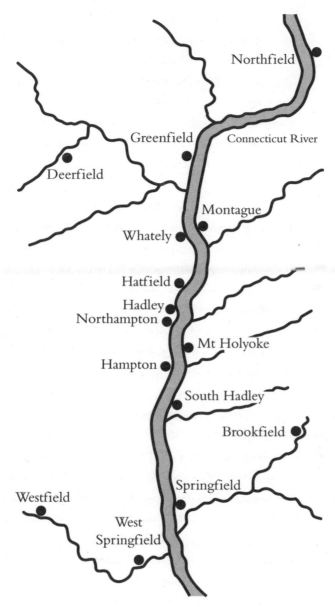

Figure 6. Map of King Philip's War

Edward Randolph's regicide fixation

Between 10 June and 30 July 1676 the colonial administrator Edward
Randolph had arrived in Boston and was residing there, having been
sent from England with instructions that the colonies should send
agents to Whitehall to answer questions, and report back, on recent
events in Massachusetts Bay and the surrounding area. Randolph was
also to gather any information he could about the situation across
the Atlantic. The colonists' protection of Whalley and Goffe did not
escape Randolph's notice, and neither did the law which (he claimed)
had been in operation in Massachusetts Bay by which the regicides had been welcomed and entertained.[46] Though Goffe had lost his
father-in-law and spiritual companion, he remained a fugitive who
was still of some interest to the Restoration authorities in England;
quite how much interest remains debatable. During the summer of
1676, Randolph noted that 'Goffe the old rebel' was 'still in the country',
and had 'narrowly escaped capture by Major Savage in the southern
parts where he and others are harboured by their anti-monarchical
proselytes'.[47] In July 1677, the Massachusetts agents William Stoughton
and Peter Bulkeley were summoned to Whitehall to respond to
Randolph's observations that Whalley and Goffe had been protected
in Cambridge and Boston in 1660. The agents merely said that they
had no authority to answer, but as private individuals they could
report that the Massachusetts authorities 'had issued warrants for their
arrest as soon as the royal proclamation had been received, but they
had escaped to other colonies'. In other words, they did what the
colonial authorities had been doing for almost two decades: dodging
and dithering.[48]

Randolph never gave up his fixation with the regicides, in the
context of his gripes with Massachusetts Bay, but this was not necessarily a reflection of royal policy. In April 1678 Randolph reported
that Daniel Gookin had harboured the regicides. In October of the

same year, the Massachusetts general court responded to Randolph's accusations by insisting, by this point with some bored irritation, that 'there was no neglect in trying to arrest Goffe and Whalley'. In 1682, Randolph made further accusations against Gookin and said that he would enquire after the 'great stock' Gookin had held for the regicides. In addition, in 1683, Randolph reported that the Massachusetts colonies had received Whalley and Goffe with 'great civility'.[49] Just two months before Charles II's death, Randolph was still trying to discover what had happened in Massachusetts in the early 1660s. Like so many before him, Randolph hit a brick wall: Simon Bradstreet from Boston simply informed him that Whalley and Goffe 'were never hid or secured' there, that warrants for their arrest had been issued as soon as Charles II's proclamation had arrived, and that, if they had been apprehended in Massachusetts, they would 'undoubtedly have been sent prisoners to England'.[50]

Randolph clearly had a keen interest in the regicides and their circumstances in New England. But far from being a concerted attempt by Charles II—through Randolph—actually to find and *capture* the regicides, this was rather a series of gripes about past events in Boston and Cambridge between eighteen and twenty-three years previously—a long-established objection to the freedoms exercised by the Massachusetts Bay colony. As Increase Mather reported in 1687, Randolph was 'well known' for making complaints about the colony, 'because in their lawbook it is declared, if men fly thither, being persecuted, they shall find favour'.[51] Randolph brought a defamation case against Mather for his comments: he lost the case and, subsequently, had to pay costs. Even when Randolph complained to the lords of trade in London about the Massachusetts authorities' protection of Whalley and Goffe in 1660, they considered it 'insignificant'.[52] Randolph was, in effect, merely sniping about events in 1660 rather than making any serious attempt to find the regicides in the 1680s, and there was little or no support from Whitehall, beyond occasionally hearing Randolph's by now irrelevant fulminations.

Hartford

Meanwhile, Increase Mather, with the help of a Hartford minister, Reverend John Whiting, had continued to facilitate Goffe's correspondence. On 8 September 1676, Goffe even wrote to Mather that he 'much desire[d]' to read Mather's *Brief History* of King Philip's War, maybe to see whether his angelic presence merited a mention.[53] Just two days before Randolph's arrival in Boston, Goffe mentioned that it was a 'great comfort' to him that he could still hear from his 'far distant and dear relations'.[54] Nonetheless, he expressed frustration that it was 'difficult to attain any solid intelligence of what is done abroad'. His solution beautifully summarized his predicament both metaphorically and literally: he shut one eye, he said, and peeped through the other, 'through the crevices of my close cell to discern the signs of my Lord's coming'.[55]

By this point Goffe had travelled to Hartford, a town through which the regicides had already passed in the early months of 1661. Samuel Nowell of Charlestown, a chaplain who had been in Hadley in 1675, assisted his move. Goffe now lived with the Bull family—either Thomas Bull or Jonathan, his son—and took the name 'Duffell' (the maiden name of his mother-in-law). Though it is not entirely certain what caused his departure from Hadley, Goffe may have felt it necessary to leave Hadley once he had appeared in public to save its residents. He may simply have become wary of staying in a town like Hadley that was crawling with soldiers during King Philip's War. Or he may have been alarmed by Randolph's appearance in Boston (though Hadley and Hartford were almost equidistant from Boston). Not that Hartford itself was a completely safe haven: Goffe was told that it was difficult to send him money there, because there was not a 'safe hand to convey it'.[56]

In April 1680, John London, a resident of nearby Windsor, testified that he had spotted Goffe at Bull's house in Hartford in May the previous year. London also claimed that Goffe had changed the name 'Duffell' to 'Cooke': the surname, appropriately enough, of Goffe's co-regicide who had led the prosecution of Charles I in 1649, and who had been executed in October 1660. London alleged that the regicide received support from the Bull family through trade and also from goods sent by James Richards of Hartford.[57] He recognized Goffe, he said, because he had known him twenty years previously in England. London claimed that he was intending to kidnap the fugitive. Thomas Powell, one of London's neighbours, learnt of his plan and promised to assist him. But instead Powell took London to the Hartford magistrates John Talcott and John Allen. London himself was arrested swiftly, was not allowed to leave the county without a licence, and was accused of conspiracy against the colony for which he 'deserved to be hanged'.[58] London was able to spread the news that Goffe had been seen in Hartford, though, by slipping away to Boston. From there he rode to Somerset County, Maryland, where he told his brother and a Colonel Colburne in the hope that the news would then be conveyed to England.[59]

It was at this point that two features of the regicides' lives in New England in 1661 reappeared: the first was the fear, communicated to Goffe, that a general governor of New England was to be appointed by Charles II; if this were to happen, Goffe was advised, he should 'judge it convenient to remove' himself from the town.[60] The second was the reappearance of a familiar figure. Governor William Leete, who had been so assiduous in preserving the fugitives' liberty in 1661, once again emerged in the regicide story in 1680. The governor of New York, Sir Edmund Andros, wrote to Leete with news of Goffe having been spotted by London in Hartford. Leete received the letter on 10 June 1680. On the same day he signed a warrant that instructed Hartford's constables to search the town for Goffe. Perhaps Leete had learned the error of his former ways and had now become swift and ruthless in the prosecution of orders to capture the surviving regicide.

Perhaps there is another explanation: Goffe was already dead and Leete knew it. The last letter sent to Goffe—or the last letter we know about—was penned on 30 July 1679. Written by Peter Tilton, who

lived six doors away from Russell in Hadley and who had visited the
regicides frequently, the letter had a curiously final air to it. '*Vale, vale*',
Tilton signed off, echoing the final farewell spoken to the dead at
Roman funerals.[61] He may have suspected that this would indeed be
his final 'farewell' to the regicide. It is possible, even likely, that Goffe
had passed away during the eleven months between this last letter
and Leete's receipt of Andros's orders.[62] Goffe had written as early as
April 1677 that his 'trials' were 'considerable' and that he should be
pitied and remembered in friends' prayers because of his 'weakness'.[63]
This may have been spiritual weakness—the cries of a man now
engaged in a psychological struggle after spending seventeen years
largely incognito. It is more probable, however, that his health was
deteriorating and continued to decline until his death sometime
between August 1679 and June 1680.

With Goffe safely beyond discovery, Leete could assume once more
the mantle of a man assiduous in following due process. The deceased
man would remain undisturbed and Leete could face the Restoration
authorities with a clean bill of health, if not a clear conscience. Leete's
reply to Andros was a disingenuous defence of his colony in which
he attempted to clear it of any wrongdoing, while attacking those
who questioned the loyalty of the people of Hartford. Leete insisted
that they were 'much abused' by the false reports of Goffe's residence
in the town. He asked for the names of the informers who 'acted
under gross mistakes', maybe to 'delude' Andros and 'cast reproach' on
Hartford. The people of Hartford themselves were 'amused that any
such thing' could be suspected of them—amused, perhaps, because
they knew Andros was chasing a ghost.[64]

A paper-chase?

By plotting apparent attempts to capture the regicides after 1660, and
the network of colonists who protected them, an intriguing picture
emerges of colonial administration and its complex dealings with the

British government in London. Efforts by Charles II's government to capture the regicides in America usually amounted to little more than infrequent bursts of rhetorical enthusiasm or vague instructions tacked onto the end of other commissions. Charles II's government had to be *seen* to be doing something about capturing the fleeing regicides; many colonial officials felt the need to be *seen* to be doing something to help. But the veneer covered up the political realities on both sides of the Atlantic.[65]

There was a delicate balance between crown and colonies. The crown realized that it did not have the wherewithal actually to capture the regicides in America; it did not wish to provoke overt colonial disloyalty; nor did it want to disrupt lucrative trade routes by heavy-handedly imposing on them a retributive royal will. The Massachusetts Bay authorities found an effective way to 'spin out' their dealings concerning the regicides as they were preoccupied with their own trade with the Old World and did not want to risk provoking possible retribution from Whitehall that would undermine their independence. Yet they did not wish actually to compromise that independence by bowing to missives from Whitehall or to endanger the godly regicides with whom they had much sympathy. So they paid lip service to the execution of Whitehall's warrants, while putting little effort into measures that might stand a chance of catching the regicides. This was essentially a paper-chase with crown and colonists going through the motions. The former sent letters and declarations across the Atlantic, with little (if any) realistic hope that they would result in the regicides' capture. The latter received the letters and declarations, promulgated them, and acted on them with just sufficient delay and lack of application for the regicides to remain safe.

The New Haven colonial officials could be more brazen in their dealings with Whitehall as they expected little support for their colony from London. They were unapologetic, therefore, in their measures to protect the regicides. The lives of Whalley and Goffe were only in real danger for a short period in May 1661 but even then only two men were assigned to capture them and they were hardly the most determined bounty hunters—they were easily tricked by the colonial authorities and gave up their search almost as soon as it had begun. Even the arrival of Edward Randolph, a man frequently painted as a pantomime villain hell-bent on infringing American liberties, posed little threat to the regicides. He was interested in them and the history of their protection in New England, but his contributions to the 'hunt' were a series of bad-tempered fulminations rather than any meaningful moves to capture them and return them to England.

In essence, because the regicides were in hiding for fifteen or more years, we assume that they were being chased. But the imagined threat to their lives was almost always more serious than the real threat. It is quite possible that they were not captured, not only because of the network of colonists who protected them, but also, as time progressed, because of a lack of enthusiasm and interest from Charles II's government in capturing them. Very few early accounts of the regicides in America refer to William Leete's 'depression', mentioned in a letter from John Norton to Richard Baxter in September 1661—the letter in which Leete might be interpreted as rewriting New Haven history to save himself from retribution by Charles II and his court. This letter might have been considered distinctly impolitic anyway because it reminded the British authorities that Leete and company had been so troublesome in the first place and highlighted the fact that, following a flurry of decrees and letters in 1661, serious interest in capturing Whalley and Goffe had dwindled by September of that year.

Charles II's letter to Massachusetts in June 1662, excepting the regicides and their protectors from pardon and indemnity, was not accompanied by any manpower, while the colonies' evasion and procrastination were met with notable leniency from Charles's government. In effect, that government could not afford to alienate the American colonies and allow them to disrupt England's place in the lucrative trade networks of the Atlantic basin.[66] Thus half-hearted attempts to capture the regicides may have been a tacit admission that trade concerns and cordial relations with the colonial authorities, who were protecting the regicides, took precedence over an ideological witch-hunt. Charles, for the moment at least, was being a pragmatic imperialist keen to exploit trade opportunities and to expand territorial control in the New World. He also had to deal with a complex chain of independent colonial authorities that had been sympathetic towards his great enemy, Oliver Cromwell, in the past. Suspicious, stubborn, jealous of their own autonomy, and separated by 3,000 miles of ocean, they were remote from government communication and control.[67]

In any case, the regicides in America were difficult to find, and any further failed or abortive attempts to capture them would have resulted in further loss of face for the British government. This anxiety might explain the subtle wording of the 1664 commission that 'due inquiry' would be made into the regicides but no arrests made of any protectors; they would be encouraged simply 'to take the more care for their future behaviour'. It might also explain why, in their efforts concerning the regicides, the commissioners only managed to confiscate a bunch of cows. So far, then, we have a much subtler picture than that of a vengeful king sending bloodthirsty agents to America to hunt down the men who had signed his father's death warrant. The manhunt in America was not 'unrelenting'.[68] There were long periods of inactivity for good reason: Charles II and his courtiers were preoccupied with events at home; they realized the complicated realities of colonial governance; they knew previous attempts to capture the fugitives had proved lacklustre and unsuccessful; and perhaps their enthusiasm for revenge had waned. It was one thing to issue directives from Whitehall; it was quite another to put real manpower behind the threats, especially when it became clear that the New England magistrates were old hands at smiling and nodding, agreeing wholeheartedly to the king's face but actually doing very little to capture Whalley and Goffe.

PART II

Afterlives

4

Thomas Hutchinson and the regicides' rediscovery

Shout at the grave...
Triumphant joys that reach the skies.

George Coade, *A Letter to a Clergyman, Relating to*
His Sermon on the 30th of January (1773), 67

Following Goffe's death in 1679—then the death of John Dixwell, the third regicide in America, ten years later—the story of the regicides went unheard beyond the tales told furtively by their friends and supporters in Hadley, Hartford, or New Haven. American history progressed for eighty or so years with little, if any, wider interest in the fugitive signatories of Charles I's death warrant. In 1685 Charles's second surviving son, James, had become the first openly Catholic British monarch since 1558. His short-lived establishment of the Dominion of New England—along with its insensitive royal governor, Sir Edmund Andros, the prospect of whom had exercised Leete so much in the 1660s—pointedly challenged local autonomy in places like Connecticut, Massachusetts, New Hampshire, and Rhode Island. However, the overthrow of James II in the Glorious Revolution of 1688–9 brought an end to this particular brand of encroachment of royal power over the American colonies; more fundamentally, it provided another model for deposing a monarch.

The colonies' economic and political independence was further nurtured during Robert Walpole's tenure as first minister under Kings George I and II (1721–42), which was characterized by a relatively indulgent approach to the territories across the Atlantic. Yet the colonies' crucial role as a theatre of war in the conflict between England and France—the Seven Years' War in Europe and the French and Indian War in America (1754–63)—had more serious consequences. It brought to the fore claims that the British government, in its financial demands on the colonists for their military defence, once again was trespassing on their rights and liberties. The colonists' successes in the war against the French and Native Americans also kindled a sense of self-confident nationalism that would soon be turned against their colonial overlords across the Atlantic. The colonies' assemblies, meanwhile, had been using their power to enact legislation and to vote on taxation and spending, countering the authority of colonial governors, thus setting a course for self-government that would become enshrined in the Declaration of Independence of 1776. It was against this backdrop of increasing colonial self-confidence and burgeoning independence that interest in Whalley and Goffe reawakened.

Forgetting and remembering the regicides

In 1793 the president of Yale College, Ezra Stiles, published his *Poem, Commemorative of Goffe, Whaley, & Dixwell* (1793). Writing under the pseudonym 'Philagathos', he noted that figures like Nathanael Greene and Richard Montgomery, major generals in the American revolutionary war, had been given memorials, while other American heroes had given their names to garrisons: Alexander Hamilton, Henry Knox, Benjamin Franklin, and Thomas Jefferson. 'Yet scarce are mention'd in the historic page', Stiles lamented, 'Thy mother Britain's best-deserving sons'. These sons, who fled from the 'second Charles's rage', were William Goffe, Edward Whalley, and John Dixwell. Stiles was not the only one to perceive this neglect. Aedanus Burke, chief justice of

South Carolina, wrote to Stiles suggesting that subscriptions be requested for the erection of a monument to Whalley, Goffe, and Dixwell which could be placed in front of Yale College to provide 'the youth a good lesson, and conspicuous example, that the fame of great men, who undergo hazards and suffer in the cause of public freedom, is not to perish utterly'.[1]

For Stiles and Burke, the English regicides who had fled to America represented not only the successful fight against Charles I's 'tyranny' in the 1640s but also the effective resistance to Charles II's renewed allegedly 'tyrannical' efforts after 1660. Whalley and Goffe, in particular, were seen as defenders of liberty on both sides of the Atlantic. The implication of Stiles's poem was that the regicides' fame might disappear without a monument, as the names of Whalley, Goffe, and Dixwell were not readily on the tongues of the American Revolutionaries. The Massachusetts delegation to the First Continental Congress in Philadelphia—John Adams, Samuel Adams, Thomas Cushing, and Robert Treat Payne—had made a visit to Dixwell's grave in 1774, yet we should not attach too much weight to this fact. Adams's diary for 17 August of that year suggests that this was only one brief stop on a more extensive tour of New Haven which also took in three congregational meeting houses and the library and chapel at Yale. No ink is spilt lauding Dixwell as one of Adams's heroes. He was more concerned with considering whether the Parliament of Great Britain had any right to legislate in the colonies.[2]

We can garner from the biography of Ezra Stiles, the first man to write a full-length account of the regicides in America, some reasons why they may not have received more attention up to this point. When the regicides were still alive, many colonists judged it prudent not to advertise knowledge of their existence or to inform Royalist agents of their location as they wished to avoid implicating themselves in illegal protection of the fugitives. This secrecy continued into the eighteenth century, observed Stiles's biographer, because the regicides' 'ashes [were] liable to violation' if they were discovered. Any detailed and open research into the regicides was described as 'impracticable'.

Very little had been committed to paper; 'The select few, to whom the secret was originally entrusted, handed it down with singular care, by verbal tradition'.[3]

It was a little odd, then, for Stiles to complain under the pseudonym 'Philagathos' that the regicides had not yet been commemorated publicly—few people would have known or would have openly admitted to knowing who Whalley, Goffe, and Dixwell were. This was not a simple case of neglect: it was a combination of ignorance, feigned ignorance, and covertness. In the aftermath of the American Revolution, though, 'the graves of the enemies of tyrants were sure of protection, if not of veneration', so 'the difficulty of obtaining the history of these judges became sensibly diminished'.[4] The argument went, then, that a full and open account of the regicides in America could not be written safely until after the Revolution.

Thomas Hutchinson's 'lesson in obedience'

Reading Stiles's biography, we might be tempted to think that he was the first to 'rediscover' the regicides in America after their disappearance from public memory. His biographer had a hagiographical interest in promoting his subject's originality. Yet in fact there had already been interest in the regicides decades before the publication of Stiles's poem or his *History of Three of the Judges of Charles I* (1794). In the years running up to the American Revolution, material about the regicides on the run in New England was collected and printed. Much of this information focused on events in 1661. In 1769, for example, came the publication of the report made to Governor Endecott by the Royalist agents Kellond and Kirke that gave a precise account of their pursuit of the regicides in the summer of 1661. Readers in the late 1760s would learn of Kellond and Kirke's departure from Boston on 7 May 1661; their arrival in Hartford on 10 May; their meeting with Governor Winthrop; their first encounter with Deputy Governor Leete on 11 May; their reports about the protection of the fugitives in New Haven by

Davenport and Jones; and the humiliating treatment suffered at the hands of Leete. Also available in print in 1769 were two letters to William Leete: the first from 4 July 1661 informing him that 'the non attendance with diligence to execute the King's majesty's warrant for the apprehending of Colonel Whaley and Goffe will much hazard the present state of these colonies', and the second about the public appearance in New Haven of Whalley and Goffe. Furthermore, in 1769 readers could peruse the Declaration of the Commissioners of the United Colonies about the fugitives, signed at Hartford on 5 September 1661, which stated publicly that 'all such person or persons, that since the publication of his Majesties order have wittingly and willingly entertained or harboured... Whalley and Goffe, or hereafter shall do the like, have and will incur his Majesty's highest displeasure'.[5]

Two years later, *A Chronological Table of the Most Remarkable Events in the Province of the Massachusetts-Bay, from the Year 1602 ... to the Year 1770* (1771) included incidents relating to Charles I and the regicides. In 1634, it was noted, Charles I had prevented troublesome MPs—John Pym, John Hampden, Arthur Haselrig, and Oliver Cromwell—from travelling to New England. Even more significant for our purpose here was the table of 'remarkable events' which included the arrival of Whalley and Goffe in America, their concealment outside New Haven, their residence in Hadley, and the appearance of the 'deliverer of Hadley', Goffe.[6]

It was the loyalist Thomas Hutchinson, lieutenant governor and later governor of the Province of Massachusetts Bay, author of *The History of the Colony of Massachusetts-Bay* (1764), who had described the story of the regicides, which had then inspired much of this material.[7] 'The story of these persons has never yet been published to the world', Hutchinson declared. Yet Hutchinson had an interest in how Whalley and Goffe—and their protectors—were portrayed. From their first appearance on the printed page, the regicides in America became political pawns whose story was filtered according to the agenda of the author telling that story. Once the Mather library papers—including Goffe's diary—had been scattered or destroyed at the time of the Stamp Act in 1765, Hutchinson's account of the fugitives became the principal source for the regicides' time in America. Hutchinson took advantage of this short-lived print monopoly (there were contrasting oral histories, as we shall see) to fashion 'a lesson in obedience' and 'to quell resistance to king, Parliament and his own authority'.[8] Hutchinson was loyal to George III in the same way, he tried to argue, that New England colonists had been loyal to the Stuart monarchy.

Hutchinson had his own political troubles in mind when delivering his lesson on Whalley and Goffe. By the time the first volume of his *History* had been published, Hutchinson was becoming increasingly alienated from what has been called the 'liberating, meliorating, freshening spirit of the time'—a spirit embodied by James Otis in the 1761 Writs of Assistance case.[9] Great Britain had been granting writs to customs officers that allowed them to search property at their own whim without taking any responsibility for damage caused during the search. Such writs expired on the king's death; so George II's death in October 1760 provided an opportunity for Otis to challenge the writs as a violation of the British constitution, of Magna Carta, of natural law, and of the colonists' rights as British subjects. John Adams enthusiastically—if romantically—suggested that 'then and there the child Independence was born'.[10] Hutchinson disagreed with Otis's view of the writs. At the same time, he was mulling over the seventeenth century, the regicides in America, and the historical relationship between crown and colonies. As one commentator puts it, 'if seventeenth-century New Englanders...could support the right of the king to seize the regicides, Hutchinson's contemporaries needed to grant *their* king the right to issue writs for the seizure of contraband from New England warehouses'; 'the Puritans of the 1660s and 1670s became the antecedents of conservative and loyal whigs a century later'.[11]

Hutchinson therefore portrayed the regicides as individuals with few friends in the colonies and described them as men suffering wretchedly for their crimes in the 1640s and 1650s. 'They were in constant terror', he noted, 'their lives were miserable and constant burdens'. They were not Puritan heroes keeping alive the values of the English Republic among disloyal colonists by evading the Stuart authorities, but miserable fugitives hiding from strangers who would happily claim their bounty and return the regicides to London to face justice.[12] Peter Oliver, one of Hutchinson's loyalist contemporaries, concurred with him and called Hutchinson a man with 'an acumen of genius united with a solidity of judgment and great regularity of manners'. Oliver, former chief justice of the superior court of Massachusetts Bay and one of the judges in the trial after the Boston Massacre of 1770, argued that Goffe 'chose to breathe away a wearisome existence in the lonely hermitage of a dreary wilderness'; there was more of the 'enthusiast' in Goffe's diary, he claimed, than the 'great man'.[13]

In essence, Hutchinson was trying to excuse his colonial predecessors from complicity in the shelter of criminals and to give the impression that they were loyal to the crown in the seventeenth century, just as his contemporaries were in the eighteenth. For a start, Hutchinson argued, Whalley and Goffe were not 'among the most obnoxious' of Charles I's judges. This assertion, however, demonstrates ignorance, wilful or otherwise, of the events of the late 1640s and especially Goffe's hostile behaviour towards Charles I at the Putney Debates and at the Windsor Prayer Meeting. Furthermore, Hutchinson noted, the regicides 'appeared grave, serious and devout, and the rank they had sustained commanded respect'. Who could blame the Massachusetts Bay authorities, then, for welcoming the regicides so warmly? This warm reception, Hutchinson continued, was not 'any contempt of the authority in England'. Even though Whalley and Goffe were known to have been two of his father's judges, Charles II had not yet been proclaimed king 'when the ship that brought them left London'. This was also wishful thinking on Hutchinson's part: warmly welcoming Whalley and Goffe was a tacit—or not-so-tacit—snub to the Stuart dynasty, whether or not Charles had been proclaimed. There had already been rumours circulating in New England about the fall of the English Republic.[14] In any case, why, the colonists might have wondered, were Whalley and Goffe in New England instead of safely ensconced at home? Because, as the regicides surely would have informed them, the king was returning.

Moreover, Hutchinson claimed, it was thought in Massachusetts that only seven regicides would be put on trial and it was not until the end of November 1660 that the colonies received the news that Whalley and Goffe were excluded from the Act of Indemnity and Oblivion. While Hutchinson admitted that there were those in Boston who would 'stand by' the regicides and offer them 'pity and compassion', he preferred to hail those who were not loyal to Whalley and Goffe and who actively sought to capture them. He wrote of the information conveyed to London by Thomas Bredon, the 'hue and cry' that went up in the colonies to detain the regicides, and the warrant dated 8 March 1661 to secure them. Following the royal mandate of 5 March, Hutchinson insisted, 'there is no doubt that the court were now in earnest in their endeavours to apprehend them'. Kellond and Kirke were appointed to capture Whalley and Goffe, Hutchinson noted, as he attempted with a certain degree of desperation to demonstrate the historical loyalty of the Massachusetts Bay colonists to their British overlords: the colony had not surrendered its charter to England in 1638 and it did not expect to do so in subsequent years as no one was causing a fuss; the colonists had not proclaimed Charles II king in 1660 merely because, Hutchinson claimed, they did not know the appropriate ceremonial protocol.[15]

Hutchinson gave less attention to the behaviour of the New Haven magistrates. Admittedly, he was writing the history of Massachusetts Bay, yet he made a curious decision in his account of the regicides to gloss over the behaviour of William Leete and the lack of assistance extended to Kellond and Kirke at the point when Whalley and Goffe were closest to discovery and capture. His history, in fact, relegated the fugitives' treatment in New Haven to a footnote and mentioned Leete only cursorily, when Whalley and Goffe appeared openly in New Haven ostensibly to surrender on 22 June 1661: 'They let the deputy governor Mr Leete know where they were, but he took no measures to secure them'.[16]

Hutchinson also tried to redeem the colonists by pointing out that few of them were willing to aid and abet the regicides' flight: in New Haven, he argued, they remained undiscovered 'by the fidelity of their three friends'. Hutchinson himself listed four names—John Davenport, William Jones, Richard Sperry, and another farmer named Burrill—but overlooked other highly placed men like William Leete and Matthew Gilbert who were crucial to their protection. After Whalley and Goffe had moved to Hadley, Hutchinson claimed, 'very few persons in the colony' knew about their presence. Furthermore, Hutchinson was keen to mention that those who had once entertained the fugitives later repented, thought they had left America, or simply did not know where Whalley and Goffe had gone. Mr Mitchell of Cambridge, who fraternized with Whalley and Goffe on their arrival in America in 1660, later reflected, 'Since I have had opportunity by reading and discourse to look a little into that action for which these men suffer [the trial and execution of Charles I] I could never see that it was justifiable'. Governors Endecott and Bradstreet claimed, respectively, that Whalley and Goffe 'went towards the Dutch at Manhadoes and took shipping for Holland' and that 'after their being at New-Haven he could never hear what became of them'.[17] Hutchinson did not point out that these alleged penitents were very few among the wider network of individuals who had protected the regicides. Nor does he consider the possibility that Mitchell, Endecott, and Bradstreet were covering their backs and trying to avoid retribution from London either by expressing repentance or by feigning ignorance.

It was no accident that Hutchinson printed the August 1661 declaration of loyalty from the colony of Massachusetts Bay to Charles II above the footnote that contained the story of the regicides on the run:

FORASMUCH as Charles the second is undoubted King of Great Britain and all other his Majesty's territories and dominions thereunto belonging, and hath been some time since lawfully proclaimed and crowned accordingly: we therefore do, as in duty we are bound, own and acknowledge him to be our sovereign lord and King, and do

therefore hereby proclaim and declare his sacred Majesty Charles the
second to be lawful King of Great Britain, France and Ireland, and all
other the territories thereunto belonging. God save the King.

In response to Hutchinson's *History*, a wag contributor to the *Boston
Gazette and Country Journal* of 20 November 1769 wrote a letter
from the long-dead Whalley and Goffe, on 'the 30th of October. We
had almost said the 30th of January': 'We mean soon to send a letter
to a late historian, to set him right, *if he inclines to be set right*, in
regard to some transactions in our day, which have been greatly
misrepresented to the world'. The letter left blanks instead of nam-
ing Hutchinson outright but readers knew the figure in question
and annotated their copies accordingly. Hutchinson has been described
as 'the most hated man in all of North America' in the late eighteenth
century; his treatment of Whalley and Goffe may have helped to set
him on that course.[18]

Commemoration and sedition

The Boston Gazette's contributor wrote 'We had almost said the 30th
of January' because that was the date of Charles I's execution, and by
invoking this date they brought to the fore a key reason why the
regicide, and regicides, remained a recurring feature of American
life—but not necessarily in a way that Hutchinson would have supported. That date was now supposed to be marked each year by a day
of contrition and humiliation. In 1662 a statute was passed in essence
stating that 'every thirtieth of January shall be set apart to be observed
in all the churches in England and Ireland, and Wales as an anniversary
of fasting and humiliation'.[19] The statute also pointed to 'all your
majesty's dominions', including those colonies across the Atlantic.
Virginia, for example, set aside 30 January as a fast day so that 'our sor-
rows may expiate our crimes and our tears wash away our guilt'.[20] The
date also provided opportunities for 30 January sermons to lament
former disobedience and reflect on current disloyalty to the monarch.

Ezra Stiles noted, for example, that 30 January sermons were preached at the Episcopalian Trinity Church, Newport, Rhode Island, until 1769.[21]

There was also an interest in the American colonies in printing 30 January sermons that had originally been preached in England. Charles Moss's sermon of 30 January 1769 was delivered at Westminster in London before later being printed by Joseph Crukshank in Philadelphia. This sermon was read against the backdrop of colonial affairs as an anti-rebellion, anti-revolutionary treatise. 'Domestic union', it argued, 'was never more ardently to be wished than at present, when our fellow-subjects in the New World have been withdrawing their affections and their duty from their mother country'.[22] True to its 30 January roots, Moss's sermon contained an implied warning that affection and loyalty to the king could be withdrawn, just as it had been in the 1640s. Charles's character was attacked in 1750, for example, prompting Boston Episcopalians to respond with a series of contributions to the *Boston Evening Post*. Traducing Charles's reputation and celebrating his execution, one argued, was a threat to episcopacy and monarchy, and a 'great danger of the state'.[23] In New England, however, there were very few Episcopalians: they constituted about 0.2 per cent of the population c. 1700, rising to approximately four per cent by the 1770s.[24]

Crucially, not everyone lamented rebellion or remembered Charles I with a tear in their eye, and the commemoration sermons only proved provocative to those who looked back to the regicide with admiration. Puritans especially were less predisposed than Episcopalians to follow the rulings of Anglican monarchs and bishops, including those concerning the executed king who was now fashioned as 'King Charles the Martyr'. Puritan America, in contrast, was inclined to view the 30 January commemoration with hostility rather than enthusiasm, and they looked to their seventeenth-century history with pride in their ancestors' actions against the crown: many Puritans had emigrated to America in the first place because of antipathy to the Stuarts; during the 1640s and 1650s, American Puritans, especially in New England, sympathized with the Parliamentary cause, the regicide, the Commonwealth, and the Protectorate; in 1650 John Cotton preached to his Boston congregation and justified Charles I's execution in the context of the civil wars; regicide fitted the end-of-the-world-view of Congregationalists who saw it as a precursor to the advent of Christ's Kingdom; Puritan colonists regarded Oliver Cromwell with respect and affection because they considered him to be doing God's work; then John Endecott in the 1650s paid Cromwell what he called an 'anniversary acknowledgement of our obligation', an ironic precursor to the annual act of commemoration that would soon take place for Charles I.[25]

The problematic and contentious nature of remembering regicide and regicides in sermons would persist in America for at least 150 years. When the Restoration authorities tried to introduce the 30 January commemoration across the Atlantic, it was in Massachusetts that one of the most dramatic examples of resistance occurred. Waite Winthrop—member of the Massachusetts governor's council and major general in the Massachusetts militia—called in the warrant which gave instructions for the January observation and 'suppressed' it. New Hampshire, too, in 1684 saw resistance to the royal commemoration. Furthermore, in 1688 when the sheriff of Suffolk County and the constables of Boston were instructed to enforce the 30 January statute, riots ensued.[26] In 1708 the Puritan Samuel Sewall was given the almanac of Edward Holyoke, future president of Harvard, in which the 30 January fast had simply been crossed out.[27]

This sedition was also reflected in American colonists' interest in subversive 'commemorations' of the regicide back in England. James Peirce's sermon, preached at Exeter on 30 January 1717, was printed in Boston around a decade after its original delivery.[28] It is no wonder that Boston readers would have been interested in Peirce's sentiments, as he questioned the validity of the 30 January sermon as a whole. Though Peirce was by no means a republican, some of his ideas would feed into American revolutionary theories about opposition to tyrants. Peirce expressed dissatisfaction with the essential premises and assumptions behind the commemoration, reflecting the complexities involved in remembering the death of Charles I: such 'remembering' revisited painful debates over whether it was treasonable in 1649 to execute a king who had shed the blood of his own subjects.[29] If Peirce were compelled to commemorate the day, then he would do it in his own subversive manner. Peirce's first complaint was with the notion that he and his congregation were complicit in regicide and should therefore lie prostrate in humble penitence. 'The curse is causeless', he argued, 'when the person against whom 'tis levelled is innocent'.[30]

This would have had some resonance with residents of Boston, about eighty years and a few thousand miles removed from the regicide. The people who *were* complicit in Charles's death were those who 'put the king upon invading the rights of his subjects'.[31] Peirce shifted attention to Charles's evil counsellors, while still implicating the king in the infringement of his subjects' liberties. Parliament, he continued, was the 'bulwark of our civil liberties, against the encroachments of an arbitrary power'; 'it was the duty of...subjects to stand by them and defend them' against 'the arbitrary power of our kings'.[32] Kings were to be obeyed, but resisted when they became tyrants.[33] Peirce's sermon was 'earnestly desir'd by many of the hearers to...appear in the world',[34] which it did, quite literally, when Bennet Love, a Boston bookseller, had it printed in the New World.

'Unkinging' kings

Jonathan Mayhew adopted similar ideas in 1750 in the West Meeting House in Boston, in a sermon that has become one of the most celebrated from the colonial period. Mayhew was moved to challenge the 'slavish doctrine of passive obedience and non-resistance' which was usually 'warmly asserted' in 30 January sermons,[35] and he addressed the central issue of national culpability. 30 January was meant to be a day of national, indeed international, penitence. In contrast, Mayhew argued that the rebellion and regicide—if they could even be given those terms—were not 'national' acts. Furthermore, they had little to do with mid-eighteenth-century America: descendants of so-called 'rebels' could not be implicated in their ancestors' crimes, especially if they were not crimes in the first place. God's 'permission of providence' permitted civil rulers to govern, he argued, and obedience to them was necessary when they worked for 'the good of society'. But there were limits to this obedience: 'when humble remonstrances fail...and when the public welfare cannot be otherwise provided for and secured', subjects should 'rise unanimously even against the sovereign himself...to vindicate their natural and legal rights'.[36] This had been the case, Mayhew implied, under Charles I, a ruler who was 'a terror to good works' and who had acted 'directly counter to the sole end and design of [his] office'.[37] The doctrine of non-resistance to 'hereditary, indefeasible, divine right' kings was 'fabulous and chimerical'.[38] Nations had the right to resist and, if necessary, dethrone their monarch to vindicate 'their liberties and just rights'.[39]

From this perspective it was nonsensical to Mayhew that every January people continued to regard Charles I with 'warmth and zeal' and to view the regicides with contempt.[40] Charles had paid 'no regard to the constitution and the laws of the kingdom'; he had a 'natural lust for power'; he employed 'wicked counsellors', including the 'fiend' Archbishop Laud; he raised taxes 'without the consent of Parliament'; and he contravened his coronation oath by 'assuming a power above the laws'.[41] Thus, Mayhew argued, Charles had become a tyrant, 'unkinged himself', and 'forfeited his title to the allegiance of the people'. The 1640s, therefore, technically had not witnessed a rebellion against a *king*; the regicide was not actually *regicide*, and Mayhew was unsure if it even counted as murder.[42] So Mayhew issued a fundamental challenge to the 30 January commemoration: Charles could not be a martyred king if he were neither king nor martyr. Mayhew's sermon became famous because his theory of limited submission was applied to the American Revolution. His arguments about the withdrawal of loyalty to 'unkinged' tyrants were used against George III, two decades after the sermon's original delivery. John Adams viewed Mayhew as a 'prime mover' for American liberty.[43]

'If the orators on the 4th of July really wish to investigate the principles and feelings which produced the Revolution', Adams argued, 'they ought to study . . . Dr Mayhew's sermon'.[44]

This provocative and ultimately revolutionary sermon was prompted by the annual ceremony of a conservative and fawning 30 January commemoration. Interest in the revolutionary concept of regicide persisted because Americans were obliged by statute to think about the act every January. Nevertheless, the conservative nature of the 30 January sermon could provoke reactions very different from those that were intended; the very foundations of the sermons were challenged and these challenges could prompt revolutionary ideas. Ritualized grief had been exported over 3,000 miles to British Americans, many of whom would rather celebrate than lament Charles I's demise. On 30 January 1766, for example, a crowd of several hundred people assembled in Marblehead, Massachusetts and set fire to effigies of English MPs. They demonstrated that the day could be used for rebellious gestures against the mother country rather than humble contemplation of the heinous act of killing a king. And many took the opportunity, when invited to meditate publicly on the regicide, to do so with delight. Fast days, by the 1770s, were viewed by Thomas Gage, a British army officer stationed in America, as 'an opportunity for sedition to flow from the pulpit'.[45]

In New York in 1773 there appeared a sermon from the 1740s in which the Exeter merchant George Coade had responded 'to all the sermons that ever have been, or ever shall be, preached' on 30 January.[46] His pamphlet was initially a reply to a sermon delivered by Bishop Benjamin Hoadly at Westminster on 30 January 1721 and it was first published in England in 1747. The Library of Congress copy of Coade's treatise has the annotation 'Jonathan Hedges His Book 1773', which suggests that it was being purchased and read in the years preceding the American Revolution. Coade, like the other preachers and writers discussed above, had heard and read many 30 January sermons and felt moved to counter their claims. He shook the very foundations of those sermons by declaring that Charles was 'a staunch bigot';

he infringed 'the rights of his subjects' and violated 'the fundamental laws of the realm'; he used his 'despotic power against the constitution'; he 'declared his encouragement of Popery'; he treated MPs in a way which was 'illegal and arbitrary'; and he raised money without the 'consent or authority of Parliament'.[47] Because of these despotic actions (and more), Coade noted that 'a multitude of people began to take refuge in . . . foreign plantations'.[48] The descendants of these refugees were now buying and reading Coade's views on the monarch who had driven their forefathers away and whose memory they were compelled to remember with remorse and humiliation. Coade's response to the 30 January sermons pre-dated Mayhew's more famous treatise but its central premise was the same: if the prince subverted the constitution, if he violated the fundamental laws of the nation, then he forfeited his office—he *unkinged* himself—and could be resisted and deposed.[49]

As the New York publication of Coade's pamphlet showed, discussions of loyalty to an allegedly tyrannical king and parallels between Charles I and George III became especially relevant in the 1770s. During this decade Charles I did not just feature as a villain in colonial sermons on 30 January: he became an all-year-round *bête noire*. For example, John Allen's sermon from 3 December 1772, at the Second Baptist Church of Boston, went to seven printings and five editions within two years. Its dedication claimed that Charles's 'violat[ion of] the people's rights' cost him his life. Allen, in the sermon itself, maintained that Charles had fallen 'into the hands of wicked men'. Following their love of liberty inscribed in Magna Carta, 'people and Parliament' fought against Charles and demonstrated that they 'rever'd their rights and liberties, above his life, power and prerogative'. Allen included a barely disguised threat that any monarch acting like Charles I—under the influence of evil counsellors— would suffer a similar fate.[50] Abraham Keteltas, on 5 October 1777, at the First Presbyterian Church of Newburyport, Massachusetts, invoked the British tradition of standing up to tyrants, including Charles I, who had 'invaded the rights of his people'.[51] Other pamphlets published in America made a direct comparison between George III and Charles I. In a satirical dialogue between George and the Devil, the Devil suggested that the king's subjects' desire for liberty could 'blast' his great designs, 'as happened to . . . Charles'.[52]

Loyalty and disloyalty

Even those 30 January sermons that purported to be loyal were not necessarily straightforward in their praise of Charles I. Charles Inglis, rector of Trinity Church, New York, took a conventional text for his commemoration sermon in 1780: 'Fear God. Honour the King'.[53] There was much in the sermon that was predictable considering Inglis's loyalist stance in the wake of the American Revolution: 'there must be some who preside', he preached, 'and others, over whom that presidency is exercised'.[54] Subjects, therefore, were obliged to respect the authority of monarchs, to obey their laws, and to support their peaceful and stable reign.[55] Yet it took Inglis half an hour to mention Charles I in a sermon commemorating the king's martyr- dom. When he eventually mentioned the name of the king whose sacrifice he was meant to be remembering, Inglis deliberately chose not to give a detailed account of the 'rise, progress and effects' of the civil wars.[56] Inglis may have been more concerned to discuss immediate political events in colonial America; perhaps it was more important to pay reverence to the congregation or to implore them to be more religious, as was happening in eighteenth-century 30 January sermons in England.[57] Most likely, Inglis was avoiding reopening the debate about Charles's role in the 'rise' and 'progress' of the civil wars.[58] Among the colonists the general view of the civil wars and regicide centred on a king infringing the liberties of his subjects, either of his own volition or at the behest of evil counsel- lors. Either way, invoking the reasons for his execution reopened the uncomfortable question of why Charles had been executed in the first place.

By 1780, Inglis noted, the obligation to mark Charles's martyrdom had been 'disregarded by some people'.[59] Indeed, in 1770 Ezra Stiles had expected that there would be a 30 January sermon at Trinity Church, Newport, just as there had been in previous years. But, he noted, George Bisset, assistant minister at Trinity, 'declined and omitted it this day'.[60] Stiles was not upset by the omission. He argued that 30 January 'ought to be celebrated as an anniversary thanksgiving', not of a king but of a nation that 'had so much fortitude and public justice, as to make a royal tyrant bow to the sovereignty of the people'. Stiles proceeded to list Charles's crimes: ruling without Parliament; forcing loans; imposing harsh fines and arbitrary imprisonments; promoting Archbishop Laud, 'that scourge of justice, religion and humanity'; and placing the colonies under 'episcopal and military government'. In short, Stiles was questioning why anyone should commemorate the 'martyrdom' of a king who had 'established maxims of civil and religious polity utterly subversive of all the principles of Runnymede [Magna Carta] liberty and the English constitution'. Through his own policies, the 'despotic deluded' Charles had forfeited his throne, and his life, to his people.[61]

5

Ezra Stiles, the regicides, and the American Revolution

The root of all bitterness...was the unhappy rebellion in England, against the noble prince...King Charles the First. The virulent ferment of that measure excited the seeds that were sown before, and hereby an anti-monarchical spirit, and prejudice against the king, his person and government, became so strongly rooted in the country as not to be easily or speedily, if ever, totally eradicated.

Gershom Bulkeley, *Bulkeley's Will and Doom, or the Miseries of Connecticut by and under an Usurped and Arbitrary Power* (1692)[1]

Between the Declaration of Independence, the military defeat of the British in 1783, and the publication of the first full-length study of the regicides in America in 1794, America was preoccupied with taking its first steps as an independent nation. This independence had come about through a potent combination of imperial misman-agement, complaints about trade, grievances concerning colonial taxation without representation in Parliament, ideologies promoting individual freedoms and rights and the overthrow of 'tyrannical' rulers, and a deepening sense of national 'American' consciousness. The shackles of George III's rule had been shaken off, just as Charles I's and James II's had been in Britain the previous century. But this political *carte blanche* soon became overwritten with debates over America's social, economic, political, cultural, and diplomatic future.

The Constitutional Convention of 1787 betrayed disagreements over the share of power between the nation, the locality, and the individual. The most appropriate transition from monarchy to republic varied according to different commentators. Also open to conflicting interpretations was America's recent history, with the blame for British imperial tyranny sometimes laid squarely at the feet of the king, and sometimes at those of his Parliament. From these debates about America's past, present, and future arose Ezra Stiles's *History of Three of the Judges of Charles I* (1794)—a mix of political philosophy, historical research, gossip, and myth—the eccentricity of which appropriately reflected the excited and sometimes contradictory rediscovery of Whalley and Goffe in the eighteenth century.

Considering Ezra Stiles's strongly critical view of Charles I and the 30 January commemorations, it makes sense that he was the author of the first full-length study of the regicides in America. Stiles spent several years researching his book, began writing it in January 1793, finished it that April, then published it in 1794—exactly three decades after Whalley, Goffe, and Dixwell had appeared in the first volume of Hutchinson's *History of Massachusetts-Bay*. Stiles's work was not the first response to Hutchinson, but it certainly became the most comprehensive. His approach to the regicides and the colonists who protected them was very different from Hutchinson's. Once again the story of Whalley, Goffe, and Dixwell was interpreted through a personal ideological lens, and Stiles did so to re-explain the loyalties of seventeenth-century colonists and to place the regicides among the American and French revolutionaries of the late eighteenth century. While Hutchinson saw the regicides as miserable outcasts and strangers among a vast majority of colonists loyal to the crown, Stiles portrayed them as 'martyrs of freedom', heroes, and proto-revolutionaries in colonies sympathetic to their brand of rebellion.[2]

Stiles was convinced that Hutchinson could not have offered his readers the full story of the regicides because he had relied on incomplete documentary evidence. The clandestine nature of the regicides' existence in America would not have lent itself to an extensive and complete paper trail. Furthermore, Hutchinson's focus on the *History of Massachusetts-Bay* would have allowed him to ignore much of William Leete's behaviour and to gloss over the regicides' friends in other colonies. Stiles himself could not make use of much documentary evidence about the regicides because so much of it had been destroyed or dispersed when Hutchinson's house was ransacked in 1765. Stiles's response was to embark on a different kind of research by visiting as many places related to the regicides as possible and meeting as many of their friends' descendants as he could. By employing the methodology of oral history, Stiles was able to gather more information than his predecessor and to shift the interpretative focus from Hutchinson's allegedly loyalist Boston towards the more troublesome and proto-republican New Haven.[3] Yet it was a notoriously difficult approach that perhaps gave undue prominence to misremembered 'facts', folk myths, or individuals who self-servingly and inappropriately exaggerated their ancestors' roles in the regicides' story.

Ezra Stiles's regicide myths

One commentator has summarized *A History of Three of the Judges of Charles I* as 'Stiles at his worst...a tedious hodgepodge of fact and fancy, compounded mainly out of dim recollections by old men and women of things their grandfathers had told them fifty years before'.[4] On 16 July 1785, for example, Stiles met Captain Tim Bradly of Woodbridge, who as a boy had lived with the son of Richard Sperry, the owner of the farm near West Rock just outside New Haven, where the regicides had sheltered in 1661. Richard Sperry's son had often told Bradly the story of the regicides and the location of the Judges Cave near to the Sperry farm. Stiles was shown the remains of the old Sperry farmhouse where he noted the ruins of its chimney and cellar. Two days later, Stiles visited Joseph Sperry who told him more about the 'traditions of the regicides' and directed him to a cave about half a mile from Sperry's house. He noted, however, that Sperry's story was not 'sufficiently discriminative' to provide a full account of the regicides' movements, so he tried to piece together what he could: Whalley and Goffe had fled from New Haven, first to Richard Sperry's house, then to a 'thicket of woods and wilderness behind the mountain'. Sperry would occasionally entertain the fugitives in his house, until 'one day or night some persons riding up to the house', who were thought to be enemies, caused the regicides to flee to some nearby woods and then to the cave atop West Rock. There was some talk, too, of their residing at a '*lodge* and *fort* four miles distant northwest' and at 'a rivulet in Meriden' twenty miles from New Haven.[5]

It was Stiles who was in large part responsible for the early myth-making that emerged in the regicides' story. A number of factors conspired to create these myths about the regicides. First, Stiles relied heavily on oral tradition in the towns where Whalley and Goffe had once resided, and spoke to families who were keen to associate their forebears, whether accurately or inaccurately, with the regicides. These families had received stories of the two men and had handed them down in a narrative chain with each link adding embellishments and distortions. By the time Stiles got to hear them, these tales had been circulating for over a century. Second, so much of the regicides' story in New England was, and is, incomplete and obscure. The myths of the regicides originated from a time long before more detailed discoveries about the regicides came to light: so little was known about their time in New England that something had to be put in its place. This lack of certainty, therefore, left plenty of scope for writers to indulge their imaginations and fill the vacuum provided by historical obscurity.

Third, the regicides became key historical figures in the birth of modern America: they had fought for liberty and, in turn, had received protection from the forerunners of the American Revolution who had guaranteed the regicides' own personal liberty. Such an unsubtle narrative works best if Whalley and Goffe are credited with swash-buckling heroic deeds and spells of intense danger, rather than the real story of prolonged periods of spiritual introspection, boredom, cold, and survival through handouts and a little trade. We can never know for sure whether all the features of the regicide myths have a basis in reality; so we need to test the veracity of the details by comparing their likelihood to our more concrete knowledge of Whalley and Goffe, their movements, and their personalities.

At least three of Stiles's myths concern Kellond and Kirke's pursuit of the regicides to New Haven, an episode replete with opportunities for dramatic embellishment as it was the point at which the regicides were closest to being captured. Whalley and Goffe were in New Haven between March and August 1661. Kellond and Kirke were sent to pursue and capture them in May and they travelled from Boston through Hartford and Guilford. Deputy Governor Leete delayed them; and they arrived in New Haven on 13 May. On the day Kellond and Kirke were due to arrive, one story in Stiles's *History* goes, Whalley and Goffe had gone for a walk to the 'neck bridge' which Kellond and Kirke would have to cross if they were to enter New Haven. According to the story, the town sheriff (a Mr Kimberly), eager to arrest them, overtook them 'with a warrant to apprehend them' but, somewhat laughably, the regicides hid behind a tree, before defending themselves 'with their cudgels', because they were 'expert at fencing'. While Kimberly ran away to get back-up, the regicides ran off into the woods.[6]

The story, however, does not tally with our knowledge of actual events and common sense. Leete's successful attempt to delay Kellond and Kirke's arrival in New Haven had given Whalley and Goffe plenty of time to leave. It is true that they may have waited until 13 May (a Monday) to avoid travelling on the Sabbath. But if they were to leave on that day, they would have left as early and discreetly as possible without choosing to walk brazenly across a major route into New Haven. We also have no evidence that the New Haven magistrates had already issued a warrant for the regicides' apprehension. In fact, they delayed matters until 17 May, by which time Whalley and Goffe were long gone and Kellond and Kirke had given up the chase. Whalley and Goffe are sometimes viewed as warlike figures, principally because they

had held the title of 'major general' and had fought with distinction
in the English civil wars. It is easy to assume, therefore, that they were
fencing experts, swinging their cudgels with devastating effect. But a
brief perusal of Goffe's diary (see Appendix III) suggests that the
regicides' concerns were spiritual now rather than military. Finally, we
know that William Jones of New Haven accompanied Whalley and
Goffe from Westville to their cave at West Rock on 15 May. It is rea-
sonable to suppose, therefore, that Jones would have assisted them
in their journey from New Haven to Westville two days earlier. No
mention of Jones is made in the Kimberly myth.

The regicides' absence from New Haven during Kellond and Kirke's
search of the town undermines the veracity of two other myths. The
first relates to 13 May 1661, when the agents approached the town and,
about a mile from New Haven, allegedly passed over the aforemen-
tioned 'neck bridge' under which Whalley and Goffe were now hiding.[7]
The close proximity of hunters and hunted makes for a tense and
dramatic episode but this part of the story is only credible if we make
two assumptions. First, that the regicides were still in New Haven and
had not left the town earlier than this, as soon as news of the royal
commissioners' impending arrival became known. And, second, that
Whalley and Goffe stayed on main thoroughfares, despite the likelihood of encountering Kellond and Kirke travelling in the opposite
direction. The regicides may not indeed have had many, if any, alternative roads on which to travel. But this view does require us to believe
that both commissioners and regicides were following somewhat
contorted routes to their destinations. The regicides would have travelled west from New Haven to Westville while the commissioners
were travelling west from Guilford to New Haven: their paths need
not have met at all. Ezra Stiles suggests that the only time of day that
the regicides could have hidden under the bridge, without drowning
in up to eight feet of water, would have been noon,[8] which would
also have been a sensible time for Kellond and Kirke to be crossing
the bridge, after travelling nearly twenty miles from Guilford that
morning. But it is an unlikely time for the regicides to be leaving

New Haven, when they knew that the royal commissioners were on their way. As early as 1831, it was noted that accounts of the bridge myth were 'extremely contradictory'.[9]

Even more improbable is the section of the myth that has the regicides returning to New Haven that night to go back to William Jones's house. According to tradition, this was 'a preconcerted and contrived business, to show that the magistrates at New Haven had used their endeavours to apprehend them before the arrival of the pursuers'.[10] Quite why Whalley and Goffe hiding under a bridge would have exonerated the New Haven magistrates from their deliberate inability to catch the regicides is unclear. Also, the magistrates must have known that Kellond and Kirke would wish to search the town, in which case, if we follow the myth, they must have expected the commissioners to do this, and then depart, remarkably quickly—so quickly that the regicides could return safely that same night. But we know that the New Haven magistrates, led by Leete, were in fact planning to challenge and stall Kellond and Kirke. In any case, Whalley and Goffe would have expected the commissioners to search Jones's house; so they would have been unlikely to return there quite so soon.

This expectation makes a third myth even less likely. This tale, too, has the regicides returning to New Haven and discovering that they need to evade Kellond and Kirke, who are still searching the town. Whalley and Goffe apparently had to shift their residence because the commissioners were in close pursuit and the regicides did not want to implicate their hosts, such as Davenport or Jones, in the sheltering of fugitives. They therefore went to the home of a Mrs Eyers, 'a respectable and comely lady', but she saw Kellond and Kirke approaching her house and ushered the fugitives out of the back door towards the woods. Whalley and Goffe, however, returned to the house immediately and were concealed by Mrs Eyers. In good conscience, then, Mrs Eyers could tell Kellond and Kirke truthfully and politely that she had seen Whalley and Goffe earlier that day walking towards the woods. She failed to add, of course, that she had also seen the regicides return to her house.[11] Or so the story goes.

Mrs Eyers does not appear in any other sources associated with the regicides. Nor is it likely that the regicides, when given the opportunity of disappearing into the woods, would return immediately to a house which they knew Kellond and Kirke were approaching and about to search thoroughly. The fact they were not actually in the town of New Haven also undermines the Eyers myth, as dramatic and comic as it might be.

One final myth needs debunking: it relates to the regicides' arrival in Boston after their journey across the Atlantic and it has a feature in common with one of the New Haven stories: the regicides' fencing prowess. The presence of fencing in two different tales might be considered to corroborate them: if two groups of people are talking about the same skill in two different places, we might consider that both groups are responding to something they have both witnessed. Equally, we might err on the side of scepticism and prefer to view the recurrence of one feature as the result of New Haven residents receiving the story from Boston (or vice versa) and attaching it to their own local folklore. Folklore is in fact what the Boston fencing myth appears to be. Allegedly the regicides encountered a 'gallant gentleman' who had set up a stage on which he challenged other men 'to play with him at swords'. One of the regicides, apparently disguised in 'rustic dress' and armed with a cheese wrapped in a napkin as a shield and a dirty mop as a sword, mounted the stage. The regicide used the cheese to defend himself from the gentleman's sword and employed the mop to give him 'a pair of whiskers'. When the gentleman attempted a second thrust, his opponent once again employed the cheese to good effect and wiped the man's eyes with the mop. When the gentleman made a third thrust, the same thing happened: the cheese stopped his sword and the dirty mop slowly wiped his face. Understandably irked, the gentleman threw down his small sword and lunged at his adversary with a broad sword. The regicide, however, stopped him with the words, 'hitherto you see I have only played with you, and not attempted to hurt you; but if you come at me now with the broad-sword, know, that I will certainly take your life'.[12]

This last quotation does not ring true. It is hardly credible that a devoutly religious man, enjoying the protection of Bostonians, would threaten mortal injury to a man he had just goaded with cheese and a mop. As the regicide was in disguise, it suggests that this event may have happened towards the end of 1660 or in the first two months of 1661 when Whalley and Goffe, though known to be wanted men, were still in Boston until advised to leave by Daniel Gookin. Furthermore, if the regicide were in disguise, he surely realized the danger he was in and the need to keep a low profile. It is scarcely likely, therefore, that he would stand on a public stage and humiliate a Bostonian in a comic manner that would be sure to gain wide circulation. The myth is simply a fabrication based on a few superficial details gleaned about Whalley and Goffe: that they had been accomplished soldiers a decade and a half earlier; that they had been resident in Boston at some point; and that they might have had the need to disguise themselves. It follows the predictable structure of an adventure story and includes comic features to encourage the story's dissemination. The story of a mysterious figure bringing public attention to himself is internally inconsistent and culminates in a threat of murder delivered by a man we know was extremely godly and grateful for the protection he had been given by the people of Boston.

Stiles's 'martyrs of freedom' in context

Following Stiles's *History*, other early first histories of Whalley and Goffe included some adventure-stories, though use of phrases like 'the tradition is' and 'the report is' suggests that there were some reservations about treating the stories as gospel truth.[13] Even the earliest narrators of the regicides' flight were not able to approach the New Haven stories with complete seriousness. One referred to their 'original quaintness' and submitted that they might 'perhaps afford some amusement to the curious'.[14] Another dismissed them as 'not all congruous, or otherwise credible; but they are worth the use of

a leisure hour'.[15] But, as we shall see, the following century authors
like Margaret Sidney and W.H. Gocher had fewer reservations as they
happily used Stiles's stories in their own works[16] and mixed them with
historically accurate characters and events, which caused myth to
become fact in the undiscerning mind.

The importance of Stiles's study, however, does not rest on amusing
folklore. It was written and published against the background of the
revolutions in British America and France; it would have taken a particularly myopic and tedious antiquarian to have missed the relevance
of the English regicides to Stiles's own revolutionary period. Deeply
sympathetic to both revolutions, Stiles presented Whalley, Goffe, and
Dixwell as prophets and heralds from an earlier age. Hence Stiles's
lengthy essay on tyrannicide and his enthusiastic and sympathetic depic-
tion of the regicides,[17] describing them as moving 'in a great sphere'
and acting in a 'great cause'.[18]

While Stiles was clearly preoccupied with undermining Hutchinson's
interpretation of the regicides, he was also researching and writing
during a period characterized by debate and anxiety over the possibility of monarchy in America. There were fears in the 1787–8 debate on
the proposed constitution that the new republic would give way to a
monarchical tyranny in the form of a president who was not yet subject to any democratic control. There were those who supported some
form of monarchy to curb the more impetuous democratic ambitions
of post-Revolution Americans. Those who had read their classical
history would have known that there were powerful precedents for
republics turning into monarchies. And those who viewed George
Washington's early presidency would have seen elements that smacked
of monarchy: a king-like procession from Mount Vernon to New York
in 1789; an inauguration referred to as a 'coronation'; several pseudo-
monarchical state portraits; and a court with routines and etiquette not
dissimilar to those found in London or Versailles. Republicans like
Thomas Jefferson and James Madison were aiming, it has been argued,
'to prevent the United States from becoming a . . . British-backed
monarchy' led by Federalists like George Washington, John Adams,

and Alexander Hamilton. The 1790s has been described as 'one of the most passionate and divisive decades in American history'.[19] It was also the decade in which Stiles was researching, writing, and publishing the history of three prominent anti-monarchists.

Stiles may also have been reacting to the trend among some prominent revolutionaries over the previous two decades to reinterpret the history of the Stuarts: seventeenth-century *Parliament* had become the enemy, a forebear to the eighteenth-century Parliament that was passing legislation like the Stamp Act that provoked the colonies by infringing their liberties.[20] In this interpretation, Charles I was a *victim* of Parliamentary tyranny, rather than himself an historical parallel to a tyrannical George III. Parliament had 'usurped' Charles's prerogatives; now it was tyrannically doing the same to the colonies. These colonies had not historically been under Parliamentary jurisdiction, so they were not now. As domains of the crown, they were 'dependent' solely on the person of the king; but the crown, through contracts with the original colonial proprietors and chartering companies, in the seventeenth century had bestowed upon the colonies a guarantee that they would govern by their own laws. The early Stuarts became constitutional models for the likes of Benjamin Franklin, when he wrote to Samuel Cooper in June 1770 that Parliament seemed 'to have been long encroaching on the rights of their and our sovereign', or for Alexander Hamilton in *The Farmer Refuted* (1775) when he argued that the colonists were 'losing sight of that share which the king has in the sovereignty, both of Great-Britain and America'.[21]

English Revolution to American Revolution

This interpretation of Charles I as victim was at odds with the prevalent view that had otherwise been developing in the mid to late eighteenth century. While there had been some criticism of Oliver Cromwell in America for infringing civil liberties in England through his use of a standing army (the presence of which was feared in the colonies),[22] by the 1760s Cromwell received more praise than vilification, and Charles I vice versa. This in part reflected a Puritan reaction to the rise of the Church of England in the colonies, while Great Awakening ministers from the 1740s had seen in Cromwell's 'zeal and enthusiasm' the qualities of a model Christian as they evangelically promoted personal spiritual introspection above church hierarchy and ceremony.[23] But, more importantly, the civil war and its leading characters were invoked in direct parallel to the American experience in the years leading up to the American Revolution. In the 1770s Samuel Sherwood observed 'tyranny and oppression' being exercised by the British government, just as it had been previously during 'the reign of the Stuart family', while the Boston Sons of Liberty hailed Cromwell as a 'glorious fellow'.[24] The lawyer James Otis wrote under the pseudonym John Hampden—the man who had challenged Charles I's Ship Money levy in 1637—when attacking the 'arbitrary and wicked proceedings of the Stuarts' in his *Rights of the British Colonies Asserted and Proved* (1764). John Adams damned 'the execrable race of the Stuarts', and saw himself as a descendant of the seventeenth-century Parliamentary cause, in his *Dissertation on the Canon and Feudal Law* (1765).[25]

These were not isolated examples. In the wake of the Stamp Act in 1765, which imposed a direct tax on the colonies by way of revenue stamps on printed documents, Patrick Henry, another Son of Liberty, told the Virginia burgesses that Julius Caesar had his Brutus, Charles I had his Cromwell, and 'He did not doubt but some good American would stand up, in favour of his country'.[26] In the same year, when the Anglican Church in Connecticut refused to observe a fast day, a 'comic liturgy' was printed and acted out, in which 'We beseech thee, O Cromwell to hear [our prayers]' replaced the customary 'We beseech thee to hear us, good Lord'. Between 1774 and 1775 *The American Chronicle of the Times* was published, the fourth book of which had Cromwell appearing as 'lord protector of the Commonwealth of Massachusetts Bay', mustering his loyal generals Thomas Fairfax and John Lambert, and the rest of his 'brave warriors'. The Son of Liberty Joshua Brackett was the proprietor of the Cromwell's Head inn in

Boston, the exterior sign of which hung sufficiently low that its visitors had to lower their heads in reverence to the lord protector's visage.[27] John Dickinson, the 'penman' of the American Revolution, could not fully explain the events of the 1770s without looking back to the reign of Charles I.[28] Other seventeenth-century republican heroes like Algernon Sidney and John Milton became required reading for the Founding Fathers. Thomas Paine's *Common Sense* owed a debt to Milton, whom George Washington also read;[29] Sidney's *Discourses Concerning Government* inspired Thomas Jefferson, among many others.

While there was not necessarily a direct causal link between the English and American Revolutions, the Anglo-American memory of regicide and the regicides in the late seventeenth and eighteenth centuries contributed a model of resistance to tyrants. The political philosophy that developed in this environment and crossed the Atlantic did not make the American Revolution inevitable, but it did offer a framework of thought and language for that Revolution. A number of connections were made between the seventeenth-century Anglo-American experience of repression, civil war, revolution, and Restoration, and the eighteenth-century American experience of resistance and revolution.

First, the independent, proto-republican spirit of seventeenth-century Puritans fleeing, then resisting, the repression of British monarchs was seen as sowing the seeds of American political independence a century and a half later. In 1797 Benjamin Trumbull published the first volume of his *Complete History of Connecticut* which, 'published in conformity to act of congress', included the story of the regicides and—crucially—referred to 'the spirit of republicanism' displayed by many of the New Haven magistrates. The regicides and their proto-republican protectors could scarcely have been portrayed in a more positive fashion. Whalley and Goffe were described as 'gentlemen of singular abilities' who had 'moved in an exalted sphere'; 'their manners were elegant, and their appearance grave and dignified, commanding universal respect'.[30] They were 'universally esteemed, by all men of character, both civil and religious' in Boston and Cambridge.

Furthermore, Trumbull noted, when it became clear that Whalley
and Goffe were wanted men and Governor Endecott assembled his
magistrates to discuss their apprehension, 'their friends were so numer-
ous, that a vote could not...be obtained to arrest them'. Some of these
'friends' continued to stand by the regicides; others advised Whalley
and Goffe to abscond. Upon their arrival in New Haven, Trumbull
continued, the regicides continued to enjoy unstinting hospitality:
'the more the people became acquainted with them, the more they
esteemed them, not only as men of great minds, but of unfeigned
piety and religion'. Even when the colonists' personal safety and the
'liberties and peace' of their country seemed to be at risk from a
vengeful Charles II, William Leete and his friends viewed Whalley
and Goffe as 'the excellent in the earth, and were afraid to betray
them, lest they should be instrumental in shedding innocent blood'.[31]

Trumbull's knowledge of the dates of the regicides' travels and
his reference to the myths found in Stiles's *History*, published three
years previously, suggest that Stiles was Trumbull's principal source
for his history of the regicides. As with Stiles, Trumbull's focus on
the warm admiration for the regicides in New England suggested
his enthusiastic sympathy towards Whalley and Goffe, as well as a connection between the English and American revolutionaries. Indeed,
the colonists' spirit of resistance, independence, and republicanism
had arguably been fomented by the English civil war. As early as 1692,
Gershom Bulkeley noted that the rebellion against Charles I had
excited 'an anti-monarchical spirit' in America, which had become
so 'strongly rooted...as not to be easily or speedily, if ever, totally
eradicated'. That spirit had led to the 'admiration' and 'entertainment'
of some of the king's 'murderers here and there in the country'.[32]

Second, the post-civil war political philosophy of the seventeenth-
century English philosopher John Locke further provided an ideological
basis for resistance. Locke argued that there was a contract between
ruler and ruled: a contract into which subjects entered to grant them
security and protection from harm, to save them from the violence
and instability that were inherent in the state of nature. But subjects
did not give away all their rights to a central authority, and that

authority had to respond to subjects' wishes and necessities. If the authority failed in its responsibility to protect its subjects, or if it over-reached its power, then the contract was broken and subjects had a right to rebel, instituting a new authority that would guarantee civil order and provide subjects with the protection necessary to pursue their individual goals. Locke had begun writing in the reign of Charles II, a reign preoccupied with the sinister shadow of the English civil war: Charles was determined that the miseries of the 1640s would not be experienced again but he also recognized that the nature of govern-ment fundamentally had changed. Kings could lose their crowns and their heads by the judicial will of their subjects.

John Locke's views on civil liberty were adopted by American revolutionaries and then attacked by the English minister Jonathan Boucher as 'new-dressed principles' that had been 'industriously revived and brought forward with great zeal' in the reign of Charles I. 'There is hardly a principle or project or any moment in Mr Locke's Treatise', Boucher argued, 'of which the rudiments may not be traced in some of the many political pieces which were then produced'.[33] Boucher's views of the causes and effects of the American Revolution were delivered in 'thirteen discourses' in America between 1763 and 1775, then published after the Revolution once he had returned to England. Boucher was 'avowedly hostile' to the Revolution and noted a number of parallels between England in the 1640s and America in the 1760s–70s. Benjamin Franklin's admirers defended him, Boucher commented, in just the same way that the regicides had been defended.[34] More fundamentally, Boucher observed that 'the history of the last century, and what then passed among ourselves, is a perpetual lesson, at least to British subjects, to leave off contention before it be meddled with'. The English civil war had begun, as the American Revolution had, 'about matters which, comparatively speaking, were but of little moment'; it had erupted due to the interference of 'persons unknown to the laws, who began their reformation by overturning the estab-lished church'. That is, once Puritans had meddled with the church in England, it was not long before they meddled with the state. The implication was that the same thing had happened in America.[35]

Third, some commentators viewed the American Revolution as another English civil war, but one transplanted to the colonies. They may have been 3,000 miles away from England, but the rebellious colonists were arguably still *English*: 'of the same language, the same religion, the same manners and customs, sprung from the same nation, intermixed by relation and consanguinity', with 'the manners, habits, and ideas of Britons... the same laws, the same religion, the same constitution, the same feelings, sentiments and habits'. For some, the American colonists were actually purer Englishmen than their corrupted cousins across the Atlantic; their quest for a constitution undefiled by Hanoverians (or the Stuarts and other monarchs before them) made them 'undegenerated descendants of their British ancestors... desir[ing] a constitution perfectly English'.[36] Others, most famously Thomas Paine, pointed out the flaw in the 'second civil war' line of reasoning: by the 1770s, he argued, not a third of the colonists were of English descent, so they did not have a mother country in England, but a mother continent in Europe more widely.[37]

Fourth, for those writing in the post-revolutionary period, it was not just the English civil war, Commonwealth, and Protectorate that provided seventeenth-century inspiration for resistance to George III, but also the politics of the reign of Charles II. And to some observers one case study was unavoidable: that of the regicides on the run in the American colonies. In celebrating the principles espoused by seventeenth-century New Englanders that underlay the events of the 1770s, they hailed especially the story of Kellond and Kirke's fruitless pursuit of the fugitives in 1661 and the royal commission sent to New England and New Netherland by Charles II in 1664.

Revisiting the royal commission of 1664

In 1799 Hannah Adams's *Summary History of New-England, From the First Settlement at Plymouth* was 'published according to Act of Congress'. It included the story of Whalley and Goffe and described them in terms very similar to Trumbull's: 'gentlemen of distinguished abilities' who had 'moved in an exalted sphere'.[38] Adams, a distant cousin of President John Adams, retold the story of the regicides' arrival in Boston, their time in the cave outside New Haven, their journey to Milford, their return to New Haven, and their later residence in Hadley. Fundamentally, she linked their time in hiding to the colonists' fear that Charles II would remove their liberty and privileges. Adams was convinced that Charles was determined to rule like his father. The colonists' enemies in England, she argued, 'gave exaggerated accounts of every interesting occurrence, and the king was prejudiced by their representations'.[39] One such 'interesting occurrence', presumably, would have been the case study of Whalley and Goffe and their protection, through a variety of means, by colonial authorities.

For Hannah Adams, when Charles II sent the 1664 commission with its four officials—Nichols, Carr, Cartwright, and Maverick—the king's primary intention was not to advance English claims over Dutch colonies but to reduce the English colonies to 'the plan of twelve royal provinces, according to the ideas adopted by his father in 1635, and to have a viceroy over the whole'.[40] As we have seen, the reality was a little subtler than this. Although the question of jurisdiction was present, neither king nor colonial authority was prepared to concede sovereignty, and each side initially was careful to ensure it did not significantly rile the other. The warships and soldiers that arrived in the summer of 1664 were targeted ostensibly at New Netherland. Although New Englanders might fear that Charles would use this military force against them, the king could always argue that this was a deluded and wilful misinterpretation. After all, his pursuit of the regicides at the time—if we can call it a real pursuit—was careful and measured. The commissioners were to discover who had protected the regicides but not to arrest them. The 'protectors' were simply to be encouraged to 'take the more care for their future behaviour'. This was potentially a sinister threat but it was not an overtly aggressive and intrusive one.

But Hannah Adams allowed no such subtlety in 1799. The 1664 commission was just another example, she suggested, of the British government threatening the independent sovereignty and jurisdiction of New England. The colonies 'disrelished' this threat because of their 'strong aversion to arbitrary power'. Moreover, Adams argued, 'the inhabitants of New England may emphatically be said to be born free. They were settled originally upon the principle... that "all men are born free, equal and independent"'. The 1664 commission, she argued, 'excited the irritability natural to a people jealous for their liberty'.[41] There can have been few more overt claims to a direct connection between the seventeenth-century European settlement of New England and the American Revolution.

So, in addition to Stiles's *History* of Whalley, Goffe, and Dixwell, the decades following the American Revolution clearly witnessed a resurgence of interest in the regicides in America. Once independence from Great Britain ensured there would be no retribution for sheltering fugitives who had committed treason on British soil, the story of the regicides appeared in all manner of different places—not just traditional histories or collections of historical documents. Jedidiah Morse's *American Universal Geography* in 1796, for example, featured Whalley and Goffe alongside a discussion of turnpike roads. Morse not only noted the cave north-west of New Haven in which the regicides lived when they were hiding from Charles II's agents; he also conveyed the wider story.[42] Yet, as we have seen, the implications of the regicides' story, and of its wider political and historical context, were far greater in this post-revolutionary period than Morse's geographical digressions might suggest.

The 'rediscovery' of the story of Whalley and Goffe provided a ready interpretative framework for the events of the 1770s. The regicides may not yet have been given the architectural monument that Aedenus Burke desired but, as the eighteenth century progressed, they were increasingly remembered in print. Authors looked back to the seventeenth century to find historical evidence of the British government infringing the rights of America's independent colonies. In the context of the American Revolution, there seemed to be some striking parallels to the history of the regicides in the 1660s. Indeed, whenever the regicides in America were invoked—before, during, and after the Revolutionary years—interest focused on two key episodes: first, the period in 1661 when it became clear that Whalley and Goffe would not be exempt from prosecution, the colonial authorities had to decide whether to protect them, and Kellond and Kirke were sent to look for them; and, second, the 1664 commission from England, which was concerned ostensibly with advancing claims over New Netherland but might be interpreted as a renewed attempt to capture the regicides.

Both the 1661 and 1664 episodes went beyond the immediate issues and implications of capturing men who had been protected by significant individuals in the New England colonies. Both arguably involved an attempt by the British government to interfere directly in colonial affairs. The events of 1661 invoked the sinister spectre of a 'governor of New England', which reinforced the propensity of the New Haven authorities to give Charles II's government the run-around; the 1664 commission was concerned not only with the capture of Whalley and Goffe but also with control of jurisdiction and territorial disputes in New England. Both episodes were seen to culminate in colonists resisting this interference either subtly or overtly. It was not such a surprise, therefore, even if it was rather unsubtle, for these episodes later to be seen as precursors to the struggle between 'liberty' and 'arbitrary power' during the American Revolutionary years. Yet such interference was exaggerated to provide 'evidence' of America's deep-seated love of liberty and independence in the face of British tyranny. So it was in the eighteenth century that the seeds of the prevalent, if misleading, interpretation of the regicides in America were sown.

6

The spirit of the regicides, liberty, and American national identity

Memory plays many pranks with history. Its products are attractive, but as a rule unreliable, as like a snowball on a warm day in winter, the volume increases with each revolution on the hill of time. Still it supplies the gloss and spangles used to dress statistical matter...By blending fact and fancy it is possible to weave a narrative which entertains and at the same time instructs the reader. Those who believe it can; those who doubt it may;—so let it go at that.

W.H. Gocher, *Wadsworth: or The Charter Oak* (1904), 48

The election of Thomas Jefferson in 1800 represented a victory for those who had spent the previous two decades exalting the regïcides in order to drive out the vestiges of monarchism in the new American Republic. Jefferson's simple inauguration—he was the first president to walk to the ceremony and he wore plain clothes—shunned the pseudo-monarchical pomp of previous Federalist administrations. He now appealed for conciliation between Federalists and Republicans, the hostility between whom had raged through the 1790s, providing the political backdrop for some of the more excitable rediscoveries of the regicides. At first sight, the early decades of the nineteenth century were not ripe for continued interest in Whalley and Goffe. Newly freed American minds were looking optimistically westwards, not back across the Atlantic to English (now somebody else's) history. The Louisiana Purchase of 1803 provided Americans with over 800,000 square miles into which they could expand; the Lewis and Clark expedition commissioned in the same year afforded an opportunity to map and explore potential trading routes to the west of the Mississippi River. Independence from Great Britain also brought freedom from colonial restrictions on trade, manufacturing, and shipping; a new spirit of optimism was reflected in economic growth, the pursuit of new career opportunities, excited resettlement through westward migration, and the development of a new urban environment. Perhaps this explains why, by April 1819, the graves that were thought to belong to the regicides had become so neglected and overgrown that Ezra Stiles's grandson, Jonathan Leavitt, only stumbled across them in search of a lost ball.[1]

We need not be so pessimistic. Leavitt had read his grandfather's *History*, had previously tried to find the regicides' graves, and thought that he had come across 'the bones of the mighty'. And beyond the confines of the New Haven burial ground, Whalley and Goffe were not shunned from a new American consciousness that looked increasingly westward towards the Pacific Ocean rather than the former English colonies on the Atlantic coast. Several factors combined to ensure that two old English Puritans from the mid to late seventeenth century played a prominent role in the development of a new American national identity. From June 1803 when Reverend Isaac Jones, a descendant of William Jones, was the first to etch on the Judges Cave an inscription, 'Opposition to tyrants is obedience to God',[2] to G.H. Durrie's painting of that very cave fifty years later, the regicides played an important role in American culture. The association between regicide and revolution remained of especial interest among those whose nation was forged in its own revolution against an English king. The drive westwards also inevitably brought further conflict with the indigenous populations, evoking echoes of King Philip's War, and affording a new relevance to the story of the Angel of Hadley. Authors', readers', and artists' taste for the supernatural and republican liberty further ensured that English regicides found their place within a framework of American literature and art.

British to American literature

Early nineteenth-century British representations of the regicides in America were not overly celebratory. Even Ebenezer Elliott, the strident political reformer and author of *The People's Anthem* ('When wilt Thou save the people?...Not thrones and crowns, but men!') in *Kerhonah* (1835) portrayed a John Dixwell disturbed by nightmares of being Charles I's executioner: 'Forgiveness! Oh, forgiveness, and a grave!' Dixwell's thoughts are not restful, whether he be awake or asleep: 'Ne'er shall I be at peace/Till in the grave'.[3] It is only through helping the eponymous chief, Kerhonah, that Dixwell might find redemption for his regicidal crime.[4]

Other early nineteenth-century British portrayals hinted at an overenthusiastic religiosity and impulsive radicalism at odds with the British establishment of the time.[5] Poet Laureate Robert Southey's *Oliver Newman*, one of the earliest British imaginative portraits of Whalley and Goffe, was not wholly critical of the regicides, but it presented Goffe's son as the judicious hero, with an impetuous and Native-threatening Goffe relegated to a bit-part. Southey first thought in 1811 of an *Iliad*-style epic set during King Philip's War, and he began writing it in 1815, but *Oliver Newman* was never completed.[6] We do know of Southey's intentions, though, from a letter of January 1811 and an appendix to the poem in 1845, replete with references to Whalley and Goffe, their time in Hadley, and the pursuit by Edward Randolph.[7] Goffe's son, Oliver Newman, was to be a hero who buys a Native American woman and her child, Elizabeth, in order to return them to their tribe; who prioritizes this mission above his own search for his father; who tends to a wounded Mohawk; who is accused of being a spy by Native Americans, but suffers the ensuing violence with patience and fortitude; who, upon discovering his regicide father, stands by him, and even saves his enemy Edward Randolph from a murderous fate at the hands of the Native Americans. The regicide Goffe, meanwhile, was to be a hot-headed soldier who assembles some forces against the Native Americans, takes some prisoners, and is about to execute them when his son, Oliver, appears to save them. Even Goffe's nemesis Randolph was to be portrayed in an unusually positive light, agreeing not to divulge Goffe's whereabouts and requesting a grant of land for Oliver.

A similar reticence towards Goffe may be identified in Sir Walter Scott's *Peveril of the Peak* (1822), which was written at around the same time as the composition of Southey's *Oliver Newman*. Scott has Major Bridgenorth contemplating one benefit of a national calamity: some talented individuals 'slumber' in society's 'bosom' until 'necessity and opportunity call forth the statesman and the soldier from the shades of lowly life to the parts they are designed by Providence to perform'. Oliver Cromwell and John Milton are two names that spring to Bridgenorth's mind. Another is the Angel of Hadley, whom Bridgenorth calls Richard Whalley, a fictional pseudonym for William Goffe. Bridgenorth relates a story from his time travelling in America, which is essentially a recapitulation of the Angel of Hadley, with a greying hero appearing to save Bridgenorth and his colonial hosts: 'such was the influence of his appearance, his mien, his language, and his presence of mind, that he was implicitly obeyed by men who had never seen him until that moment'.[8] In view of Scott's position as a member of the conservative establishment, it is surprising that the regicide is presented in such positive and heroic terms. Or, at the very least, there is little sense of the Angel of Hadley being denounced as a criminal.[9] But we might pause and question Scott's sympathy for the regicide story when the judgement of its narrator is questioned elsewhere in the novel for being undermined by the 'insane enthusiasm of the time'.[10]

Instead it is to nascent American literature that we need to turn for more overtly positive representations of Whalley, Goffe, and Dixwell.

By the 1840s, such was the confident enthusiasm for the regicides in America that one British visitor to New Haven was warned not to call them 'regicides' at all—the term implied criminality—but 'the judges'.[11] Regicides had appeared in American novels with such frequency in the 1820s and 1830s that it was not uncommon to write a novel with a cameo appearance, even if that cameo was sometimes rather forced. One reviewer of John C. McCall's *Witch of New England* (1824), for example, was puzzled by Whalley's presence since the author did 'nothing with him, except to kill him in defiance of physiology, representing him as being found dead, with his body erect, intent on his book, and looking as if he were alive'.[12] As the English regicides became a dominant feature of nineteenth-century American literature, historical fiction and historical fact existed in a symbiotic state. Each had a productive effect upon the other: research on the regicides prompted fictional portraits of them; fictional portraits invigorated interest in what really happened; and the real historical story encouraged even more creative literary accounts. In the process, the regicide myths from the eighteenth century were perpetuated, or new ones were founded.

American history is replete with myths, especially those surrounding American independence; they have been a binding force, helping to create a unifying American national identity. It has been argued that the demands of patriotism, the desire for good stories, and the longing for a collective identity have all combined to produce mythological stories centred on opposites: heroes and villains, wit and foolery, good and evil, David and Goliath. Cast in the forge of nineteenth-century Romanticism, these myths arguably subverted the democratic and communitarian impulses of the American revolutionaries and compressed the Revolution's story and ideals into those of comic-book superheroes. These characters, almost always military, were found in isolated stories, with neat beginnings and ends, to provide appropriate moral instruction to successive American generations.[13] This style of writing was, in part, a reaction to the bloody realities of the Revolutionary War. Those who had lived through it, and their immediate descendants, concealed the miseries of warfare; their descendants then devised white-washed stories with carefully selected plots that were suitable for patriotic public consumption. The Romantics were fortunate to find in the regicides a tale that could be portrayed as 'clean' and capable of celebrating the revolutionary values of the 1770s, while transplanting them into sanitized stories much less harrowing than the warfare that had been witnessed only too recently.

Furthermore, in the half-century after the American Revolution, when the new American nation was being forged, a new national identity needed to be forged alongside it. America was an adolescent nation with disparate threats to that national identity. As its territory expanded westward, there was the danger that unifying national bonds might be loosened, and that those more interested in focusing on the distinctiveness of their local region might undermine a cohesive American character.[14] A significant part of America's new national identity consisted of its history, not least that of its founders, some of which needed to be recalibrated and mythologized to underline the idea that America's possession of independence and liberty was inevitable and timeless.[15] Literature became a key vehicle for the creation of a distinctive, independent, cultural identity, especially once the War of 1812 provoked a further surge of American nationalism.[16] American authors who imitated European writers were accused of 'denationalizing the American mind' and of 'enslaving the national heart'.[17] Instead, American history was to feature in American literature to highlight a proud, distinctive, separate nation and to entertain, inspire, and educate readers in desirable habits, tastes, and principles. Episodes from American history were to be selected that would instruct readers in 'great moral truths'; and the most prominent episodes were to be stories about adventure and freedom in seventeenth- and eighteenth-century America.[18]

There were few stories from the colonial period that combined adventure and freedom more entertainingly than those of regicides on the run in America. But there were tensions here: the colonial history that nationalistic American authors were meant to adopt could not avoid including a significant European element. Europeans, who were crossing the Atlantic and settling in America throughout the colonial period, did not sever their links completely with the Old World. Moreover, despite this call for American cultural independence and superiority, there was still a residual Anglophilia. As Orestes Brownson observed in 1839, England still 'continued to manufacture our cottons and woollens, our knives and forks, our fashions, our literature, our sentiments and opinions'.[19] In the case of the regicides in America, these became creative tensions: the Anglophiles could read about Whalley, Goffe, and Dixwell, and remember the regicides were English, but enjoy the fact they were not subject to the morally and politically inferior governance represented by English kings. The advocates of American cultural independence and superiority could adopt the regicides as honorary proto-American revolutionaries, protected by colonial authorities who embodied the values of the American Revolution more than they did the political culture of Restoration England. Whalley, Goffe, and Dixwell were un-English in the sense that they were not welcome in their native land after the Restoration of the monarchy and had no sympathy with the values promoted by Charles II and his supporters. It mattered little that, in reality, Goffe admitted he always felt a stranger in America. More important was the incorporation of the regicides into an early republican, nationalistic, American literary framework.

The spirit(s) of the regicides

The regicides were associated with several Romantic characteristics that made them attractive to early nineteenth-century American authors: a sense of history, nationalism, liberty, individual bravery, and—the one that first reached prominence—the supernatural.[20] The Puritan obsession with the activity of God and the Antichrist on earth underlaid a preoccupation with Satan's influence among early Americans. This fixation led to the most famous of the witch trials at Salem in 1692 that, in turn, perpetuated interest in the presence of the Devil and his agents in the New World. It was impossible to look back to seventeenth-century America without thinking of the witchcraze; thus many early American novels, set in the colonial period, featured the supernatural. The story of the regicides in America neatly dovetailed with this literary interest in the paranormal as Whalley and Goffe, like spectres, appeared and disappeared from view. The regicides and their protectors adopted a mode of disguise that was plausible to their superstitious contemporaries; they could appear and move about small parochial communities in supernatural guises. The Angel of Hadley, in particular, was a ghostly figure that provided a useful spectral meta-phor for liberty for those penning novels about the regicides.

James McHenry's *The Spectre of the Forest* (1823), for example, pre-sents Goffe as a tall, slender figure aiding his adopted community in moments of peril. To provide security 'from the grasp of the law', Goffe is 'obliged to assume the character of a supernatural being'. His appearance is made all the more mysterious by his apparel. Wearing surplice-like garments of black fur with a black hood, he carries a bible in one hand and a white staff in the other. He appears to New Englanders to assure them: 'a servant of God will meet you, and from him you will learn that the Redeemer of Israel is mighty to save you'. McHenry's Goffe survives into the 1690s, when King William and Queen Mary pardon him. Mary declares that Goffe 'must have suf-fered much amidst those savage deserts...his old age might, without any injury to the cause of royalty, or any appearance of disrespect to our grandfather's memory, be allowed to enjoy peace in that remote country, where he has been so long concealed'. William agrees in a cod-Dutch accent, so long as he receives confirmation that Goffe is not an enemy to *their* monarchical government.[21]

A similar ghostly and heroic figure appears in J.N. Barker's play *The Tragedy of Superstition* (1826). Sir Reginald Egerton—a clear fictional representation of Edward Randolph—is sent by Charles II to find the regicides, because the king 'finds it decorous to grow a little angry with the persons that killed his father' and has heard that the people of New England have been giving the fugitives 'food and shelter'. Goffe, who is known only as the 'Unknown', appears at times of danger, like McHenry's spectre, to protect the people of New England. Barker makes the Unknown appear like the Angel of Hadley to coordinate the defence of his adopted town against the Native Americans: 'Turn back for shame...I am sent to save you', he implores.[22]

Goffe appears in a comparable fashion in James Fenimore Cooper's *The Wept of Wish-ton-Wish* (1829), but this time he is called 'Submission', which Cooper claimed 'savoured of the religious enthusiasm of the times', and which denoted the regicide's readiness to submit to God's providential design. In a nod to the Angel of Hadley, Submission remains unmoved by the threat from Native Americans, insisting that 'peril and I are no strangers'. He is central to the defence of Wish-ton-Wish during a number of attacks and is cast as a vigorous military hero: 'he parried, at some jeopardy to one hand, a thrust aimed at his throat, while with the other he seized the warrior who had inflicted the blow, and...buried his own keen blade to its haft in the body'. In a later attack Submission disregards his own safety to call the colonists to their square and urges them to 'be firm'; he struggles 'manfully' against his 'luckless fortune'.[23] As a novel, *The Wept of Wish-ton-Wish* was not much of a success,[24] but as a play it enjoyed more positive fortunes. Goffe became one of the most prominent stage characters in nineteenth-century America. In its theatrical form, *The Wept of Wish-ton-Wish* was described as a 'burletta', a musical drama akin to comic opera, and, for much of its stage-life, it featured the famous French ballet-dancer Celine Celeste. It opened in London in November 1831, toured America at the height of its popularity in the 1830s to 1850s, and was still in production on both sides of the Atlantic until at least 1878.

In Delia Salter Bacon's *Tales of the Puritans: The Regicides* (1831), it is not Goffe who appears as a spectral vision but his wife, who is also Whalley's daughter. Moving the supernatural lens away from Hadley, Bacon focuses instead on the Royalist agents Kellond and Kirke, who arrive in New Haven in search of the regicides and then meet with

William Leete. A fictional character, Samuel, is sent from Leete's household to warn Whalley and Goffe of the agents' presence in New Haven. The regicides retire to the cave at West Rock and tales are spread of a supernatural 'beautiful being' living in the cave—'strange sights and unearthly voices had been seen and heard at midnight'—to ensure that no one visits it and discovers them. This 'beautiful being', known as the Lady of the Mist, is none other than Isabella Goffe. As Kellond and Kirke get closer to their quarry, a pessimistic William Goffe concedes to Isabella that their time on the run has come to an end; that they will be caught and must face the inevitable penalty of death. Nonetheless, Whalley and Goffe leave the cave at West Rock, just moments before Kellond and Kirke arrive. Following the gaze of Isabella, who is watching her father and husband leave, Kellond and Kirke pursue the regicides down the hill, only to be tricked by the fugitives, who hide under a footbridge (the neck bridge from Stiles's *History*). Whalley later dies in his bed, wrapped in the 'peaceful beauty of holiness', while Bacon's Goffe is free to re-appear in New Haven as Walter Goldsmith, a benevolent yet reserved gentleman, lately arrived from England.[25]

Four years after the publication of Bacon's *Regicides*, a new generation of Americans was introduced to Stiles's *History*, with its coverage of the Angel of Hadley, thanks to its inclusion in S.L. Knapp's *Library of American History* (1835). This came in the wake of William Leete Stone's—note his name—*Mercy Disborough* (1834) in which supernatural happenings had once again been portrayed keeping people away from the regicides. In this novel, stories circulate of low sounds and voices and shards of light appearing and disappearing in an isolated storehouse owned by William Leete. The voices belong to Whalley and Goffe but no one dares approach the storehouse for fear of encountering paranormal beings. Whenever the inhabitants of New Haven mention the rumours to Leete, he shakes his head and cautions them 'not to throw themselves within the charmed circle of Azazel, by approaching too near'. As the story progresses and tales of unnatural occurrences spread around the New Haven community, claims about the storehouse become even more exaggerated. Demons are described howling 'pitifully in the night... causing blue flames and sudden flashes of light to issue from the crevices in the walls'. Towards the conclusion of *Mercy Disborough*, the author introduces some false history by imagining that in the mid-eighteenth century the 'haunted' storehouse was razed and an inscription on the stone walls discovered:

> Stranger, if thou art a friend to unpolluted liberty, look upon the names of two of its humble and constant, but unfortunate defenders, who, having assisted in openly and fairly adjudging a tyrant to death, were afterwards compelled, like Lot, to flee to the caves and the mountains of this howling wilderness, to escape the vengeance of the tyrant's son. But, even in these distant ends of the earth, the Philistines were upon them, and they must have perished but for the kindness of the governor, who put his life in his hand, and cherished them for many months in this dreary abode.
> EDWARD WHALLEY. WILLIAM GOFFE
> Opposition to tyrants, is obedience to God.[26]

Bacon's—and Whalley's?—rebellion

William Leete Stone had been inspired by the actual text inscribed on the Judges Cave by Isaac Jones in 1803. Indeed, aside from the combination of the regicides and the supernatural, the dominant theme that emerged from nineteenth-century portraits of Whalley and Goffe, in history books, novels, and plays, was the association between the regicides and liberty. Leonard Bacon, for example, declared that he knew of no other example from history that exhibited 'a more admirable combination of courage and adroitness, of fidelity to friendship, of magnanimity in distress, and of the fearless yet discreet assertion of great principles of liberty'.[27] Bacon wrote a preface for Israel Warren's full-length history of the regicides, in which Warren hoped that 'our young readers will find in the narrative a source of instruction in the principles of civil and religious liberty'.[28]

In W.A. Caruthers's *The Cavaliers of Virginia* (1834–5), indeed, the English revolutionary becomes the American proto-revolutionary. Because Whalley represents liberty, Caruthers places him—now called 'the Recluse'—in mid-1670s Virginia so he can be associated with the rebellion led by Nathaniel Bacon. The traditional view is that Bacon's Rebellion, an armed insurrection by Virginian settlers against Governor William Berkeley, was a precursor to the American Revolution because it involved a challenge to the authority of the colonial governor exactly one hundred years before the Declaration of Independence. While, in reality, Whalley had died by 1676, Caruthers includes him in *The Cavaliers of Virginia* and initially portrays him in sympathetic terms, with an admirable military bearing and stoic suffering in the face of exile and ignominy. He is described as having 'weatherbeaten' features, but he is 'eminently handsome'; he is 'perfectly proportioned', with a presence that is 'intellectual and commanding in the highest degree'. His cave outside Jamestown, a loose rendering of the real Judges Cave in New Haven, leads to a glittering arsenal that the Recluse has collected to aid the forces of liberty. The Recluse has kept a diary of the previous three decades, with 30 January 1649 bereft of text; only a bloodied handprint records the events of that day.[29]

The Recluse appears in *The Cavaliers of Virginia* whenever the young Nathaniel Bacon requires assistance, and Bacon's struggles are cast in terms of a fight for liberty against tyranny: either from nearby Native Americans or the encroaching excesses of European aristocracy as represented by Governor Berkeley. There are some complications: Bacon himself is not fully a Roundhead heir, descended as he is from both Royalist and Parliamentarian stock. Then, having discovered the death of his own fictional son, the Recluse is presented as repenting at length about his actions in the English civil wars and regicide, actions that had caused his lengthy exile: 'Retributive justice pursues and overtakes the guilty to the ends of the earth... Oh God, how just and appropriate are thy punishments!'[30] Caruthers's worn-down regicide may seem repentant, but the author presents the rebellion the Recluse supports as worthy of celebration: 'Here was sown the first germ of the American Revolution...Exactly one hundred years before the American Revolution, there was a Virginia revolution based upon precisely similar principles. The struggle commenced between the representatives of the people and the representatives of the king'.[31]

Despite the chronological and centennial convenience, the reality was more complex than this apparently straightforward rehearsal of American liberty versus British colonial tyranny.[32] Even before Nathaniel Bacon had arrived in America, tension had been increasing in Virginia. As the farming and sale of tobacco reaped massive profits, English colonists appropriated land in Virginia already occupied by Native Americans. By the end of the 1660s, around 10 million pounds of tobacco was being produced per year. Tobacco plantations took over more and more land occupied by Native Americans, who responded by destroying plantations and murdering settlers. The typical settler, too, exacerbated the tension felt in Virginia: they tended to be independent, competitive, and ruthless since tobacco plantations were tough to run, were thousands of miles away from England, and were situated in a harsh environment where death could strike suddenly through disease or murder. Men struggled to survive in these rough conditions and those who did were tough—they had to be: society was male-centred and unstable; life expectancy was short; the work was very hard; and they had guns.

Charles I appointed William Berkeley governor of Virginia in 1641. For fifteen years he ensured that Virginia's administrators were his supporters and friends. He imposed heavy taxes on tobacco growers, in part to pay his generous salary of £1,000 per year, and gave the best land to his friends. Many men who had left England for Virginia had done so because they hoped to own land and gain great wealth; Berkeley was thwarting this ambition. Furthermore, there was a rumour that Berkeley would tax settlers 1,000 pounds of tobacco to pay for forts and troops against the Native population. By 1665, the tension had increased still further as vast quantities of tobacco were being produced which flooded the market in England and caused prices to fall. Incomes in Virginia declined and taxes were heavy. To make matters worse, England was at war with the Dutch in 1665–7 and 1672–4; so the Dutch destroyed English tobacco ships.

At this point, Nathaniel Bacon, an inflammatory character, appeared in this potentially explosive situation. Bacon was the son of a Suffolk gentleman and a cousin of Governor Berkeley. He had been expelled from the University of Cambridge for 'extravagancies' and had been involved in a fraud-scheme; so his father sent him to America to join the hundreds of other ambitious and frustrated young settlers with questionable past lives. Bacon gained over 1,000 acres of land in Virginia, close to some Native Americans. Settlers like Bacon, in pursuit of more land to grow tobacco, were frequently aggressive towards these neighbours. But they encountered opposition from Governor Berkeley who punished them for such aggression.

In August 1675 Nathaniel Bacon took prisoner some Appomattox Native Americans for, he claimed, stealing corn. Berkeley criticized Bacon publicly for this rash action, because it would strain relations between Native Americans and English settlers even further. Then, in September, a thousand settlers surrounded Native American forts to punish them for their alleged behaviour the previous month. Native American chiefs were led away and murdered; some managed to escape, however, and ten settlers were killed. The following summer, when poor weather ruined the tobacco crops, some settlers blamed this misfortune on the 'sorceries of the Indians'. In June 1676, therefore, 400 men on foot, and 120 on horseback, marched with Nathaniel Bacon to Jamestown. Bacon demanded that Governor Berkeley make him general 'of all the forces in Virginia against the Indians'. Berkeley refused, stormed out of his house to meet Bacon, bared his chest, and shouted 'Here! Shoot me, foregod, fair mark, shoot!' Bacon set fire to Jamestown, but four months later died from dysentery. One thousand government troops made sure that the rebellion was put down. None of this had anything to do with Edward Whalley, who by 1676 was almost certainly dead. But historical accuracy was not allowed to impede imaginative representations of American history, like that offered by Caruthers, which looked back over a hundred years before the Revolution to identify struggles for liberty which, in turn, looked forward to the outbreak of the American War of Independence.

The regicides and liberty

The majority of nineteenth-century authors inspired by the regicides placed Whalley, Goffe, and Dixwell on this continuum of American liberty, but a few demurred. George Bancroft, in his six-volume history of America, wrote tersely and cryptically that Goffe was 'a good soldier, but ignorant of the true principles of freedom'.[33] Bancroft did not expound the precise nature of these 'true' principles or the precise flaws in Goffe's character that led him to fall short in his appreciation of them, but he was being consistent in his distinction between celebrating the American Revolution while deriding rebellion. Bancroft saw the American Revolution as a providential step in mankind's divinely ordained, organic path towards perfection; upstart rebels like Goffe were primal, explosive, and destructive.[34]

Barker's *Tragedy of Superstition* followed the interpretation of the regicides that had been favoured by Thomas Hutchinson and Peter Oliver in the eighteenth century: that Goffe was a lonely criminal with very few political sympathizers.[35] Then, three years later, J.A. Stone's *Metamora* (1829) displayed a similar restraint towards the regicides. Stone provides the familiar figure of a regicide, Mordaunt (or Hammond of Harrington—an echo of the seventeenth-century English republican James Harrington), evading Charles II's agents by hiding in burrows. Mordaunt, however, is not the heroic figure provided by the likes of McHenry. Instead, he is a character who tries to force his daughter into a socially advantageous marriage and who dies at the hands of the courageous Metamora rather than being a heroic saviour like the Angel of Hadley. Moreover, Mordaunt's role in the execution of Charles I actually foments the attempted overthrow of tyrannical Puritan governance in King Philip's War; he is a cause of the Hadley-style attack, not a valiant solution.[36]

While his character represented an unusual portrayal of a regicide in America, Mordaunt was one of the most prominent regicides on the nineteenth-century American stage. *Metamora*, like the stage version of Fenimore Cooper's *Wept*, became very popular, especially in the 1830s and 1840s, and, in fact, outlasted *Wept*, with performances until at least 1887: 'lines from the play became household words, "as familiar upon the public's tongue as the name of Washington"'.[37] Stone had subverted the popular view that an English regicide had thwarted the threat of tyranny posed by Native Americans in King Philip's War, and had thus preserved the lives and liberties of the colonists.

But these sceptical authors were in the minority. As with Caruthers's *Cavaliers of Virginia*, a frequent literary presence at moments of crisis was an English regicide. Nathaniel Hawthorne's 'The Gray Champion' (1835), for example, focuses on the reign of James II and the adminis-tration of Sir Edmund Andros, 'governor of the Dominion of New England' between 1686 and 1689.[38] The governor of New England that Leete had feared so much in 1661 had been imposed by 1686, and Hawthorne notes that Andros's administration 'lacked scarcely a single characteristic of tyranny', as it undermined the freedom of the colonies of New England. There is great excitement, then, in Hawthorne's tale, when rumours spread that William of Orange is preparing to overthrow James II, the king who had sent Andros to New England.

In response, Andros and his councillors—including Edward Randolph—attempt a show of strength, appearing on the streets of Boston along with the high churchmen and the red-coated governor's guard. A crowd appears on King Street made up of veterans from King Philip's War and, indeed, some old Parliamentarians. As reports spread that Andros is going to order a massacre of the Bostonians, a voice cries from the crowd, 'Oh! Lord of Hosts . . . provide a champion for thy people'. At this point the figure of an old, grey-bearded Puritan appears, wearing a dark cloak, and carrying a sword and staff. He walks alone along the middle of the street to confront Andros's assembled soldiers. As the old man advances, the soldiers' drumming intensifies, until he ends up marching in step to the beat. He stops sixty feet from

Andros and his companions, holds out his staff, and shouts, 'Stand!'
The drumming ceases, the old man stares at Andros, and the soldiers
stop their advance, despite Randolph's cries for them to continue.
The old Puritan addresses Andros: 'I have staid the march of a king
himself, ere now ... I am here because the cry of an oppressed people
hath disturbed me in my secret place'. He adds that James II has been
deposed and Andros's governorship has ceased. Andros stares at the
old man but orders a retreat before the 'Gray Champion' disappears.

The old man is, of course, William Goffe, and he appears to save
the colonists from tyranny in Boston, in much the same way that his
'Angel' had appeared to save them from a different kind of tyranny
in Hadley. That the real Goffe was long dead by 1689 was irrelevant.
The regicide figure appears, says Hawthorne, 'whenever the descendants
of the Puritans are to show the spirit of their sires'. So, he is present
on King Street at the Boston Massacre in 1770, then five years later
as the first revolutionaries fall at Lexington, then at Bunker Hill. The
English regicide embodies America's revolutionary spirit and appears
whenever there is the threat of oppression by tyranny, either from
America's own rulers or from an external enemy. As Hawthorne puts
it, the regicide 'is the type of New-England's hereditary spirit ... New-
England's sons will vindicate their ancestry'. Indeed, Hawthorne's
account was one of the first to depict the regicides as explicit representatives of the values of the American Revolution long before the
Revolution had occurred.

This idea was adopted seven years after Hawthorne's 'Gray Champion',
by the anonymous author of *The Salem Belle* (1842). In this novel, too,
the writer considered the link between the seventeenth-century
Puritans and their eighteenth-century descendants: 'The fathers of those
times sleep in the dust. The sons, too, are silent as the fathers; but
on the ears of the third generation the hymn of liberty poured its
strains of gladness, and the name of Washington was borne on every
breeze and enshrined in every patriot's heart'. The 'tyrant' against whom
these seventeenth-century Puritans were fighting was not Washington's

George III, but Charles II. While *The Salem Belle* does not include a regicide as a central character, a journey through Hadley provides an opportunity for meditation on 'the venerated Gen. Goffe', who was 'loved' by the whole town which protected him from 'the tyrannical Charles [II]'. Somewhat intriguingly, the author expresses compassion for Charles I, 'the only Stuart who commands the sympathy and affection of posterity', but, even if Goffe's regicidal actions had been 'misguided', his name was held in Hadley 'in honored and grateful remembrance'. For it was individuals like Goffe who led the way for America to become a country 'where no kingly prerogative tramples with its iron foot on the sacred rights of man'.[39]

H.W. Herbert's *Ruth Whalley* (1845) takes a different approach to the regicides' fight against tyranny. As with McHenry's *Spectre*, *Ruth Whalley* has a regicide surviving long into the 1680s. As with Hawthorne's 'Gray Champion', it has a proto-republican Massachusetts Bay suffering under the tyranny of Edmund Andros. This regicide, though, is not William Goffe, but an octogenarian Edward Whalley. He sits erect yet mute in the corner of a house owned by his son, Merciful Whalley. He never smiles or takes any notice of events going on around him. He does not stir until his son is struck by a Native American girl, Tituba, and Merciful attacks her in return. Ruth Whalley screams at her father, Merciful, to stop his violence, fearing that he will murder Tituba. Edward Whalley grabs a steel-hilted sword, and rushes towards his son. Edward Whalley thinks, however, that he is back in the English civil war, that the screams come from his wife, and that Charles I's Cavaliers are attacking her. Edward rebukes Merciful for attacking the girl and for being a 'persecutor'. On the national stage or in the domestic setting, Edward Whalley upholds liberty against tyranny, whether that tyranny originates from the Stuarts and their colonial officers or from his own violent son.[40]

Republican enthusiasm was taken a step further by J.K. Paulding in *The Puritan and His Daughter* (1849). Subverting the tradition of dedicating books to monarchs, Paulding instead dedicated his novel to 'the most high and mighty sovereign of sovereigns, King People'. He hoped that generations would be taught the lessons illustrated in the book, 'insomuch that it shall go through as many editions as the *Pilgrim's Progress* or *Robinson Crusoe*: that all members of Congress, past, present, and future, shall be furnished with a copy'. Paulding's central character, Harold Habingdon, flees England at the Restoration and later encounters an old, white-haired man whom he has not seen since the Battle of Marston Moor in 1644. This regicide informs Habingdon that he has 'been hunted like a wild beast' and forced to hide in various locations. The two contemplate Charles I's claims to martyrdom and agree that an earthly tribunal rightly condemned the king for abusing his power and oppressing his people. The grey-haired man hopes that the New World will do justice to the regicides' memory, for it is here that there are 'no impregnable bulwarks of oppression . . . no bristling bayonets pointed at the heart, to quell the throbbings of liberty'.[41]

For Paulding, there was something innate in America that made it a crucible for freedom. He envisaged a blank social and political slate on which a new administration and polity, based on liberty, could be drawn. The first letters had been etched by individuals like the English regicides, who had insisted that they—not God—would judge Charles I, before transplanting these ideas of liberty to the New World after they had been undermined in the Old. But there is an important caveat to add here: by tracing the origins of American liberty back to the age of the Puritan settlers, far before 1776, American authors could celebrate that liberty without celebrating the mob-led, demagogical, anarchic excesses that many observers saw resulting from the American Revolution.[42] In some interpretations, this 'harvest of Puritanism' had within it revolutionaries like Whalley and Goffe, who themselves now represented *American* Puritanism in its foundation of a wise, patient, stoic, respectable revolution, instead of the *English* Puritanism that had been explosive and bloody—even if, in reality, their signing of the king's death warrant in 1649 had, temporarily at least, helped turn the world upside down.

Writing Randolph

Some authors were preoccupied with individuals from this Old World who were on the regicides' tails, and who represented a new generation of Stuart oppression that was attempting to quash the republican ideals embodied by Whalley and Goffe. One such prominent individual was Edward Randolph. As Nathaniel Hawthorne had done in 'The Gray Champion', G.H. Hollister presented Randolph in a very negative fashion in *Mount Hope* (1851). Randolph, years after he pursued the regicides, had become a *bête noire* in America. Charles II, with Randolph's encouragement, had revoked Massachusetts Bay's charter in 1684; then Randolph had been a prominent member of Edmund Andros's administration of the Dominion of New England. It is unsurprising, therefore, that authors like Hawthorne and Hollister should have cast Randolph's earlier anti-regicide behaviour in a simi-lar critical light. Randolph is described as 'a vampire in human shape' and a 'name so associated with tyranny and overreaching power in the mind of every colonist'.[43]

While *Mount Hope* includes the standard appearance of the Angel of Hadley, Hollister reserves the greater action for fictional face-to-face conflict between Randolph and the regicides. On one occasion, Goffe ascends a rock platform just above Randolph, who shoots his rifle directly at the regicide's chest. The shot misses, and as Randolph storms towards Goffe for hand-to-hand combat, Randolph—distracted by 'the glittering spurs of knighthood and the visions of a successful political career'—is stabbed in his side. Even more dramatically and improbably, the denouement of *Mount Hope* has Hollister imagining many of the principal actors in the regicides' story assembling for one final skirmish. John Dixwell arrives to inform Goffe that Randolph is still on their tail. Channelling his inner Hamlet, Randolph appears, announcing that the regicides are 'dead—for a ducat!' before crossing swords with Goffe. Dixwell starts shooting. A young man named William Ashford bursts in to fight Randolph. Kellond and Kirke, of all people, turn up to attack Goffe, but without success. Kellond is killed; Kirke begs for mercy. Ashford wounds Randolph, but not mortally, so Randolph is able to escape to England.[44]

In Hollister's *Mount Hope*, William Ashford is actually William Goffe Jr, who is reunited with his father after a period of estrangement and the younger man's journey through America, meeting Dixwell, Winthrop, and Russell en route. Indeed, it was common for pro-regicide novelists to give Whalley and Goffe their own children based in America. In J.R. Musick's *A Century Too Soon* (1893), Goffe's daughter is betrothed to Robert Stevens, one of Bacon's 'republican' rebels: Robert's 'meeting with General Goffe and his love for Ester had more strongly cemented his love for liberty'.[45] Goffe has a daughter, Maria, in Grimm's *The King's Judges* (1892), while in McHenry's *Spectre of the Forest*, Goffe is the father of Ester Devenart. Edward Whalley, too, has a son, Merciful, in Herbert's *Ruth Whalley*, as well as his eponymous granddaughter. In fictional terms, therefore, the regicides are imagined as bestowing a biological legacy: revolutionary names and revolutionary genes that form a direct genealogical link between 1649 and 1776. The regicides' revolutionary spirit did not merely live on in some intangible and undetectable form until its re-emergence during the War of Independence. Instead, pro-regicide authors portrayed them as proto-Founding Fathers who not only transplanted revolutionary ideas to America in the 1660s but also provided the *American* descendants in whom those ideas would germinate a century later.

Beyond fiction

Whalley, Goffe, and Dixwell did not just appear in novels in the nineteenth century. In Britain, the incendiary British socialist George Julian Harney invoked John Dixwell in his periodical *The Democratic Review* (1849–50). Harney had been imprisoned for selling the unstamped *Poor Man's Guardian*; he was a founder of the republican East London Democratic Association; he was a Chartist who urged the use of physical force to achieve universal suffrage; he was an advocate of a General Strike; he met Karl Marx and Friedrich Engels; and his journal, *The Red Republican*, published the first translation of *The Communist Manifesto*. Harney's *Democratic Review* carried an article prompted by the opening of Dixwell's grave in New Haven and the erection of a monument to the regicide. Dixwell had died in New Haven on 18 March 1689 and his remains had been deposited in a grave on (or before) 1 April. *The Democratic Review* hailed Dixwell as one of those who had acted as a 'champion' of the Good Old Cause in the 'revolutionary conflict' and who had been confident to his dying day that 'the Lord will appear for his people . . . and that there will be those in power again who will relieve the injured and oppressed'.[46] Writers in America had no need to foment revolution in the same way as George Julian Harney: they had already shaken off the shackles of British rule and few would have followed Harney down the path of revolutionary socialism.

In 1850 John and Elizabeth Barber considered the story of Whalley and Goffe hiding in a cave to be of use for 'moral and religious' instruction. Citing the inscription on the cave, 'Opposition to tyrants is obedience to God', they published a poem that would educate their readers about the regicides' plight. The poem compared the regicides to the 'holy men of old', struggling against the elements to preserve their liberty and their opposition to tyranny.[47] Much more famously, Henry David Thoreau, while contemplating 'solitude' in his *Walden* (1854), referred to 'a most wise and humorous friend . . . who keeps himself more secret than ever did Goffe or Whalley';[48] while Walt Whitman, in the 1860s, published the section of *Leaves of Grass* titled 'To a Cantatrice':

Here, take this gift,
I was reserving it for some hero, speaker, or general,
One who should serve the good old cause, the great idea, the progress and
    freedom of the race,
Some brave confronter of despots, some daring rebel;
But I see that what I was reserving belongs to you just as much as to any.[49]

Whitman's phrase 'good old cause' referred generically to the cause of freedom and liberty, and he used it elsewhere in the context of America's civil war. But the phrase was borrowed from the English civil war and Interregnum, and it would have been difficult by this point to read about a 'general' serving the 'good old cause', a 'brave confronter of despots', without thinking back to those 'daring rebels' Whalley and Goffe.[50]

Celebration of republican freedom was also to be found in American visual art of the mid-nineteenth century. On 24 December 1847, Prosper Wetmore, president of the American Art Union, addressed that society and refuted the assumption that republican institutions were inimical to 'the cultivation of the arts of design'; that the 'influences of a free public opinion must of necessity be indicated in something "savage and wild"'. Instead, the artwork commissioned or encouraged by the American Art Union, the artefacts of the American School, sent out 'a living school of moral beauty', a 'contemplation of the sublime, the beautiful, the true'. One of these paintings, distributed among the union's members in December 1847, was Thomas P. Rossiter's *The Regicide Judges Succored by the Ladies of New Haven* (see Figure 7).[51] Rossiter was a New Haven native and the catalogue of his paintings notes that *The Regicide Judges* was painted in 1847 and owned by a member of the banking, real estate, legal, and railroad Litchfield family.[52]

As with the recent American literature on Whalley and Goffe, Rossiter's painting was a sanitized portrayal of the regicides, and one that amended their story so it could fit the style of American national identity encouraged at the time. He may have promoted Wetmore's 'moral beauty', but not really 'contemplation of...the true'. Rossiter's painting has the elder of the regicides, Whalley, standing well dressed, poised, and dignified in front of a large opening to the Judges Cave, in contrast to the reality of a cramped and undignified existence at the mercy of the elements. To the right of the composition sit Goffe and another male figure, presumably Richard Sperry, who had assisted the regicides during their time on West Rock. To the left of the painting

Figure 7. Thomas P. Rossiter, *The Regicide Judges Succored by the Ladies of New Haven* (1847)

are four female figures, those 'Ladies of New Haven' who were offering 'succor' to Whalley and Goffe. This was in contrast to the documentary evidence of the regicides' time in the cave, but it enabled Rossiter to place the scene of the Judges Cave more firmly in the context of artwork that promoted American national identity through celebration of its colonial past, shifting the focus away from the English regicides and towards the American colonists. Whalley may stand at the centre of the composition, but the muse-like ladies of New Haven are the heroic protectors in a sturdy yet serene American landscape. The importance Rossiter ascribed to the Judges Cave can be gleaned from the other, now much more famous, iconic historical figures he incorporated into his oeuvre: Christopher Columbus; the Mayflower pilgrims; the signatories of the American constitution; and paintings of George Washington in various settings.[53]

Approximately two years after Rossiter painted *The Regicide Judges*, a regicide took a more dramatic role in what has become the iconic canvas associated with the regicides in America. F.A. Chapman's *The Perils of Our Forefathers* is an intense and theatrical portrayal of Goffe's appearance as the Angel of Hadley (see Figure 8). Chapman, first president of the Brooklyn Art School and leading spirit in its foundation, had been born in Old Saybrook, Connecticut, thirty miles east of New Haven and ninety miles south of Hadley. He was interested in the history of his native region and claimed descent from Puritan colonists of the area. *The Perils of Our Forefathers* portrays these Puritans cowering in the Hadley church, with Reverend John Russell in his pulpit looking at first resigned, but on closer inspection taking hold of a gun. Through the church doors we glimpse a chaotic scene outside, with houses on fire, colonists panicking, and Native Americans about to storm the colonists' safe haven. But in the centre of the composition

Figure 8. J.C. McRae, engraving of F.A. Chapman, *The Perils of Our Forefathers* (c. 1850)

stands William Goffe: aged and hoary yet upright and determined, fearlessly coordinating Hadley's defence. From 1859 J.C. McRae greatly expanded the audience for Chapman's dramatic rendering of the Angel of Hadley story by making engravings that were very popular and sold widely.[54] A similar engraving, E.H. Corbauld's *Goffe Repulsing the Indians*, had already been in circulation, though in this rendering the inhabitants of Hadley are mid-battle, with Native Americans drawing their bows and arrows in the foreground, and a more cartoon-like Goffe stands in the centre of the action with sword drawn and his left hand in the air directing the colonists' resistance (see Figure 9).

The 1850s also witnessed G.H. Durrie's contributions to the visual culture of the regicides with his paintings of *West Rock* (1853) and *Judges Cave* (1856) (see Figures 10 and 11). As with Frederic Edwin Church's *West Rock, New Haven* (1849), Durrie's paintings did not feature a visual representation of the regicides themselves, but they did combine two related interests. The first was the beautiful and dramatic territory of New Haven, the portrayal of which on canvas promoted the rugged and peaceful American landscape, a contribution to a distinctive American

Figure 9. E.H. Corbauld, *Goffe Repulsing the Indians* (1856)

Figure 10. G.H. Durrie, *Judges Cave* (1856)

Figure 11. G.H. Durrie, *West Rock* (1853)

national identity through the visual arts. The second was the ghost of the regicides: they did not need to be physically present on canvas for the viewer to make their connection between the New Haven landscape and the dramatic story of the escape of Whalley and Goffe. The very name, *Judges Cave*, evoked their plight when looking at the iconic New Haven scene. The empty cave was almost biblical in its dramatic emptiness: a timeless and immovable symbol of liberty against tyranny, with the spirit of Whalley and Goffe living on there, · even when their physical bodies were gone. By America's own civil war, then, heroes from England's civil war were prominent features on page, stage, and canvas. They were real or spectral figures who were modified to entertain, to educate, and to celebrate within a nascent American national identity that had to find ways to come to terms with its European origins.

7

The regicides' revival, rise, and decline

The conscience of an honest man,
Is full as royal as a king.

John Leete, *The Family of Leete* (1906), 170

Talk of freedom and liberty in early nineteenth-century America did not, of course, apply to the almost 4 million African-American slaves in southern slave-owning states. As Americans continued to drive westwards, the question of whether the new states would be slave-owning or free brought North and South into a civil war that would lead to the deaths of over 600,000 combatants. Amidst such devastation, the fate of three Puritan regicides in colonial America might easily seem irrelevant. Indeed, at first sight, *Mount Hope*'s publication in 1851 marked the beginning of the end of interest in the regicides in American literature, with that interest disappearing totally by the outbreak of the civil war a decade later. After decades of processing the cataclysmic violence wrought during the French Revolution, perhaps authors now found it too difficult to celebrate the bloody regicide that had occurred just across the English Channel.[1] We might also consider the effect of 'angel saturation': a popular motif had become too widespread and those authors who strived for originality would move gradually away from the increasingly stale story of Goffe and Hadley.

On the contrary, though, with the exception of the years following the assassination of Abraham Lincoln in 1865, interest in Whalley and Goffe persisted. The reminder in Lincoln's 1863 Gettysburg Address that America was a nation 'conceived in liberty' would have evoked memories of the circumstances of that conception, including the revolutionary inheritance bestowed on Americans by their seventeenth-century English ancestors. The process of nation-building, both as Americans continued to push westwards and as they attempted to recover from their civil war divisions, continued to feature aspects of the American colonial past. This was especially the case towards the end of the nineteenth century when America's startling growth, the social dislocation caused by westward resettlement, rapid urbanization, and memories of the destruction augured by mechanized warfare provoked some Americans to embrace their colonial past as a simpler and more desirable time. And two figures by now inexorably associated with that colonial past were Edward Whalley and William Goffe.

America's civil war and the regicides

At 11 a.m. on Thursday, 10 December 1863—two years into the American civil war—the Massachusetts Historical Society assembled to hear its president, Robert C. Winthrop, read an extract from the diary of William Goffe, which had been found among his family papers. The following year, John Gorham Palfrey published the third volume of his *History of New England*—the part that dealt with Goffe at Hadley—even though the publication process had been interrupted by the civil war. Nathaniel Hawthorne's *Dr Grimshawe's Secret*, an unpublished romance written during the American civil war, features a possible regicide in its web of references to British and American history. The story takes place near a Salem graveyard and includes a character who dreams of an ancient English estate from which a regicidal Puritan fled to New England, where he started a family.[2]

Continued interest in the regicides at this time might be explained in two divergent ways. Retreat into colonial history may have offered

an escape from the miseries of America's own civil war; the regicides'
story was devoid of slavery and the debates surrounding it. Perhaps
those civil war soldiers who had their picture taken atop the Judges
Cave outside New Haven were indulging in their own form of escape
(see Figure 12).[3] Conversely, the story of Whalley and Goffe may have
been attractive to Union supporters, as it was rendered as a story about
liberty—albeit a different kind of liberty from the emancipation of
slaves. The way that the New England states concentrated on their
own peculiar history might also have constituted an exercise in forming

Figure 12. Henry S. Peck, stereoview of civil war soldiers at the Judges
Cave, New Haven (1860s)

their own identity—either for the Union during the war years or for America as a whole in subsequent decades.

Whatever the explanation, the regicides clearly had not left the American cultural landscape by the early 1860s. It is possible that Abraham Lincoln's assassination in 1865 temporarily reduced the American taste for literature that celebrated the deaths of national leaders. John Wilkes Booth, the assassin, claimed that he was carrying out tyrannicide, a term strongly associated with the English regicides, while Reverend Henry Smith, pastor of the North Presbyterian Church in Buffalo, New York, called the assassination 'deeper dyed in guilt than any regicide in the history of the world'.[4] The Portuguese observer Rebelo da Silva called Lincoln's assassination 'essentially, a regicide'.[5] Caroline Hayden, in *Our Country's Martyr* (1865), lamented "Tis nothing new, this crime of regicide'.[6] Warren Hathaway, also writing in 1865, went further and described Wilkes Booth as 'more than a regicide', echoing Charles I's martyrology *Eikon Basilike* of 1649, by describing Lincoln as 'sacred...in the estimation of Heaven'.[7] This might explain why James Bayard Taylor's *The Strange Friend*, arguably the only published creative piece to address the regicides in the late 1860s, had merely the faintest echoes of Whalley, Goffe, and Dixwell, as it featured a nineteenth-century fugitive hiding from the British authorities in Pennsylvania.[8] Soon, though, the Colonial Revival and centenary of the American Revolution stimulated, on the page and the stage, even more interest in proto-revolutionary regicides, their lives, and their afterlives.

Centenaries and cycles

When the regicides' letters were printed in 1868, their editor noted that this 'revived the interest' that had 'always been felt' in Whalley, Goffe, and Dixwell. But it was not until the final decades of the century that there was another surge of literature concerned with the regicides.[9] There have been suggestions that, after the 1870s, authors tended to shun the legend of Hadley: a local historian, George Sheldon, had encouraged cynicism about the Angel story in 1874 and

Goffe's hoary and theatrical appearance faded from public view because of this 'glare of realism'.[10] But we should not assume that the regicides' story as a whole disappeared from public consciousness, or that the Angel of Hadley had appeared in print for the last time.

We can explain the late nineteenth-century renewal of interest in the regicides in a number of ways. In both the North and the South, the American civil war led to a growth in nationalism: the process of reconciliation included a focus on national traditions that bound individuals and parties in a recently divided nation.[11] The regicides' story was untainted by recent debates and divisions and was one that had inspired American national pride just half a century previously. Furthermore, the regicides' revival was part of a broader cultural movement that occurred in the late nineteenth century. The Colonial Revival looked back nostalgically to a time before the American civil war, while criticizing the cacophonous, corrupt, and commercialized tone of contemporary industrialized life. An additional purpose of the movement was to heal and rebuild the nation by remembering that the colonial period had been, it was claimed, a more peaceful time of honesty and virtue. By combining European colonial styles with the patriotism inspired by a renewed interest in the lives of revolutionary figures, both Europhile and American appetites were satisfied.[12]

This was a potent combination and one that promoted a revival of interest in Anglo-American colonial subjects, especially those that pointed the way to American liberty like the stories of Whalley, Goffe, and Dixwell. Thus, in 1873 Israel Perkins Warren's book—*The Three Judges: Story of the Men who Beheaded Their King*—was published in New York. Four years later, Robert Patterson Robins wrote about 'Edward Whalley, The Regicide' for the first volume of *The Pennsylvania Magazine of History and Biography*. Another visual representation of the 'Angel of Hadley' appeared in 1883 in Augustus L. Mason's *The Romance and Tragedy of the Pioneer Life*. This rendering, much less intense and action-packed than *The Perils of Our Forefathers* or *Goffe Repulsing the Indians*, featured no Native Americans at all, focusing instead on the trepidation of the Hadley residents and a less distinctive or forceful, if still bearded, Goffe (see Figure 13). In 1884 the

Figure 13. *Men of Hadley* from Augustus L. Mason, *The Romance and Tragedy of the Pioneer Life* (1884), 133

historian Henry Howe recounted the story of Whalley and Goffe hiding in their cave.[13] Two years later George Bancroft published his cryptic observations about Goffe's ignorance of the 'true principles of freedom'.[14]

This interest continued into the 1890s. Perhaps inspired by Frederick Hull Cogswell's article on 'The Regicides in New England' for the *New England Magazine*, 'many visitors' were reported at the cave above New Haven, in which Whalley and Goffe had sheltered in 1661.[15] By 1895 Charles Knowles Bolton felt he could not write a poem of colonial romance and courtship without including a digression about Whalley and Goffe's adventures: their hiding in New Haven, Governor Endecott's pretended interest in their capture, towns being searched, and the regicides' imagined evasion of Kellond and Kirke under a footbridge.[16] While the regicides' story amounted to only a small portion of the poem—approximately thirty out of 550 lines—Bolton thought he could attract readers by advertising the poem as 'a versified narrative of the time of the regicides'. Such was Bolton's enthusiasm for these regicides that he considered William Goffe to be one of his country's 'founders' when he published a series of mini-biographies of notable individuals who had travelled from Europe to North America in the seventeenth century.[17]

There is another explanation for the increased attention given to the regicides in the late nineteenth century: some Americans were very interested in the cyclical nature of their past. Writers and readers of American history were sensitive to what they considered centennial parallels in New England history. John Gorham Palfrey noted what he called 'chronological parallelisms': between the Nichols, Carr, Cartwright, and Maverick commission of 1664–5 and the Stamp Act of 1765; between the beginning of the 'attack' on New England's 'freedom' in 1675—the start of King Philip's War and, it was thought, the liberating appearance of Goffe's 'Angel of Hadley'—and the invasion of 1775 'which led to [America's] independence of Great Britain'.[18]

There was also a chronological convenience in Bacon's Rebellion, a reaction to alleged British colonial tyranny, and the Declaration of Independence a hundred years later. This parallel was not lost on J.R. Musick, who called his novel based on Bacon's Rebellion *A Century Too Soon*: 'though one hundred years before liberty was actually obtained, the sleeping goddess seemed to have opened her eyes on that occasion and yawned'.[19] In the late nineteenth century, then, it was not unnatural for Americans to cast their minds back a century or two and to see centennial parallels between events that had happened in the eighteenth century and those that had taken place in the seventeenth. The centennial of the American Revolution provoked reflection on the causes of that revolution and meditation on the seeds sown in a colonial American soil naturally fertile for autonomy and independence.

Reflection on the seventeenth century would have involved looking back to the regicides on the run in America; the opportunity to bring seventeenth-century history into the scope of the American Revolution furnished one reason why the regicides and their protectors retained their significance into the late nineteenth century. They provided 'evidence' that the American revolutionary spirit had its beginnings in the early colonists and their love of freedom. On 4 July 1883 at an Independence Day celebration at Woodstock, Connecticut, Leonard Woolsey Bacon read a poem that celebrated those colonial Americans who had anticipated the independence of America in 1776. One of them was William Leete, famed for his protection of the fugitive regicides:

> And tell of Guilford's William Leete,
>   Who stretched the State's right arm to hide
> In many a wilderness retreat
>   The vengeance hunted regicide,
>
> And told the bearers of the ban,
>   Signed and broad sealed "that tender thing
> The conscience of an honest man,
>   Is full as royal as a king."[20]

Bacon was following in the footsteps of his father, Leonard Bacon, pastor of the First Church of New Haven, who had argued in his *Thirteen Historical Discourses* of 1839 that the New Haven colonists' protection of the regicides was a 'fearless yet discreet assertion of great principles of liberty'.[21]

Stage to page

We have already seen early nineteenth-century dramatic portrayals of the regicides on the American stage in Barker's *Tragedy of Superstition*, Stone's *Metamora*, and the play form of Cooper's *The Wept of Wish-ton-Wish*. Whalley and Goffe once again trod the boards in the late nineteenth century, in Edward Grimm's *The King's Judges: An Original Comedy*, published in San Francisco in 1892. In this play Grimm again underlined an implicit connection between the revolutionary spirit of America's seventeenth-century settlers and the revolutionary mood of the eighteenth-century colonists, while further twisting the actual events that had surrounded Whalley and Goffe in the 1660s and 1670s. Grimm's New Haven inhabitants conclude that they 'have no confidence in Kings' and that 'the colonies will have no peace until they hoist their own sails and steer for liberty'. When the play's characters hear news of the executions in London of the regicides Thomas Harrison, Thomas Scot, and Hugh Peters, they declare that 'this action of the king may cause another revolution'; indeed 'it ought to re-kindle the republican feeling, if there is a spark left in the ashes'.[22]

The story of the regicides on the run would have provided sufficient drama to keep a theatre audience entertained, even if some inventive scene changes would have been required to convey the sense of the regicides travelling from place to place. Grimm's description of his play as a 'comedy', however, stretches the imagination. Apart from some exchanges in Act II, scene iii reminiscent of Sir John Falstaff and Mistress Quickly in Shakespeare's *Henry IV, Parts 1 and 2*, the remainder of the play is a straight history (or pseudo-history) with the odd moment of romance. The central figures are cast in familiar terms: Charles II is described as 'a prince destitute of honor and virtue', who threatens the New England colonies' 'civil and religious privileges'; 'a trickster and deceiver' who is 'always ready to promise but never ready to keep his word'; and who is 'just as stupid and as obstinate as his father, who is certainly one of the most stupid asses that ever lived'. Whalley and Goffe, however, are 'men of uncommon talent, and, by their dignified manners and grave deportment, command universal respect'; they are 'upright, honorable and desirable citizens'.[23]

There are references in *The King's Judges* to genuine historical events, including the open manner in which Whalley and Goffe had arrived in Massachusetts Bay,[24] and the New Haven residents' discussion of plans to capture the regicides.[25] But while the play is set in New Haven in 1661, there is a curious twist: prominent individuals in the true story of the regicides play no part and are replaced by fictional characters. Kellond or Kirke, for example, appears as a Captain Dobson, the earl of Clarendon's former groom who is in pursuit of the regicides, is imprisoned by the colonists, and is then driven out of New Haven with the threat of a noose awaiting him, should he ever return.[26] Other elements of the play have no basis in fact whatsoever: Goffe ends up buying a farm in New Haven near the cave where the fugitives can hide if any more commissions arrive from England to search for them.

As with Barker, Stone, and Cooper in the first half of the century, not all late nineteenth-century fictional accounts of the regicides were quite so sympathetic to the regicides. John R. Musick's *A Century Too Soon* (1893), already noted for making the historical links between 1649, 1676, and 1776, was less optimistic than *The King's Judges* about the regicides' reception in New England. William Goffe arrives in Boston from New Plymouth with his six-year-old daughter, Ester. They try to find shelter at an inn but the inn's owner refuses to help them. They continue searching and think they have found refuge but a man appears to tell their would-be host to 'drive them hence. No good ever comes to one harboring such'. They arrive at a blacksmith's house but Goffe and Ester are rejected again, as 'to harbour a regicide might mean death on the scaffold'. They are 'rejected at every door', until finally a Puritan family gives them shelter.

Musick is closer to Thomas Hutchinson than Ezra Stiles in his assessment of the regicides, though his portrayal omits Whalley and overlooks the kind reception initially given them in Cambridge and Boston by Reverend Charles Chauncey, Governor Endecott, Edward Collins, Elder Frost, and John Norton. Indeed, Musick's ambivalence towards the regicides emerges in his plagiarism of the historian George Bancroft, as he calls Goffe 'a firm friend of the family of Cromwell, a good soldier and an ardent partisan, but ignorant of the true principles of freedom'.[27] Musick also suggests that Charles II was not 'a bloodthirsty man', but 'good-natured, thinking more of pleasures and beautiful mistresses than of vengeance; but it was only natural that he should feel anxious to bring the murderers of his father to the scaffold'.[28] Yet despite Musick's less sympathetic approach to the regicides and moderate assessment of Charles II, he could not avoid seeing Bacon's Rebellion as a precursor to the American Revolution and associating those two American struggles for liberty with the principles of the English Revolution, by placing the Goffe family alongside Bacon's 'little army of dauntless patriots'.[29]

There was a curious tendency for regicide-preoccupied novelists in the late nineteenth and early twentieth centuries to claim that their subject had been neglected. When Frederick Hull Cogswell came to write his account of the regicides, he observed that 'for the most part the tale has slept as undisturbed as the bones of the forefathers whose living eyes looked upon the scenes and the persons involved'. His claim was not correct: his 'tale of early colonial times', published in 1896, followed the publication of several accounts of Whalley and Goffe, whether fictional, semi-fictional, or non-fictional. Like many of those accounts, Cogswell was determined to portray Whalley and Goffe in a positive light by imagining certain characteristics that were to be admired in both men. Whalley was 'tall and soldierly in bearing, his venerable head adorned with snowy white hair'; his face 'would any- where be judged to be of scholarly taste and habit'. Goffe was 'of firm and not too heavy build, with a magnificent head rising from a strong but graceful neck and a broad pair of shoulders'.[30] Cogswell was cre- ating pen-portraits of individuals he viewed as Anglo-American heroes.

Cogswell imagines the regicides conversing with their colonial protectors and portrays the former as stoic and honourable men who refuse to put the latter in danger. 'If we remain here, we render thy position one of extreme danger', they are imagined telling William Leete, 'and we would sooner perish in the storm than betray a friend'.[31] The regicides' colonial protectors similarly are portrayed in the warm glow of admiration and adoration. Leete is described as 'wise, learned, pious, honest and industrious'.[32] In contrast, Royalist agents are cast as one-dimensional villains: Kellond is described as having a 'nature at once grasping and insatiable';[33] Charles II is called 'the jesting liber- tine' as well as a 'faithless despot' and a 'tyrant'.[34] Instead of seeing the lack of interest from London in the regicides as evidence that Charles was preoccupied or pragmatic, Cogswell interpreted the quiet inter- ludes when there were no attempts to capture them as 'the quiet of the panther that crouches hidden until the prey is off its guard'.[35] Davenport is portrayed reflecting on the regicide: 'a cruel necessity to many minds, but right or wrong, the men who decreed it were the saviours of England'. Robert Treat is imagined describing the regicide as 'one of the noblest acts in all history, in showing the world that tyrants can no longer trample on the rights of the people'.[36] The only 'absolute monarchy' in the colony is the schoolhouse; 'everywhere else the individual was sovereign, and the executive was nothing but the symbol of the universal will'.[37]

Like Cogswell, when Margaret Sidney wrote her own story centred on the regicides, *The Judges' Cave* (1900), she claimed that the topic had 'had too scant notice from the pen of novelist or poet'. Perhaps she had not read Scott, Southey, or the other twenty or so novelists and poets who had written about Whalley, Goffe, and Dixwell. Sidney had grown up next to the New Haven burial ground, where she had frequently visited what she thought were the regicides' graves. She often walked to the regicides' cave where her imagination was unleashed and her heart throbbed 'in sympathy' with the regicides' cause. Sidney's novel is an encomium to her hometown of New Haven whose own safety was jeopardized for becoming a 'bulwark of protection' of liberty.[38] Four years later, in W.H. Gocher's *Wadsworth* (1904), it was not New Haven that was the 'cradle of democracy', but another town through which the regicides had passed, in March 1661, and where Goffe was living by September 1676: Hartford.[39]

The regicides' tale had begun as one that catered to the American taste for the supernatural, but it then became, for the most part, a tale that catered to the American taste for liberty. Stories like the Angel of Hadley satisfied both palates—a spectral figure preserving the lives and liberties of New England colonists. There were some authors like Bancroft, Barker, and Stone who were less effusive about the virtues of the regicides, but they were in the minority. Wherever and whenever there was a tyrant—preferably an English one—there was a literary regicide ready to challenge him. In the American imagination a regicide could appear in any episode interpreted as a stepping stone on the road to American independence and liberty, like Bacon's Rebellion or resistance to Edmund Andros. Indeed, by 1882 the regicides and individuals like Bacon were considered to be so similar that the two coalesced visually into one another. In Charlotte M. Yonge's *Pictorial History of the World's Great Nations*, Chapman's *Perils of Our Forefathers* (engraved by McRae) was redrawn with Nathaniel Bacon replacing William Goffe. The Angel of Hadley had become the Hero of Virginia. The replacement was exactly the same figure who inspired his followers in exactly the same way, only one had greyer hair and a beard (see Figure 14).

Figure 14. Engraving of *Perils of Our Forefathers* in Charlotte M. Yonge, *A Pictorial History of the World's Great Nations, from the Earliest Dates to the Present Time* (1882)

Bodies

Following on from the myths in Ezra Stiles's *History* of the regicides, regicide myths were born from later corruptions of their story, the blending of fact with fiction, the desire for adventure consonant with heroic proto-American revolutionaries, and an appetite for caricatures of historical personalities. But such distortion did not end with histories and novels. Folklore and myth also found their way into stories about the regicides' final resting places. This is a subject of more than morbid interest; preoccupation with the regicides' bodies hints at continued interest in their fate among nineteenth- and twentieth-century Americans, and illustrates the distortion of historical truth by local folklore and family traditions. It furthers the idea that the regicides, alive or dead, have long been ripe for myth-making and appropriation by generations of Americans keen to associate themselves, or their localities, with these apparently revolutionary heroes.

Claims and counter-claims about the graves of Whalley and Goffe have been made and disputed for a number of reasons. First, there is little or no definitive documentation to prove their exact burial locations. Second, the regicides' protectors had an interest in keeping Whalley and Goffe's final resting places secret: they would not have wanted to leave the fugitives' bodies vulnerable to punitive revenge and exhumation by Royalists, as had been the fate of the corpses of Oliver Cromwell, Henry Ireton, and John Bradshaw in London in 1661. And third, they would not wish to draw attention to their own protection of the regicides and risk harsh treatment of their own communities by Charles II and his agents in America. As the decades and centuries went by, however, and the perceived threat of retribution from London receded, a number of different localities laid claim to being the final resting places of the regicides. They took pride in their history of protecting such guardians of liberty and wished to stake their claim to an intimate association with them.

Various theories have been suggested concerning Whalley's final resting place. Though some are plausible, few are convincing. One theory, which originated in the folklore of the young girls of Hadley, suggested that Whalley had been buried under a fence on the border of Peter Tilton's land in the town; that way neither he nor his neighbour could be blamed for protecting a regicide, alive or dead.[40] This was undermined in 1795 when the wall of the cellar under Reverend Russell's house in Hadley was removed. About four feet underground, under the front kitchen wall, the earth was loose. Further excavation of this area uncovered some pieces of wood, some flat stones, shards of human bone, two teeth, and the whole thighbone of a tall man. The prevalent interpretation of the discovery was that these were the bones of Edward Whalley, who had died in Hadley in the mid-1670s.[41] While this theory had its detractors (one thought that Whalley's body would not have decomposed so much so quickly),[42] the discovery appeared to undermine another tradition that Whalley had been buried on the green in New Haven under a stone marked 'E. W. 1653'. This was unlikely anyway: a regicide's grave would not have been marked in this way. The date '1653' may have been a red-herring, designed to put regicide-hunters off the scent. Or it may have been a misreading of '1673' or '1678', more likely dates for Whalley's death. Stiles thought the possible Whalley headstone so important that he included it as one of his plates in his *History*, along with a possible corruption of the '5' to a '7' (see Figure 15). A more likely explanation, however, is that the New Haven gravestone, with the inscription

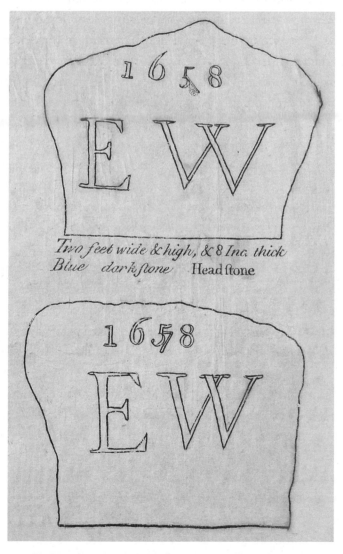

Figure 15. Illustration of gravestones from the New Haven burial ground, Ezra Stiles, *A History of Three of the Judges of Charles I* (1794), 136

'E.W.', belongs to Edward Wigglesworth, who died in the colony on
1 October 1653.[43]

The wrong Whalley?

The development of antiquarian history in the nineteenth century
brought with it renewed interest in Whalley and Goffe, those who
had assisted and protected them, and what eventually happened to the
regicides' bodies.[44] In the first edition of *The Pennsylvania Magazine of
History and Biography*, Robert Patterson Robins sought to provide a
new theory about Edward Whalley's later life, attempting to pierce the
'almost impenetrable fog of mystery' surrounding Whalley's final
years.[45] His idea was novel but wholly incorrect: Robins granted
Whalley an extra-long life that carried on beyond Hadley or New
Haven, or any of the other locations that had been suggested for the
regicide's death and burial. Instead, Robins suggested, Whalley had
fled to the county of Somerset in Maryland, where he lived until he
was 103 years old.

Even before this theory is investigated in detail, it sounds improbable. We know from the regicides' correspondence in the 1670s that
Whalley's health was failing, and that he almost certainly died in
Hadley in the course of that decade. What, then, was Robins's reasoning? First, he suggested that the bones discovered in Russell's cellar
need not have been those of Whalley. They could easily have been
Goffe's. Second, Robins relied on a letter written by Thomas Robins
of Worcester County, Maryland, in July 1769. An eager genealogist,
Thomas Robins, tracked down an Edward Middleton, whom he considered to be Whalley under a pseudonym. Middleton had arrived in
Virginia in 1681, where he was met by his two brothers-in-law. He
then travelled to Maryland, staying first at the mouth of the Pocomoke
River, before moving to Sinepuxent, where he purchased twenty-two
acres and named the property 'Genezar'. Middleton/Whalley then
moved to the southernmost point of the land—'South Point'—with
his family in 1687. It was soon afterwards, Robins claims, that

Middleton/Whalley felt safe enough to reveal his real name after the Glorious Revolution. Middleton/Whalley then lived at South Point with his family—including three sons and three daughters—until his death in 1718.[46]

Thomas Robins's letter was a curious one. At first sight, it appeared to be the work of someone keen to associate himself with a regicide and lover of liberty. The writer was laying claim to regicidal ancestry on the unlikely basis that a regicide who was close to death in the 1670s somehow managed to live for another four decades and sire six children in America. The neglect of the available historical sources and the suspension of common sense—by both Robert Patterson Robins and Thomas Robins—would be the traits of people desperate to cement a link with regicidal heroes. But the final lines of Thomas Robins's letter suggested that he was not so proud of the association: he noted that 'had he received that due to him, [Whalley] would have suffered and died on the scaffold as did many of his traitorous companions'. And just in case we were unsure of his loyalty to the British monarchy, he signed off 'Vivat rex'.[47]

Robert Patterson Robins was keener than his ancestor, it seems, to claim a genealogical link with Whalley the regicide. He took Thomas Robins's letter as sound historical proof and added further points to suggest that the man who died at South Point in 1718 was indeed Whalley and that he had good reasons to settle in Maryland: first, the renewed threat of persecution after Edward Randolph's arrival in 1686 as James II's commissioner; second, the relative safety of a proprietary government rather than a charter province; third, the warmer climate that would have eased the pain in Whalley's ageing body; and fourth, the presence of his family en route in Virginia. Robins also encouraged his readers to think that Middleton was Whalley because of his reluctance to stay anywhere 'public' where he might be discovered: first Virginia, then the mouth of the Pocomoke River.[48] Indeed, there were few places to live more remote than South Point, Sinepuxent.

Only after the Glorious Revolution of 1688, allegedly, did 'Middleton' feel safe enough to reveal his real name. But the 'Middleton' pseudonym itself enables us to unpick the Robins theory and suggest that both men have the right real name, but the wrong man. Robert Patterson Robins claims that the regicide Whalley used the name 'Middleton' as a pseudonym because it was his wife's maiden name. So it was; but it was also a name that might have been adopted by one of Whalley's children who wanted to conceal his own identity. Overexcited at the prospect that the Whalley who had settled in South Point was the famous signatory of Charles I's death warrant, both Robert Patterson Robins and his ancestor Thomas Robins over-looked the fact that there was another Whalley travelling around the American colonies in the late seventeenth century who also had rea-son to keep his real surname secret: because of his participation in Nathaniel Bacon's Rebellion in Virginia in 1676.

Indeed, from the moment it was published, readers of *The Pennsylvania Magazine* were not convinced by Robins's theory. W.H. Whitmore wrote from Boston in June 1877, suggesting a number of improbabil-ities in the Robins argument. First, if it was the regicide Whalley who died in 1718, one might expect his will to make mention of his very advanced age, which it does not. Second, the will hints that his wife survived him, but Whalley's wife (Mary Middleton) died in the early 1660s[49] and none of the surviving sources suggests that he remarried in America. Third, the will of 'Edward Wale' of Worcester County, Maryland, dated 21 April 1718, is signed with an 'x' rather than a proper signature.[50] According to the Robins theory, Whalley the regi-cide would have been around 103 by now and would have suffered decades of ill health; so perhaps he simply could not summon the strength to sign his will properly. Whalley the regicide had demon-strated in 1649 that he was perfectly capable of signing his name. Indeed, it was his signature that had got him into so much trouble in the first place. Instead, it was more likely that the Whalley who lived in South Point was a son of the regicide—Edward Whalley's sixth child (also called Edward)—or just a man who happened to share the regicide's name.

Perhaps the South Point Whalley did take part in Bacon's Rebellion of 1676. After Nathaniel Bacon's death, the rebels' last stand took place at New Kent and an Edward Whalley Jr was one of the main fomenters of the continued disloyalty. This Whalley fled from the rebellion and escaped the capital punishment that would have befallen him, had he been captured. It is plausible that between 1676 and 1681, this younger Whalley travelled from New Kent, across or around Chesapeake Bay, to Sinepuxent. Had this been the case, the younger Whalley would have avoided using his famous and inflammatory surname, opting instead for the anonymity provided by his mother's maiden name. Furthermore, he would have sought a remote settlement, somewhere like South Point, to avoid being discovered and brought to justice. By the late 1680s, the political climate had changed sufficiently for this Whalley to come out into the open: Governor Berkeley, who initially sought retribution for Bacon's Rebellion, had been away from the colonies for a decade, and the accession to the British throne of William and Mary might give rise to a political amnesty for those who had been disloyal to the Stuart monarchy both at home and overseas. One of the younger Edward Whalley's children was named Nathaniel—a tribute, it seems, to one of his former fellow rebels.[51]

Finding Goffe

Thomas Robins was not the only person to think that a regicide had spent some time in Virginia. Colonel Francis Willet of Narragansett, Rhode Island told Ezra Stiles that 'Theophilus Whalley' (who, he claimed, was actually Goffe) had moved from Hadley to Virginia. Willet then had 'Whalley' (Goffe) returning to New England to live among the Narragansett people. Thomas Hutchinson wrote to Stiles about this theory in June 1765, insisting that Willet was 'certainly mistaken'. Hutchinson alluded to an 'old woman' in Narragansett, mentioned by Stiles, whom he would visit should he find himself in the area—an insinuation that Willet's theory derived from an unreliable local oral tradition.[52] Stiles was not so quick to dismiss the idea: he included a chapter on Willet in his history of the regicides and, faced with the weight of popular belief in Willet's theory on a visit to Rhode Island in 1782, *briefly* entertained the notion that Goffe— 'Theophilus Whalley'—had travelled to Virginia and later to the Narragansetts.[53] Timothy Dwight also reported the tradition that Goffe ended up in Rhode Island, but this myth had the regicide living with Whalley's son once Goffe had left Hadley for Connecticut, and then New York, where he had apparently disguised himself by carrying 'vegetables at times to market'.[54]

After 1795, as news spread of the bones discovered under Russell's house, most observers, with the exception of Thomas Robins, were satisfied that Whalley's final resting place had been revealed. But Goffe's burial place was more open to speculation, as his final years were more obscure and his flight from Hadley could have taken him in many different directions. One theory suggests that Goffe actually remained in Hadley and was buried under Russell's house around 1685, the time when Russell felt he could leave his residence without concern and travel to Boston.[55] However, only one body was found under Russell's house; so speculation about the fate of the regicides continued.

As with Whalley, it has been suggested that Goffe was also buried in New Haven, this time under a headstone marked 'M.G. 80': the 'M' was, it was argued, an upside-down 'W'—a clever method of deception to deflect attention from the real 'William' lying underneath. Although this suggestion stemmed from a romantic desire to have regicides resting side by side (for those who thought Whalley was buried under New Haven's 'E.W.' gravestone), even one of the theory's earliest proponents admitted that it needed 'a slight stretch of imagination'.[56] The claim goes that Goffe fled to New Haven from Hartford in 1680 once Leete had ordered a renewed search for the regicide, but that Goffe died soon after.[57] Various objections, however, undermine this ingenious theory: first, Goffe was probably dead by the time Leete had ordered the search, hence the fact that he had ordered a search in the first place; second, Goffe's supporters would not have given him such a prominent burial site in case his body might be exhumed and exposed to humiliation; and third, the burial stone 'M.G. 80' almost certainly covers Governor Matthew Gilbert, who died in 1680.[58]

Much of the confusion about the final resting places of the regicides arose from the desire, especially in the nineteenth century, that the regicides should be close to one another in death, just as they had been close to one another spiritually and ideologically in life.[59] As we saw in Chapter 6, Ezra Stiles's grandson, Jonathan Leavitt, was almost overcome with emotion on 11 April 1819 when he chanced upon what he thought were the regicides' graves in the New Haven burial ground: 'Here I read the names of the judges of king Charles—men who shone in their day of glory'; beneath him, he thought errone-ously, 'lie outstretched, the bones of the mighty'.[60]

In the nineteenth century Middle Haddam, now an historic district of East Hampton, Connecticut, was a quiet hamlet with its own story to tell of the regicides. It has a fine episcopal church dating from 1786 and was the birthplace of James Brainerd Taylor, the evangelist of the Second Great Awakening. Because of these features, Middle Haddam was placed on the National Register of Historic Places in 1984. Yet Middle Haddam has an additional claim, if a rather unsound one, to historical note. *The New York Times* reported a long-standing tradition, still proudly upheld in the 1890s, that Middle Haddam was the final resting place of William Goffe. However, Middle Haddam's absence from the now well-documented account of Whalley and Goffe's travels might cause us to raise an eyebrow at the historical accuracy of this claim. Although there are still periods for which we cannot verify the regicides' location with complete accuracy, we might be suspicious of the claim that Goffe's grave is 'beneath a gnarled apple tree on a grassy hillside' in Middle Haddam, where he once lived in a log cabin 'a stone's throw' from that apple tree.[61] The apple tree was allegedly planted over the body to stop various groups finding the regicide and exhuming him, since medical students and gravediggers (apparently after Goffe's diamond-hilted sword) were interested in discovering his location. It is an attractive legend but it does not ring true.

Goffe, according to this tradition, had moved to Middle Haddam after his flight from Hadley. He had avoided Weathersfield and Middletown because they had many inhabitants who were keen to surrender the fugitive to the colonial authorities. Middle Haddam was situated deep in the forest, where Goffe could hide, with a spring of clear water from which the regicide and his horse could drink. Goffe allegedly settled here with his son, Gideon, with whom he lived until his death in 1685. This tale, however, once again stemmed from family tradition and historical hearsay. A Captain Nymphas Wright claimed that he had dismantled Goffe's log cabin as a young man and in his old age mentioned this story to Edwin A. Brainerd, who had bought what was believed locally to be 'Goffe's Lot'.

Yet the inaccuracy of the folklore and the manner of its presentation in *The New York Times* calls into question the historical veracity of this whole tale. The article reported that Brainerd was descended from the clergyman who had sheltered Goffe in Hadley, 'Rev. Mr. Robinson', whom we know was actually Russell. It also suggested that Whalley and Goffe were on the run with a regicide named 'Maxwell', clearly an inaccurate rendering of 'Dixwell'. Finally, a son named Gideon is a curious addition to the regicide story. A man named 'Gideon Goff' had indeed settled in Middle Haddam by 1710,[62] but evidently some overexcited locals took this 'Goff' to be connected with the fugitive Goffe, conveniently reinterpreting the decades before this settlement and blending together two families of similar name to suggest that Middle Haddam and its residents had an intimate connection with the regicide.

Family traditions about the regicides' burial places continued into the twentieth century. In 1953 Eleanor Smith Teesdale wrote an account of what she believed to be William Goffe's burial place—not, this time, in Middle Haddam, but in Colebrook, Connecticut, about ninety miles north-east of Hadley. Teesdale stated that she used to visit her grandfather's house in North Colebrook, before it was destroyed by fire around 1930. One of her family pastimes was visiting the 'grave of the regicide', which involved scrambling through undergrowth and vaulting fences to reach a stone on a rocky hillside, inscribed

with the words 'William Goffe, Regicide'. Teesdale surmised that
Colebrook was a likely place for Goffe to be buried because it was the
closest uncultivated area to the west of the region where Goffe was
being hunted: the flatlands around the Connecticut River. On his
death, Teesdale suggested, Goffe was carried to a remote and inaccessible
resting place safe from those who might exact revenge on the body.
She had last seen the stone in 1925, but it could not be found upon
further investigation in 1951.

The Teesdale family tradition is more credible than the Robins
theory, but there are still reasons to be sceptical. First, there is no
demonstrable evidence beyond a charming anecdote which no-one
else has ever corroborated. Second, the inscription is odd: even if
Goffe's body were laid to rest in a remote location, it would still
be peculiar to put his name on the gravestone, let alone his role as
'regicide'. Goffe's friends could not be certain that the grave would
remain undiscovered or that the body, if found, would not be dese-
crated. Other reservations have been put forward: first, it would have
been a very awkward and arduous journey to transport a bulky and
conspicuous coffin some ninety miles from Hadley to Colebrook;
second, no road existed until the 1760s to allow its transportation
through the dense forest. Perhaps, therefore, the 'gravestone', discovered
by the Teesdale family, was one of the stones placed in 1717 to mark the
boundary between Massachusetts and Connecticut, with an inscription
imagined from the lines weathered into the fieldstone.[63] The Teesdale
case study illustrates two points: first, the regicides were viewed in
such a positive way that it was considered desirable to associate oneself
and one's family with them; and second, the regicides remained of
interest to at least *some* people in twentieth-century America.

Rise and decline

Indeed, between the outbreak of World War I and the start of World
War II, the regicides had enjoyed a renewal of interest in America.
This period, the tail-end of the Colonial Revival, began with a notice

in *The New York Times*, suggesting that the Judges Cave was a 'Good Goal for Motorists': 'Good automobile roads lead to both the caves which sheltered the men, and those living in the neighborhood are always willing to point out the historic spots'.[64] In 1918 the *Saturday Chronicle* carried an outline of Whalley and Goffe's travels from Boston to Hartford.[65] Two years later, the regicide letters were published in the journal *Americana*.[66] In 1927 Aline Havard's *The Regicide's Children* was published in New York, advertised as a 'thrilling life of danger that was led in the days of the Puritans . . . told in a way to hold the interest of older and younger boys'.[67]

It was in the 1930s, though, that Whalley, Goffe, and Dixwell enjoyed a greater revival of interest, almost entirely due to one man: Lemuel Aiken Welles. From his student days at Yale, Welles was fascinated by American colonial history and, especially, the relationship between English colonists and their home country. As an undergraduate, he wrote with respect and affection about the 'sterling English qualities' early colonists had brought with them, as reflected in their 'establishment of institutions of learning, religion and government at a time when bread cost him a struggle'. The ensuing two or three centuries, though, had been characterized by what Welles saw as a diminution of these qualities: 'although many of the first settlers were men of scholarship and culture, their children could hardly write'. Welles ascribed this deterioration to the fact that the early settlers spent more time clearing forests and listening to long Puritan sermons than they did appreciating culture, while the 'finer families' intermarried with 'the inferior classes', leading to 'clods' being descended from colonial governors.[68] Welles himself was a descendant of Thomas Welles, governor of Connecticut between 1655 and 1656. So his Connecticut-based family interest, his time studying in New Haven, his later membership of the Sons of the American Revolution, and his evident enthusiasm for the Colonial Revival combined when he came across the story of Whalley, Goffe, and Dixwell.

Following a career in law, Welles published the first full modern history of the regicides in New England. Although New York's

Grafton Press only printed 500 copies, that it was printed in New York suggests that interest in Whalley, Goffe, and Dixwell extended further than the local historians of New Haven. (That said, it was the Tercentenary Commission of the State of Connecticut Committee on Historical Publications which, inspired by Welles's book, commissioned him to write a short account of the regicides in Connecticut, published in New Haven in 1935.) Yet there was a certain naivety to Welles's interpretation of the regicides. He read the available sources at face value and it was clear which side Welles supported. He called Oliver Cromwell 'one of the bravest men who ever lived' and implied that he did not sympathize with the errand on which Kellond and Kirke had been sent.[69] Welles—again, a Son of the American Revolution—was not the first observer of the regicides to sympathize with them and the revolutionary ideas they bestowed on America. More problematic was his uncritical approach to the claims of the colonists who protected Whalley, Goffe, and Dixwell. He gave the impression that Governor Endecott had been serious in his attempts to capture the regicides. He tried to explain the delay between Endecott's receiving the 5 March 1661 mandate and his appointment of Kellond and Kirke to pursue Whalley and Goffe, by arguing naively that the order 'had to be sent to Cambridge to be printed' and that Endecott could not act without first summoning his magistrates.[70] Welles also believed that the wily William Leete had wanted to write out the arrest warrant that would have allowed Kellond and Kirke to look for the regicides in New Haven, but the magistrates Matthew Gilbert and Robert Treat stopped him.[71] In addition, Welles read uncritically the reports of Leete's 'depression' about the regicides' episode,[72] without pausing to consider whether Leete was just trying to cover his back after a period of remarkable wriggling, twisting, and turning that had allowed the regicides to retain their freedom in the New World.

Nonetheless, Welles's book appears to have stimulated another period of interest in the regicides. Aside from Welles's own article for the Tercentenary Commission of the State of Connecticut, *The New*

Haven Journal Courier from June 1934 carried the tale of Whalley and Goffe and, once again, associated the regicides' story with the American Revolution. Richard Sperry, who had sheltered Whalley and Goffe, could not be mentioned without the acknowledgement of one of his descendants, also named Richard and a 'colonel in the Revolutionary Army'.[73] Generations of Connecticut schoolchildren were taught about the regicides in Lewis Sprague Mill's *The Story of Connecticut* (1932) which was still available into the late 1950s.[74] There was some academic interest, too, in the origins of the Angel of Hadley, so prominent in nineteenth-century American literature.[75] In the late 1930s, Laicita Worden Gregg painted a mural, *Planning the Escape of Whalley and Goffe*, featuring some Clark Gable-esque regicides and New Haven colonists (see Figure 16). This mural was part of the Public Works for Art Program (PWAP) which paid artists $35 per day to produce artwork accessible and visible to ordinary people. Gregg's mural was displayed at Woolsey School in Fair Haven for generations

Figure 16. Laicita Worden Gregg, *Planning the Escape of Whalley and Goffe* (late 1930s)

of pupils to shuffle past and maybe glance up at. Then, in 1939, Karl Anderson painted *Pursuit of the Regicides* for the lobby of the Westville Post Office in New Haven.

The outbreak of World War II understandably appears to have reduced curiosity in Whalley, Goffe, and Dixwell. By 1953, when Eleanor Smith Teesdale wrote her version of Goffe's burial, interest in the regicides had become more and more specialized, eccentric even, and the subject of hazy genealogical conjecture instead of wide public interest and healthy historical investigation. Struggling to explain the reception of the regicides to an audience unfamiliar with seventeenth-century politics, one author in 1964 invoked an historical context he thought would be more familiar: 'imagine...that John Wilkes Booth [Lincoln's assassin] escaped safely to Virginia, to be warmly greeted by Jefferson Davis [president of the Confederate States], prayed over in Richmond churches, and sumptuously dined by the president of William and Mary College'.[76] Such a trend is perhaps puzzling when we read the words of Louis B. Wright, who discussed the role of British history in American culture in his lecture *The British Tradition in America* (1954). Wright insisted that:

> what went on in western Europe in the sixteenth and seventeenth centuries, especially what went on in England, is critically important for an understanding of American cultural history...we have remained essentially British in the quality of our civilization...we have inherited a great tradition which we have made our own and we are often not aware of its British origins...The civilization developed within the British Isles between 1485 and 1715...had such extraordinary vigor that it had not yet lost its dynamic power. It carried over to the New World and became the assimilative force which created the American people as we are.[77]

In Wright's terms, then, American culture was forged in the crucible of seventeenth-century British history, which had civil war and regicide at its heart. Wright's view was an Anglophilic and inappropriately monochromatic Caucasian representation of American culture. Wright was delivering his arguments in 1954 in Birmingham, Alabama, which within a decade would become the focus of the Civil Rights Movement. Narrowly defined interpretations of American culture like Wright's would soon be dismissed. As the historiographical lens widened to incorporate the diversity of American history and culture, English Puritans like Whalley, Goffe, and Dixwell lost their once-central position in the American consciousness. Instead, they became subjects fit for little more than children's books like Myra Clarke Crandell's *Molly and the Regicides* (1968).

By the 1960s, the trauma of the assassination of John F. Kennedy on 22 November 1963 (followed by that of Martin Luther King on 4 April 1968 and Robert F. Kennedy on 5 June 1968) may have further deterred American readers from thinking about those who kill their leaders. In the same way that there was little published interest in the regicides after the assassination of Abraham Lincoln, if we look beyond *Molly and the Regicides* the once-popular American regicide industry dwindled after the assassination of Kennedy. Obviously there is a difference between an allegedly tyrannical leader dying judicially after a trial in the seventeenth century (however distressing that may have been to his supporters) and a democratically elected leader being murdered in cold blood in the twentieth. But meditation on the former would have led to dwelling on the latter at a time of national trauma, a trauma intensified by the ubiquity of Kennedy's assassination. Media coverage made the event unavoidable, as it was replayed on television in people's front rooms and permeated their magazines and newspapers. As with Lincoln's assassination, reflections on Kennedy's death used the term 'regicide' to refer to the act of the killing or to refer to the individual doing that killing. Leo Sauvage in March 1964, for example, referred to the president's assassin Lee Harvey Oswald as 'a psychopathic regicide'.[78] That Kennedy's presidency had the monarchical overtones of dynasty and personal glamour at the so-called court of Camelot would have made parallels between presidential assassination and regicide all the more potent.

8

Conclusion

Nowadays when Englishmen do not flee to America because of religious persecution and do not fight their king because of tyranny, the politics of the time of the regicides seem singularly remote. The principles of government for which they fought have become established as a matter of course in the civilized world, and the doctrine of the 'divine right' of kings has gone forever. Yet we have only to remind ourselves that today Italy has a dictator as strong as Cromwell, and, like him, stimulating his people to intense earnestness and industry, to realize that times have not changed altogether.

Lemuel A. Welles, *The History of the Regicides in New England* (1927), 121–2

To investigate the lives and afterlives of Whalley and Goffe is to investigate some of the key moments in American history. While we may start with the English civil wars of the 1640s and the execution of Charles I in London in 1649, we end up travelling through the colonies, then states, of north-east America, glancing at King Philip's War, Bacon's Rebellion, the American Revolution, the American civil war, Lincoln's assassination, and the Colonial Revival, before ending up with a play published in San Francisco. The view taken of the regicides depended on the political loyalty of those reading, writing, painting, or learning about their time on the run. Interest in the regicides' fate may have waxed and waned according to contemporary political and cultural anxieties, or individuals' interest in reviving Whalley and Goffe in their own time. But, with the exception of Thomas Hutchinson and a handful of his followers, most observers saw the regicides in America as heroes outwitting tyrants, presaging the Revolution of 1776. The regicides were ripe for distortion in the ideological battleground of the American Revolutionary years, and in the hands of nineteenth-century authors trying to forge an American identity that was both independent and yet somehow in thrall to its European forebears. As Jill Lepore has put it, 'All nations are places, but they are also acts of imagination', and America's national imagination for a long time had English regicides as some of its key characters.[1]

The regicides and their protectors did foreshadow American independence, but not necessarily in the breathlessly heroic way suggested by Stiles and those nineteenth-century novelists who followed him. Instead, their anticipation of independence was a quiet and patient one—a recognition of the limitations of colonial control. In the early 1660s Charles II's government did not have the logistical resources to descend on the New England colonies in an overbearing and tyrannical manner, or the means forcibly to extract demands and pluck individuals out of the wilderness. The colonists who protected the regicides were brave, but they had the limitations of imperial control in their favour. If Charles II wished to bring the regicides to justice, then he had to rely on colonial administrators. But the regicides survived because there were too few individuals in the colonies who wanted to give them up and too many who found various ways to protect them. The Restoration government conceded that it was powerless in such a situation. This realization dawned very early in Charles's reign, and the many domestic problems he faced only served to increase the difficulty of capturing Whalley, Goffe, and Dixwell in America and of returning them to England.

In fact, while the regicides were in America there was little danger of pursuit for much of the time. Even the most notorious figure, Edward Randolph, who has become a pantomime villain for novelists, dramatists, and historians, was reduced to moaning about the Massachusetts

Bay administration, instead of taking any real action to capture the regicides. The many observers since the eighteenth century who have tried to find something more dramatic and entertaining in the regicides' story have disguised this historical reality. But we learn a lot more about the regicides themselves, the realities of colonial governance, and the relationship between English regicide and American Revolution if we remove that cartoon veneer.

Reading the literary afterlives of the regicides after the American Revolution provides further explanation as to how the real story of the regicides in America became refashioned to interest readers and to provide a neat road from English regicide to American Revolution. In each of these cultural artefacts, the regicides' story had to be filtered to suit the agenda of the author and temperament of the audience. It is not sufficient to say that the regicides were either totally vilified or celebrated wholeheartedly as heroes. The *majority* of authors settled for the latter, especially in the second half of the nineteenth century when, prompted by celebrations of the centenary of the American Revolution, some observers considered what they perceived to be the cyclical nature of American history, which brought seventeenth-century regicides into the orbit of eighteenth-century revolutionaries. Novels followed histories; histories followed novels; paintings, plays, and poems followed both.

Ironically, it is possible that the seeds of the regicides' demise were sown in the decades of their notable popularity. In the hands of nineteenth-century authors, the regicides had become one- or two-dimensional post-revolutionary constructs lacking any subtlety, complexity, or, sometimes, accuracy. One nineteenth-century author's casual attitude to historical veracity was betrayed by her dismissive note that, in her account of the regicides, 'some slight liberties have been taken with the dates'.[2] For all of these reasons the regicides were not figures who could sustain interest beyond an elementary school standard of sophistication and, at this level, there were plenty of other American heroes who were more recognizable, had performed more notable deeds, and looked better on gift shop memorabilia: Abraham

Lincoln, George Washington, and Benjamin Franklin, among others. So in the sophomoric surge of interest in the regicides lay the beginnings of their decline: there was no longer anything sufficiently challenging for serious historians to investigate and research. The regicides became further and further removed from the realities of their seventeenth-century existence and more and more cartoon figures fit for little more than local histories, tobacco adverts,[3] genealogical studies, and movie-stories about angels.

Once the regicides had become the preserve of broad-brush educators and entertainers (or both), their personalities, views, and experiences had to become wholesome, straightforward, and uncomplicated. They had to become representatives of the growth of an American liberty that could be traced across the Atlantic, back over a century, to the English civil war. Heroic myths needed to be created if the regicides were going to fit the image later given to them as intrepid proto-revolutionaries, especially as much of their genuine experience in America was not quite so heroic as we have been led to believe. In the hands of some nineteenth-century Romantic authors, historical truth was subordinated to the demands of a good story. And the requirements of a good story also demanded elements of fiction that had little or no basis in reality, but were required to keep the reading public interested in what was already a fascinating story. Devout, spiritual Puritans do not sell many books. Puritans in the midst of a breathless chase do—even if we have to suspend disbelief while we read about their exploits.

With the exception of the Angel of Hadley, if we accept its veracity, there was little in the behaviour of the regicides in America that reflected their military heroism from the English civil wars. From existing diary entries and letters we get the impression of individuals who were in a state of spiritual and temporal anxiety. Their physical hardiness was undermined during the Judges Cave episode by their retreating in times of bad weather to unexciting domesticity. And so the regicides appeared to become much frailer as their exile progressed.

This might explain the need among the early myth-makers to invent stories involving nimble fencing and tense, dramatic pursuits. If the regicides were going to be early American heroes, then they had to be doing deeds that were more heroic than hiding in basements or prevaricating over psalms.

Over time, then, the story of the regicides belonged more and more to the hagiographical tradition of American writers who wasted no critical energy in placing Whalley and Goffe at the forefront of proto-1776ers who fought for liberty against a tyrannical British monarchy. Thereafter, they would receive scant attention from more recent historians who preferred to devote their critical faculties to topics that were more in tune with the ethical and cultural concerns of twentieth- and twenty-first-century America. It was not until 2012 that Whalley and Goffe returned to the history bookshelves, first in Christopher Pagliuco's, *The Great Escape of Edward Whalley and William Goffe*, then in Don Jordan and Michael Walsh's *The King's Revenge*. In 2014, the publication of Charles Spencer's *Killers of the King* coincided with William Goffe's first appearance on a television screen, played by James Cosmo in Maxine Brant and Peter Flannery's *New Worlds*—a programme which attracted over 660,000 viewers, but was described by one critic as 'possibly the worst-directed historic drama ever'.[4]

New generations of readers were also introduced to the regicides through historical fiction: Jack Dunn's *The Diary of General William Goffe* (first published in 1982 and reprinted in 2007) has Goffe's diary being discovered by a Hadley lawyer, Jonathan Whiting. Ric Hooban's *Off With His Head: The Story of the Fighting Whalley* (2009) presents one of Whalley's descendants trying to discover the history of the 'The Whalley pen with the King's Blood on it'. Kathleen Kent's historical romance *The Wolves of Andover* (2010) includes a labourer, Thomas Carrier, with a mysterious past: involved in the battles of the English civil war and the regicide, he flees from England to Massachusetts where, much like Whalley and Goffe, he is pursued by assassins resembling Kellond and Kirke.[5]

Up to this point, Whalley, Goffe, and Dixwell had been tarred with the 'antiquarian' brush. They had become a subject fit only for genealogy hunters determined to associate their family with revolutionary lineage. Others would have been deterred by the simplistic portraits of the regicides and their pursuers found in nineteenth-century romances. Some would have baulked at the 'local history' association of the regicides: a nice story that might appeal to the denizens of New Haven without conveying much about American or British history to a wider audience. Such critics would have been wrong to take this view. *The New Haven Journal Courier* from June 1934 carried the story of Whalley and Goffe, and rightly recognized that the lives and afterlives of the regicides 'are not only the history of New Haven, but of our country'[6]—or, indeed, any country concerned with questions of monarchies and republics, tyranny and liberty.

APPENDIX I

Dramatis personae

ALLEN, John: Hartford magistrate who halts John London's scheme against Goffe.

ANDROS, Sir Edmund: English colonial administrator and governor of the Dominion of New England, 1686–9.

BARKSTEAD, John: Major general and regicide who flees England in 1660 but is captured by Sir George Downing and executed in 1662.

BREDON, Thomas: Royalist inhabitant of Boston who takes news of Whalley and Goffe to the English court in London in the early 1660s.

CARR, Robert: Royal commissioner sent to New England in 1664.

CARTWRIGHT, George: Royal commissioner sent to New England in 1664.

CHARLES I: King of England, Scotland, and Ireland, 1625–49.

CHARLES II: King of England, Scotland, and Ireland from the Restoration of the monarchy in 1660 (though his supporters dated the start of his reign to the moment of Charles I's execution in 1649, which was later codified in law).

CHAUNCEY, Charles: President of Harvard who meets Whalley and Goffe when they first arrive in America.

CLARENDON, Edward Hyde, Earl of: Lord Chancellor of England, 1658–67.

CORBET, Miles: Regicide who flees England in 1660 but is captured by Sir George Downing and executed in 1662.

CROMWELL, Oliver: Lord Protector of the Commonwealth of England, Scotland, and Ireland in the 1650s.

DAVENPORT, John: Puritan minister who preaches a sermon in New Haven to 'hide the outcasts', hosts Whalley and Goffe in New Haven, visits them in Milford, and receives letters from William Hooke, which are passed on to Davenport and then Goffe.

DIXWELL, John: Parliamentarian and signatory of Charles I's death warrant who flees to New England after a brief stay in Hanau.

ENDECOTT, John: Governor of Massachusetts Bay who greets Whalley and Goffe on their arrival in America.

GILBERT, Matthew: New Haven magistrate who helps to delay the progress of Kellond and Kirke in May 1661.

GOFFE, Frances: Daughter of Edward Whalley and wife of William Goffe, who corresponds with her husband throughout his time in New England.

GOFFE, William: Major general and regicide who flees to New England in 1660.

GOODWIN, William: Neighbour of John Russell in Hadley and correspondent of John Davenport.

GOOKIN, Daniel: Travels on *The Prudent Mary* with Whalley and Goffe, hosts them, and is accused of holding and managing their property.

HARRISON, Thomas: Parliamentarian and leader of the Fifth Monarchists who is executed for regicide in 1660.

HOOKE, Jane: Edward Whalley's sister.

HOOKE, William: Whalley's brother-in-law, a friend and correspondent of Davenport, his letters to whom are passed on to Goffe.

HUTCHINSON, Thomas: Governor of the Province of Massachusetts Bay; his house is ransacked in 1765, at which point Goffe's diary disappears.

JAMES II: King of England, Scotland, and Ireland, 1685–8.

JONES, John: Welsh brother-in-law of Oliver Cromwell and military leader who is executed for regicide in 1660.

JONES, William: Son of regicide John Jones who travels with Whalley and Goffe on *The Prudent Mary*, and hosts the regicides in New Haven.

KELLOND, Thomas: Agent sent by Governor Endecott to capture Whalley and Goffe on an ultimately ill-fated mission in May 1661.

KIRKE, Thomas: Agent sent by Governor Endecott to capture Whalley and Goffe on an ultimately ill-fated mission in May 1661.

LAUD, William: Archbishop of Canterbury under Charles I (from 1633) who is arrested in 1640 and executed in 1645.

LEETE, William: Deputy governor then governor of New Haven who hampers Kellond and Kirke's attempts to capture Whalley and Goffe, later writes to John Norton to defend his actions, and perhaps keeps the 'Angel of Hadley' legend quiet.

LONDON, John: Resident of Windsor, Connecticut, who testifies he has seen William Goffe in Hartford in 1679.

LORD, Richard: Proprietor of Hartford who claims to be involved in a plot to capture Whalley and Goffe in the early 1660s.

MATHER, Increase: Puritan minister and correspondent of John Davenport who aids the delivery of the regicides' letters.

MAVERICK, Samuel: Royal commissioner sent to New England in 1664.

MORRICE, William: Secretary of state to Charles II.

NEWBURY, Benjamin: John Russell's brother-in-law, resident of Hadley who perhaps keeps quiet the 'Angel of Hadley' legend.

NICHOLAS, Edward: Secretary of state to Charles I and Charles II.

NICHOLS, Richard: Royal commissioner sent to New England in 1664.

OKEY, John: Regicide who flees England in 1660 but is captured by Sir George Downing and executed in 1662.

PETERS, Hugh: Puritan minister who is closely identified with New England, is a chaplain in the New Model Army, and is executed for regicide in 1660.

PINCHON, John: Deputy to the Massachusetts general court who claims to be involved in a plot to capture Whalley and Goffe in the early 1660s.

POWELL, Thomas: Resident of Hartford who stops John London capturing Goffe.

RANDOLPH, Edward: Colonial administrator and leading figure in the administration of the Dominion of New England (1686–9) who develops a fixation with Whalley and Goffe and those who protect them in the early 1660s.

RUSSELL, John: Hadley minister who is supported by John Davenport in his split from Wethersfield, hosts Whalley and Goffe in Hadley, and receives a donation for the regicides from Richard Saltonstall via Edward Collins.

SPERRY, Richard: New Haven landowner who protects Whalley and Goffe when they cannot stay at the Judges Cave.

STILES, Ezra: President of Yale College and author of the first full-length book on the regicides in America.

TALCOTT: John Russell's brother-in-law, resident of Hadley, perhaps puts a halt to John London's plot against Goffe and keeps quiet the 'Angel of Hadley' legend.

TEMPLE, Thomas: Colonel who sends information concerning Whalley and Goffe to William Morrice in 1661.

TILTON, Peter: John Russell's neighbour in Hadley who visits Whalley and Goffe and corresponds with Goffe.

TOMKINS, Micha(el): Resident of Milford who houses Whalley and Goffe there for two years.

TREAT, Robert: Meets Whalley and Goffe in Milford and allegedly stops a search of New Haven, and perhaps keeps quiet the 'Angel of Hadley' legend.

WHALLEY, Edward: Regicide who flees from England to New England in 1660.

WHITING, John: Hartford minister who helps with the delivery of Goffe's correspondence.

WINTHROP Jr, John: Governor of Connecticut who gives Whalley and Goffe a guide and hosts them in Hartford.

APPENDIX II

Timeline of the movements of *Whalley and Goffe*

1660	Month	Charles II's government	Colonial authorities	Regicides
	Apr.	4th: Charles II issues Declaration of Breda.		
	May	1st: Parliament hears letters promising to pardon those involved in civil wars and Interregnum, not 'excepted by Parliament'.		
		8th: Charles II proclaimed king.		
				12th: Whalley and Goffe board *The Prudent Mary* at Gravesend under names Richardson and Stephenson.
		14th: House of Commons orders arrest of 'all those persons who sat in judgement upon the late king's majesty when sentence was pronounced'.		14th: Whalley and Goffe set sail for Boston in *The Prudent Mary*.
		18th: House of Lords orders seizure of members of court who tried Charles I.		
		25th: Charles II lands at Dover.		

(continued)

1660	Month	Charles II's government	Colonial authorities	Regicides
	June	6th: Charles II issues proclamation summoning certain individuals, including Whalley and Goffe, to appear before him within fourteen days, or forfeit any chance of pardon.		
	July			27th: Whalley and Goffe arrive in Massachusetts Bay.
	Aug.		11th: John Davenport writes from New Haven to Governor John Winthrop at Hartford that the new arrivals in Massachusetts were Whalley and Goffe.	
		29th: Act of Indemnity and Oblivion is passed; Whalley and Goffe are excluded from the forgiveness.		
	Sept.	22nd: Charles II issues proclamation putting £100 each on the heads of Whalley and Goffe.		
	Oct.	11th: Trials of regicides begin in London.		
		16th: Hugh Peters and other co-regicides are executed.		
	Nov.		18th: Governor Francis Newman dies, leaving William Leete chief magistrate of New Haven.	
			30th: News of the Act of Indemnity reaches New England.	

1661	Month	British authorities	Colonial authorities	Regicides
	Jan.	Royal proclamation orders arrest of Whalley and Goffe.		
	Feb.	Speculation circulates that no more regicides are to be executed.	22nd: Governor Endecott calls court of assistants to discuss apprehension of Whalley and Goffe.	26th: Whalley and Goffe leave Cambridge.
	Mar.	5th: Another royal mandate orders arrest of Whalley and Goffe, addressed to 'our trusty and well-beloved the present governor, or other magistrate or magistrates of our plantation of New England'.	8th: Governor Endecott and the court of assistants issue warrant to apprehend Whalley and Goffe. News of the Jan. 1661 royal proclamation reaches New Haven.	7th: Whalley and Goffe reach John Davenport's house in New Haven, having passed through Springfield and Hartford.

(continued)

1661	Month	British authorities	Colonial authorities	Regicides
		11th: Thomas Bredon reports to Council for Foreign Plantations that Charles II's proclamation against the regicides is 'vilified' in Massachusetts Bay.		27th: Whalley and Goffe travel to Milford and make their presence known publicly; they return to New Haven that night.
				30th: Whalley and Goffe leave Davenport's house and move to William Jones's house nearby in New Haven.
	Apr.		28th: News of Massachusetts Bay arrest warrant reaches New Haven.	
	May		6th: Endecott signs the 5 March royal mandate.	
			7th: Kellond and Kirke are given letters by Endecott to pursue regicides. They leave Boston in search of Whalley and Goffe.	
			10th: Kellond and Kirke meet with Governor Winthrop at Hartford.	

11th: Kellond and Kirke meet with Deputy Governor Leete at Guilford. Leete reads their letters aloud. Warrant is issued to search Windsor. Leete refuses to let Kellond and Kirke continue their pursuit on the impending Sabbath. Dennis Crampton gives Kellond and Kirke information about the regicides being in New Haven.

13th: Kellond and Kirke arrive in New Haven. Leete arrives there two hours later. The acting governor refuses to issue arrest warrant, or let Kellond and Kirke search houses, until the freemen are assembled. The magistrates assemble for five or six hours, then still say they cannot do anything until a general court of freemen is assembled. Accounts differ as to whether Leete wants to issue warrant and is stopped by Matthew Gilbert and Robert Treat, or whether this is a cover-up for Leete giving Kellond and Kirke the run-around.

11th: Whalley and Goffe leave Jones's house, possibly for a nearby mill.

13th: Whalley and Goffe move again, perhaps to 'Hatchet Harbour'.

(continued)

1661	Month	British authorities	Colonial authorities	Regicides
			14th: Kellond and Kirke leave for Manhattan.	15th: Whalley and Goffe move to a cave (West Rock) on Providence Hill.
			17th: General court of New Haven meets and Leete signs warrant for search of regicides.	
	June		10th: Massachusetts Bay general court ratifies report insisting that Whalley and Goffe should be apprehended.	11th: Whalley and Goffe leave cave, resolving to give themselves up to Deputy Governor Gilbert.
			19th: Massachusetts Bay general court declares that fugitives from English justice should not expect shelter in that colony.	22nd: Whalley and Goffe appear publicly in New Haven but escape again.
				24th: They return to their cave.
			After 24th another search is made for regicides, following their public appearance in New Haven.	

July

4th: Secretary Rawson writes to Governor Leete from Boston, advising him to arrest regicides.

15th: A postscript is added to the letter, informing Leete that the regicides' appearance the previous month is known.

Aug.

1st: Leete assembles general court and responds to Boston letter claiming that their lack of action was not due to antipathy towards Charles II or sympathy for the regicides. He expresses concern about the prospect of a 'general governor'.

19th: Davenport writes letter of 'apology' to Thomas Temple, who sends it to Secretary Morrice in London.

19th: Whalley and Goffe leave cave and travel to house of Michael Tomkins in Milford.

20th: Thomas Temple, following information from John Pinchon and Richard Lord, informs Secretary William Morrice that Whalley and Goffe are still in America.

(continued)

1661	Month	British authorities	Colonial authorities	Regicides
	Sept.		5th: Commissioners of United Colonies of New England (Massachusetts Bay, Plymouth, Connecticut, New Haven) meet at Plymouth and issue warning against sheltering Whalley and Goffe.	
			23rd: John Norton writes to Richard Baxter claiming Leete's distress at the regicide saga.	
	Oct.	28th: It is reported that the Restoration authorities are taking little notice of any alleged attempts to capture the regicides, as so far New England magistrates have done 'nothing'.		

1662	Month	British authorities	Colonial authorities	Regicides
	Mar.	Okey, Corbet, and Barkstead are arrested in Delft.		
	Apr.	19th: Okey, Corbet, and Barkstead are executed.		
	May			15th: Davenport visits Whalley and Goffe in Milford.
	June			20th: News reaches Whalley and Goffe of the arrest and execution of Okey, Corbet, and Barkstead.

	Month	British authorities	Colonial authorities	Regicides
	Aug.	28th: Charles II writes letter to Massachusetts Bay, still excepting from pardon those guilty of treason, and those who harboured them. 14th: John Lisle shot in Lausanne, Switzerland.		Following Lisle's death, rumours spread that Whalley and Goffe have also been killed in Switzerland.
1664	Apr.	25th: Instructions issued to four royal commissioners to travel to New England colonies and New Amsterdam.		
	July	20th: Two royal commissioners arrive at Portsmouth. 23rd: Two more royal commissioners arrive at Boston.		
	Oct.			Hearing of arrival of royal commissioners, Whalley and Goffe return to cave for just over a week. 13th: Whalley and Goffe leave with John Russell for Hadley.

	Month	British authorities	Colonial authorities	Regicides
1665	Feb.			10th: John Dixwell meets regicides at Hadley.

	Month	British authorities	Colonial authorities	Regicides
1674	Dec.			Whalley dies around this time.

	Month	British authorities	Colonial authorities	Regicides
1676	Mar.	30th: Edward Randolph leaves England for Boston.		
	June	10th: Randolph arrives in New England. He notes in his report home that Massachusetts Bay by law encourages protection of fugitives, including Whalley and Goffe.		
		17th: Randolph notes that Goffe 'the old rebel' is still in America.		12th: Goffe appears as the 'Angel of Hadley' in King Philip's War (theory put forward by Douglas C. Wilson).
	July	30th: Randolph returns to England.		
	Sept.			8th: Goffe has moved to Hartford by this date; he lives with Thomas or Jonathan Bull.

1678	Month	British authorities	Colonial authorities	Regicides
	Apr.	Randolph reports that Gookin had harboured the regicides.		
	Oct.		Massachusetts Bay general court responds to Randolph's accusations, claiming 'there was no neglect in trying to arrest Goffe and Whalley'.	

1679	Month	British authorities	Colonial authorities	Regicides
	Apr.			2nd: Goffe writes last surviving letter.
	July	Massachusetts agents are summoned to Whitehall to respond to Randolph's claims about the regicides being protected by Massachusetts authorities in 1660; the agents claim that the said authorities issued the arrest warrant as soon as it had been received, but the regicides had fled.		30th: Last surviving letter written to Goffe. It is likely that Goffe dies around this time, hence Leete being willing to order a search of Hartford the following year.

1680	Month	British authorities	Colonial authorities	Regicides
	Apr.		20th: John London testifies to New York authorities that he saw Goffe at the Bulls' house in Hartford the previous May. London claims that he planned to apprehend Goffe, but he was stopped by Hartford magistrates.	
	May		18th: Governor Andros of New York writes to Leete, now governor of Connecticut, informing him of Goffe's presence in Hartford.	
	June		10th: Leete receives Andros's letter and orders search warrant for Hartford constables to search Bulls' house and surrounding area for Goffe.	
			11th: Leete replies to Andros, complaining about lies spread about his colony.	

APPENDIX III

The diary of William Goffe

This excerpt was discovered among the Winthrop Papers by Robert C. Winthrop and presented to the Massachusetts Historical Society on 10 December 1863 (*Proceedings of the Massachusetts Historical Society*, vol. 7 (1863–4), 281–3). The full diary, covering 1660 to 1667, was passed to the Russell family in the late seventeenth century, before being added to the Mather library in 1758. Thomas Hutchinson was in possession of the diary in 1765, when his house was attacked at the time of the Stamp Act. It is presumed that the diary was destroyed or dispersed at this time. The following is the only extract that has survived; the spelling and punctuation have been modernized where appropriate.

★ ★ ★

12d 3m.—The King was proclaimed at Gravesend; there was much rejoicing among the people, but God's people lamented over the great profaneness with which that joy was expressed. It was observed that many dogs did that day run mad; and died suddenly in the town.

13d 3m.—We kept Sabbath aboard. To a good minister's church in the town was stuck up near the pulpit a broom; in token as was by all conceived, that the minister should shortly be swept away from them.

27d 5m.—We came to anchor between Boston, and Charlestown; between 8. & 9. in the morning: All in good health through the good hand of God upon us: oh! That men would praise the Lord for his goodness…as psalm 107. 21, &c.

29d 5m.—Lord's day; we had opportunity of waiting upon God in his public ordinances, which were solemnly performed by Mr. Mitchel. I handed Mr. Mitchel a paper,—which I here insert, to mind myself hereafter of my present purposes to cleave to the Lord, and to love him, and serve him forever, which the Lord by his own grace and spirit enable me to do, now and always.

Having received much mercy from the Lord, at his leaving his native country, and in his passage through the great deeps; as also in this land;

wherein he is a stranger; Now before the Lord in the congregation of his people, doth humbly desire that the praises due unto God,—may be rendered on his behalf. And that the Lord may be entreated yet to follow his poor unworthy servant with goodness and mercy; that he may walk as becomes the gospel, and forever cleave to the Lord; and love him, and serve him, in all conditions.

9d 6m.—Went to Boston lecture, heard Mr. Norton on Hebr. 2. 16. Went afterwards to his house, where we were lovingly entertained, with many ministers, and found great respects from them. But were threatened by one that came in the Scotch vessel,—he said, if it had not been for those that walked with us, he would have had us by the hair of our heads: but when I heard of it, I said all the hairs of our heads were numbered by the Lord.— Luc. 12. 6: 7.—At night, Major Gookin showed us a printed paper that was brought in the Scotch ship, wherein the Lords do order 66 members of the High Court of Justice to be secured, with their estates,—it is dated 18d May 1660. But I will meditate on Hebr. 13. 5. 6.

10d 6m.—The Lord was graciously pleased to refresh my soul with his presence, in reading the word, and prayer, in my private morning exercise; and I felt some sensible affections moving towards Christ; and resolutions to cleave to him more for the future.

13d 6m.—I was in some measure quickened in my approach to God in prayer, in the morning.

15d 6m.—Supped at Mr. Chauncey's; the good old servant of the Lord, still expressing much affection, and telling us, he was persuaded the Lord had brought us to this country for good both to them and ourselves.

18d 6m.—The Lord was pleased to help in some measure in my preparation for the Lord's supper, and to give me some sense of the greatness of his love in giving Christ, and to show me my great need of him; both in reference to the guilt of sin, and power against sin; and to work in me some sensible affections towards himself, and earnest longings, and thirstings after communion with him in the ordinance unto which I was approaching.

19d.—The Lord was pleased very graciously to appear in his ordinances.

Oh! How gracious is God to his poor servants that gives us in the land of our pilgrimage such blessed entertainment. I am banished from my own house; but feasted in the house of God; oh, that I might dwell therein forever.

23d 6m.—In the evening we visited Elder Frost, who received us with great kindness and love esteeming it a favour that we would come into their mean habitation; assured us of his fervent prayers to the Lord for us:—a glorious saint makes a mean cottage a stately palace; were I to make my choice, I would rather abide with this saint in his poor cottage than with any one of the princes that I know of at this day in the world.

24d 6m.—We visited G. Beale sorely afflicted with the stone. He complained that he could not in the extremity of the pain submit with cheerfulness to the will of God; and told us that God spake many things to him under this exercise. Among other things he said he was now much convinced of evil, that he had not blessed God when he could make water with ease—and so for other common mercies—a useful lesson!

26d 6m.—Mr. Mitchel with divers came to visit us; our discourse tended to provoke to give up ourselves wholly to Jesus Christ and make him the whole delight of our souls.

4d 7m.—My first thoughts when I awaked this morning were on i. Pet. 2. abstain from fleshly lusts. My last thoughts, on my bed, were meditations on ps. 68. He that is our God is the God of salvation. 1. Such as have received Christ may come to know, and be able to say that God is their God—2. the believer's God is a God of salvation. 3. It's a consideration that yields much relief to the saints in time of eminent danger, that he that is their God is the God of salvation and that to him belong the issues from death.

5d 7m.—I awaked with that scripture, Math. 5. Blessed are they that hunger, &c. 1. the soul that truly hungers and thirsts after righteousness shall be made righteous. 2. to be filled with righteousness and true holiness is true blessedness.

6d 7m.—I awaked with some weak thought of some scripture but my heart being oppressed with much deadness my spirit was confused &c.—the Lord pardon my great deadness, and quicken me for his name's sake.

APPENDIX IV

The (dis)appearance of John Dixwell

In 1660, just after twenty-nine of those involved in the regicide had themselves been tried for treason, a printed account of their trials appeared: *An Exact and Most Impartial Accompt of the Indictment, Trial, and Judgment (according to Law) of Nine and Twenty Regicides* (1660). This publication included nearly 300 pages of exchanges between the court and the regicides. When the radical Puritan regicide Thomas Harrison was in the dock, Charles I's death warrant was read out to prove that Harrison had been involved in 'imagining and compassing'—thinking about and plotting—the king's death. Yet when the death warrant was reprinted in the *Exact and Most Impartial Accompt*, one name was missing: that of John Dixwell.[1]

Dixwell had been a captain in the Kent militia in the civil war before being promoted to the rank of colonel of foot. In 1646 he was elected MP for Dover in the Long Parliament and kept his seat after Pride's Purge two years later—a clear suggestion that he had supported putting Charles I on trial. He sat in the High Court of Justice that tried the king and he attended every session of the trial before becoming the thirty-eighth signatory of Charles's death warrant. While he did not reach the same heights as Whalley and Goffe during the Interregnum, his career was not without notable achievements: he was appointed to the Council of State in 1651, sat in three Protectorate Parliaments, and became governor, later lieutenant, of Dover Castle. In short, he had done enough—most notably by signing the king's death warrant—to ensure that he would not be forgiven at the Restoration.

The omission of Dixwell's name from the list of regicides in the *Accompt* may have been an innocent mistake. The *Accompt* would have been a typesetter's nightmare: it was long, dense, and produced quickly; errors were bound to creep in. Yet there might be another explanation for the omission: John Dixwell had run away and his location was unknown. Although the names of Whalley and Goffe appeared on the reproduced death warrant, it was probably known that they had fled to America when the *Accompt* went to press and this was confirmed definitively by Thomas Bredon on 11 March, a fortnight before the latest point at which the *Accompt* could have been printed.[2] The Restoration authorities could acknowledge openly that Whalley and Goffe were at large but could claim that the regicides' location was known and that moves were afoot to capture them. Dixwell's location was a mystery which would cause embarrassment to the Restoration authorities: not only had Dixwell evaded justice, he had exposed their inability to bring him to justice. A possible solution might have been to omit his name from the reprinted death warrant and hope that no one noticed or asked too many questions.

The fact is that Dixwell proved to be one of the regicides most successful at hiding his whereabouts from contemporaries and modern historians. All we know is that Dixwell hid in Hanau for five years. His precise location would remain a mystery until 10 February 1665, when he met Whalley and Goffe at Russell's house in Hadley. Whalley and Goffe may have suggested that Dixwell travel to New Haven where they had themselves received kind hospitality. Whatever his purpose or motivation, Dixwell did travel to New Haven and stayed there for over two decades under the pseudonym James Davids. He boarded initially with an elderly couple, Benjamin and Joanna Ling. Benjamin died on 27 April 1673, at which point Dixwell married Joanna in a marriage perhaps based on property rights rather than romantic love. Joanna would have wanted to ensure that Dixwell had somewhere to live in the event of her death. As it happened, Joanna died just a month after her second marriage but Dixwell continued to live in relative comfort. His 'health and comfortable being' was reported in November 1676, though he did suffer from swollen feet, the remedy for which, apparently, was to wash them in brandy. Dixwell was also provided with clothing, shoes, and books.[3] On 23 October 1677, at the age of about seventy, Dixwell married Bathsheba How, a woman less than half his age.

Dixwell's personal happiness contrasted sharply with the ordeals suffered by his co-religionists in England. On 12 January 1681, Dixwell received a letter informing him of clouds gathering 'very thick' in his mother country.[4] This was not a meteorological observation but a reference to the fate of Nonconformist Protestants in the context of the Exclusion Crisis and the development of the first political parties in England. Charles II had not sired any legitimate children; his Catholic brother, James, duke of York, was therefore due to succeed to the throne on the king's death. Since Restoration England was a virulently anti-Catholic country, the succession would prove difficult. Memories remained of the persecution of Protestants under Queen Mary in the 1550s, the threat posed by the Spanish Armada in 1588, and the Gunpowder Plot designed by Catholics to murder James I in Parliament.

Allegations were made that there was a 'Popish Plot' to assassinate Charles II and put his Catholic brother on the throne, something about which Goffe had also been informed in Hartford.[5] Moreover, for many Protestants it seemed that Louis XIV's militantly Catholic France sat menacingly just across the English Channel.

Largely in response to the spectre of the duke of York returning his dominions to the Catholic faith once he became King James II, the 'Whig' political party was born. By campaigning 'out-of-doors', and attempting to pass a law 'excluding' James from the succession, it tried to ensure that James would never become king. The latter strategy was thwarted dramatically by Charles II's abrupt dissolution of Parliament at Oxford in March 1681; he would not call a Parliament again for the remainder of his reign. Charles considered the Whig machinations to be an affront to his authority as hereditary monarch. He had witnessed what happened when Parliament meddled with the royal succession and was determined that it was not going to happen again. He also felt insulted by the disloyalty and ingratitude exhibited by many of his subjects: he had offered them widespread forgiveness in 1660 but now he thought that too many were exploiting his good nature and returning to the behaviour displayed by his father's enemies in the run-up to the civil war. 'Forty-one is come again', the cry went up, to remind Charles II's subjects to avoid the traumas of the 1640s and rally behind the king and his brother.

Many individuals associated with the allegedly ungrateful and traitorous Whigs were Nonconformist Protestants who would not subject themselves to the king's Church of England or to the true Stuart succession. It was no wonder, then, that Dixwell was informed of 'thick' clouds gathering: the Whigs were in the final throes of their attempts to exclude James from the succession, while the king's dissolution of Parliament foreshadowed a period of intense persecution of his enemies, including a renewed assault on Protestant Nonconformists. Their meetings were disrupted; they were fined and imprisoned. They were spied on and harassed in a time known as the 'Tory Reaction'—those years towards the end of Charles II's reign when the 'ingratitude' of his enemies was punished in harsh measure.[6] The persecution and the punishment increased in 1683 when the Rye House Plot was discovered, the aim of which was to assassinate the royal brothers as they returned to London from the horseracing at Newmarket.

Charles II's enemies had not forgotten about the regicides in America. John Breman served as an MP between 1679 and 1681, campaigned against the duke of York, and later supported the king's illegitimate son, the duke of Monmouth, as a Protestant alternative for the throne. During the Exclusion

Crisis, he asked after Dixwell 'most kindly'. Moreover, Breman was associated with the republican John Wildman, who likewise remembered Dixwell 'with a great deal of kindness'.[7] Their enquiries after the regicide raise the interesting question of whether they were told of his whereabouts. At the very least, Breman's enquiry suggests that he thought the regicide was still alive. We will never know whether Elizabeth Dixwell, who spoke to Breman and Wildman, revealed his precise location. It is likely, though, that Dixwell's presence in New Haven was known or suspected by his new neighbours: the residents of such a small community would have noticed the arrival of a stranger of unusual bearing, especially as he attended public worship. Well educated and dressed differently, his adoption of a pseudonym with initials exactly the same as his real name might have raised a few eyebrows amongst those already familiar with the tale of regicides on the run in their colony.

Whether they had their suspicions or not, many colonists were willing to accept the story that 'James Davids' was indeed James Davids and not the fugitive John Dixwell. Dixwell himself left a list of his closest associates in New Haven who probably knew his true identity. These men included William Jones and James Bishop, whom Dixwell described as his 'honoured friends', as well as his 'Reverend friends' James Pierpont and Samuel Hooker of nearby Farmington.[8] Furthermore, Nicholas Street, Davenport's successor as minister of New Haven, may well have known this mysterious figure's true identity.[9]

James did indeed become King James II on Charles II's death in 1685, but three years later he fled from England. James was forced to abdicate, in effect, by his subjects who could not tolerate the plans the new king was making to return their nation to the Catholic faith. James believed that his subjects would choose to return to Catholicism if they were given convincing arguments and reasons as to why the so-called 'Roman faith' was the true form of Christianity. However, James's attempts to promote a faith in which he believed devoutly were politically suicidal. The nation, which had been split in the late 1670s and early 1680s over the prospect of James's succession to the throne, now united in its desire to remove him. James alienated those Tories who previously had supported his hereditary claim to the crown: though James was going to be a Catholic king, they had argued that he would have to abide by English laws and that his accession was preferable to the potential chaos caused by subjects' meddling in monarchical succession. In any case, so long as James II had no male heir, his reign would have been a brief Catholic hiatus before the nation reverted to a Protestant monarch upon his death. This changed when James's wife, Mary of Modena, gave birth to a son in June 1688 and the prospect of a Catholic dynasty in perpetuity loomed large.[10]

William of Orange, James's own son-in-law, and Mary, James's daughter, were invited to become joint sovereigns. Now Protestants felt that their religion would be safe and that a new era would dawn when an old regicide like John Dixwell might be able to return to England. Dixwell indeed was sent a letter in September 1689 informing him that William was 'bent to the honest part' and that his friends were trying to secure him an official pardon. Moreover, they were confident that they would be able to obtain such a pardon with an Act of Parliament to support it. Dixwell was urged to make his way with his family to Amsterdam where he could stay until everything was ready for him to return to England. Yet Dixwell was warned to travel in the 'greatest privacy' because threats had been made against the regicide and there were individuals who would do him 'a mischief'.[11] As Wildman had given the advice that Dixwell should stop off in Amsterdam before returning to England, it seems probable that he did know of the fugitive's residence in America: it would have been odd if Wildman did not know the direction from which the regicide would be returning. Dixwell, however, never made it home and his friends' plans were fruitless: he had died on 18 March 1689.

Notes

PREFACE

1. Henry T. Blake, 'Cut Ninety Years Ago', *New Haven Register* (September 1893), cited in Colin M. Caplan, *Westville: Tales from a Connecticut Hamlet* (Charleston, SC, 2009), 15–17.
2. *The New York Times* (15 July 1894).

CHAPTER 1

1. Full text available online through the Liberty Fund at http://oll.libertyfund.org/pages/1647-the-putney-debates.
2. C.V. Wedgwood, *The Trial of Charles I* (London, 1964), 189–93.
3. Jordan and Walsh, *King's Revenge*, 167.
4. Ibid., 63.
5. 'English Heritage Battlefield Report: Naseby [14 June] 1645' (1995), 13.
6. Thomas Birch (ed.), *A Collection of the State Papers of John Thurloe*, vol. 4 (London, 1742), 509.
7. John Rushworth, *Historical Collections of Private Passages of State*, vol. 7: 1647–8 (London, 1721), 874; Robert Patterson Robins, 'Edward Whalley, the Regicide', *The Pennsylvania Magazine of History and Biography*, vol. 1, no. 1 (1877), 333.
8. Francis Peck, *Desiderata Curiosa*, vol. 2 (London, 1779), 374–7.
9. Christopher Durston, *Cromwell's Major-Generals* (Manchester, 2001), 44.
10. Lesley Le Claire, 'The Survival of the Manuscript', in Michael Mendle (ed.), *The Putney Debates of 1647: The Army, Levellers and the English State* (Cambridge, 2001), 31.
11. William Allen, *A Faithful Memorial of that Remarkable Meeting of Many Officers of the Army in England, at Windsor Castle, in the Year 1648* (London, 1659).
12. Patricia Crawford, 'Charles Stuart, That Man of Blood', *Journal of British Studies*, vol. 16, no. 2 (1977), 41–61.

13. Franklin B. Dexter, 'Memoranda Respecting Edward Whalley and William Goffe', *PNHCHS*, vol. 2 (New Haven, CT, 1877), 119.

14. Pagliuco, *Great Escape*, 36.

15. Oliver Cromwell, *The Writings and Speeches of Oliver Cromwell*, ed. W.C. Abbott and C.D. Crane, vol. 2 (Cambridge, MA, 1939; repr. Oxford, 1988), 324.

16. Durston, *Cromwell's Major-Generals*, 45, 48. Both Whalley and Goffe later demonstrated that they were inimical to Quakers.

17. Birch (ed.), *State Papers of John Thurloe*, vol. 3, 637.

18. Durston, *Cromwell's Major-Generals*, 20.

19. A.L. Rowse, *The Regicides and the Puritan Revolution* (London, 1994), 126.

20. BL Lansdowne MS 822, fols 3–4. I am grateful to Jonathan Fitzgibbons for this reference.

21. Durston, *Cromwell's Major-Generals*, 221.

22. John Evelyn, *Diary*, ed. Guy de la Bedoyere (Woodbridge, 1995), 105.

23. Sir George Wharton (?), *A second narrative of the late Parliament (so called) . . . by a friend to the good old cause of justice, righteousnesse, the freedom and liberties of the people, which hath cost so much bloud and treasury to be carried on in the late wars, and are not yet settled* (London, 1658), 13–14.

24. For doubts concerning this, see Jonathan Fitzgibbons, '"Not in Any Doubtfull Dispute"? Reassessing the Nomination of Richard Cromwell', *Historical Research*, vol. 83 (2010), 281–300.

25. Jordan and Walsh, *King's Revenge*, 111; Pagliuco, *Great Escape*, 51.

CHAPTER 2

1. *PMHS*, vol. 7 (1863–4), 282.

2. William Gordon, *The History of the Rise, Progress, and Establishment of the Independence of the United States of America*, vol. 1 (London, 1788), 176–8. Hutchinson had actually disapproved of the Stamp Act.

3. Stiles, *History*, 96–8.

4. A copy of an excerpt from the 1660 journal was found in the Winthrop papers by Robert C. Winthrop, and communicated to the Massachusetts Historical Society in December 1863. *PMHS*, vol. 7 (1863–4), 280. It was surmised that this brief insight into Goffe's diary later found its way into the Library of the American Antiquarian Society at Worcester, Massachusetts. See Appendix III.

5. Ibid., 281.

6. For the continental network of regicides see Gaby Mahlberg, '*Les Juges Jugez, se Justifiants* (1663) and Edmund Ludlow's Protestant Network

in Seventeenth-Century Switzerland', *Historical Journal*, vol. 57, no. 2 (2014), 369–96.

7. Robert Patterson Robins, 'Edward Whalley, the Regicide', *The Pennsylvania Magazine of History and Biography*, vol. 1, no. 1 (1877), 323, 351.

8. Philip Major, *Writings of Exile in the English Revolution and Restoration* (Farnham, 2013), 141–2.

9. Michael P. Winship, *Godly Republicanism: Puritans, Pilgrims, and a City on a Hill* (Cambridge, MA, 2012), 2, 4, 5, 184, 193–4, 203, ch. 8. Cf. David D. Hall, *Reforming People: Puritanism and the Transformation of Public Life in New England* (New York, 2011), xi, 19, ch. 3.

10. For Whalley and Goffe's views on providence, see Anthony Fletcher, 'The Religious Motivation of Cromwell's Major Generals', in Derek Baker (ed.), *Religious Motivation: Biographical and Sociological Problems for the Church Historian* (Oxford, 1978), 260–5. David Cressy, *Coming Over: Migrations and Communication between England and New England in the Seventeenth Century* (Cambridge, 1987), 144–51.

11. *Cal. S.P. Col.*, vol. 10, 1677–80 (August 1678), no. 782; Virginia DeJohn Anderson, 'New England in the Seventeenth Century', in Nicholas Canny (ed.), *The Origins of Empire: British Overseas Enterprise to the Close of the Seventeenth Century* (Oxford and New York, 1998), 198.

12. Christopher Durston, *Cromwell's Major-Generals* (Manchester, 2001), 47.

13. Douglas C. Wilson, 'Web of Secrecy: Goffe, Whalley, and the Legend of Hadley', *New England Quarterly*, vol. 60 (1987), 522.

14. *PMHS*, vol. 7 (1863–4), 281.

15. Matthew Jenkinson, 'John Crowne, the Restoration Court, and the "Understanding" of *Calisto*', *The Court Historian*, vol. 15, no. 2 (2010), 145–55.

16. Harvard MS Sparks 10, N.E. Pap., IV, 82: 'Walley & Goffe. Account of their Reception at Boston'; *Cal. S.P. Col.*, vol. 5, 1661–8 (August 1661), no. 161.

17. *CMHS*, third series, vol. 10 (Boston, MA, 1849), 39.

18. *PMHS*, vol. 7 (1863–4), 281.

19. Pagliuco, *Great Escape*, 59.

20. Harvard MS Sparks 10, N.E. Pap., IV, 82.

21. *PMHS*, vol. 7 (1863–4), 282.

22. Thomas Birch (ed.), *A Collection of the State Papers of John Thurloe*, vol. 5 (1742), 150–1. Cf. Fletcher, 'Religious Motivation', 262.

23. Howard Nenner, 'Trial of the Regicides: Retribution and Treason in 1660', in Howard Nenner (ed.), *Politics and the Political Imagination in Late Stuart Britain* (Woodbridge, 1998), 21–42.

24. For a fuller account see Matthew Jenkinson, *Culture and Politics at the Court of Charles II, 1660–1685* (Woodbridge, 2010), ch. 2, and Andrew Hopper, *Turncoats and Renegadoes: Changing Sides during the English Civil Wars* (Oxford, 2012), ch. 9 and epilogue.

25. *The Speeches and Prayers of Some of the Late King's Judges* (London, 1660); 'W.S.', *A Compleat Collection of the Lives, Speeches, Private Passages, Letters and Prayers of those Persons Lately Executed* (London, 1661); 'W.S.', *Rebels No Saints: Or, a Collection of the Speeches, Private Passages, Letters and Prayers of Those Persons Lately Executed* (London, 1661); Matthew Jenkinson, 'A New Author for the "Observations" in *Rebels No Saints* (1661)?', *Notes and Queries*, vol. 52, no. 3 (2005), 311–14; Jenkinson, *Culture and Politics*, ch. 2.

26. Carla Gardina Pestana, *The English Atlantic in an Age of Revolution, 1640–1661* (Cambridge, MA, and London, 2004), 60.

27. Harvard MS Sparks 10, N.E. Pap., IV, 82.

28. George Bate, *The Lives, Actions and Executions of the Prime Actors* (London, 1661), 22–3.

29. *Rebels No Saints: Or, a Collection of the Speeches, Private Passages, Letters and Prayers of Those Persons Lately Executed* (London, 1661), 118.

30. 'Letters and Papers Relating to the Regicides', *CMHS*, fourth series, vol. 8 (Boston, MA, 1868), 185.

31. Arthur Bryant (ed.), *The Letters, Speeches and Declarations of King Charles II* (London, 1935), 112–13.

32. 'Letters and Papers Relating to the Regicides', 167, 170, 187.

33. Ibid., 182.

34. Edmund Ludlow, *A Voyce from the Watch Tower, Part Five: 1660–1662*, ed. A.B. Worden, *Camden Fourth Series*, vol. 21 (London, 1978), 196.

35. *CNYHS*, vol. 2 (New York, 1869), 39.

36. Franklin B. Dexter, 'Memoranda Respecting Edward Whalley and William Goffe', *PNHCS*, vol. 2 (New Haven, CT, 1877), 126.

37. Mary-Peale Schofield, 'The Three Judges of New Haven', *History Today*, vol. 12 (1962), 347.

38. Pestana, *English Atlantic*, 30.

39. Ibid., 42–3; Robert M. Bliss, *Revolution and Empire: English Politics and the American Colonies in the Seventeenth Century* (New York, 1990), 48.

40. Charles M. Andrews, *Colonial Self-Government, 1652–1689* (New York and London, 1904), 37–48.

41. *DRCHNY*, vol. 3, 49–50; *Cal. S.P. Col.*, vol. 5, 1661–8 (March 1661), no. 45; *Cal. S.P. Col.*, vol. 10, 1677–80 (October 1678), no. 811; J.M. Sosin,

English America and the Restoration Monarchy of Charles II: Transatlantic Politics, Commerce, and Kinship (Lincoln, NE and London, 1980), 92.

42. *Cal. S.P. Col.*, vol. 5, 1661–8 (April 1661), no. 80.

43. Pagliuco, *Great Escape*, 66.

44. Stiles, *History*, 32; Francis J. Bremer, *The Puritan Experiment* (Lebanon, NH, 1995), 187.

45. John Davenport, *The Saints Anchor-hold* (London, 1661), 194. It has been suggested that Davenport's careful priming of his congregation betrays a potential reluctance on behalf of the New Haven community to take such a risk in welcoming and harbouring the fugitive regicides. Major, *Writings of Exile*, 151.

46. *CMHS*, third series, vol. 7 (Boston, MA, 1838), 123.

47. Charles M. Andrews, *The Colonial Period of American History* (New Haven, CT, 1939), 151.

48. Herbert L. Osgood, *The American Colonies in the Seventeenth Century* (New York and London, 1907), 161.

49. Charles J. Hoadly, *Records of the Colony or Jurisdiction of New Haven, 1653–1665* (Hartford, CT, 1858), 451.

50. *DRCHNY*, vol. 3, 41.

51. John Hull, 'Diary', in *Archaeologia Americana*, vol. 3 (Cambridge, 1857), 202.

52. *DRCHNY*, vol. 3, 41.

53. Ibid., 42.

54. Dexter, 'Memoranda', 117–46.

55. Andrews, *Colonial Period*, 158.

56. Dexter, 'Memoranda', 129.

57. Ibid.

58. Ibid.

59. Ibid., 129–30; Pagliuco, *Great Escape*, 72.

60. Dexter, 'Memoranda', 130.

61. John Gorham Palfrey, *History of New England During the Stuart Dynasty*, vol. 2 (Boston, MA, 1860), 505.

62. *CMHS*, vol. 27, 124.

63. Hoadly, *Records*, 380.

64. Welles, *Tercentenary*, 11.

65. Ibid., 12.

66. *CMHS*, series 3, vol. 8, 329.

67. Dexter, 'Memoranda', 133; Hoadly, *Records*, 419.

68. *CMHS*, third series, vol. 7, 125–6.

69. Welles, *Tercentenary*, 13.

70. Andrews, *Colonial Period*, 154–5.

71. Pestana, *English Atlantic*, 17.

72. Andrews, *Colonial Self-Government*, 57–8.

73. Hoadly, *Records*, 418.

74. Ibid., 421.

75. Dexter, 'Memoranda', 133.

76. Welles, *Tercentenary*, 14.

77. John Gorham Palfrey speculates that Temple was probably keener to apprehend the regicides than Pinchon. *History of New England*, vol. 2, 504, n. 1.

78. Pagliuco, *Great Escape*, 73.

79. Richard Baxter, *Apology Against the Modest Exceptions of Mr T. Blake* (London, 1654), 4.

80. Welles, *Tercentenary*, p. 16; Hoadly, *Records*, 419.

81. Dexter, 'Memoranda', 134–5.

82. *CMHS*, series 3, vol. 7, 328–9.

83. Letter from the Mather papers cited in Douglas C. Wilson, 'Web of Secrecy: Goffe, Whalley, and the Legend of Hadey', *New England Quarterly*, vol. 60 (1987), 528.

CHAPTER 3

1. *CMHS*, fourth series, vol. 8 (Boston, MA, 1868), 159.

2. Welles, *Tercentenary*, 17–18.

3. *CMHS*, fourth series, vol. 8, 173.

4. 'A Representation of the state of affaires in New England as Collected our of Severall Letters & by reporte of Severall persons wch Lately came from thence as followeth', *CNYHS*, vol. 2 (New York, 1869), 46.

5. Francis J. Bremer, *Congregational Communion: Clerical Friendship in the Anglo-American Puritan Community, 1610–1692* (Boston, MA, 1994), 219. Cf. Francis J. Bremer, 'Increase Mather's Friends: The Transatlantic Congregational Network of the Seventeenth Century', *Proceedings of the American Antiquarian Society*, vol. 94, no. 1 (1984), 59–95.

6. Welles, *History*, 70. Melinda S. Zook, *Protestantism, Politics and Women in Britain, 1660–1714* (Basingstoke, 2013), ch. 1.

7. Welles, *Tercentenary*, 19.

8. *CMHS*, fourth series, vol. 8, 122–225.

9. Ralph C.H. Catterall, 'Sir George Downing and the Regicides', *The American Historical Review*, vol. 17, no. 2 (1912), 268–89; Jordan and Walsh, *King's Revenge*, 271.

10. *CMHS*, fourth series, vol. 8, 198.

11. *Cal. S.P. Dom.*, 1663–4 (May 1663), no. 4.

12. *CMHS*, third series, vol. 7 (Boston, MA, 1838), 127.

13. *Cal. S.P. Dom.*, 1663–4 (January 1663), nos. 51, 54.

14. *CMHS*, third series, vol. 7, 126; HL MS Goodspeed Coll. Folder 2, Charles II to John Endecott, signed Edward Nicholas, 8 June 1662.

15. *CMHS*, third series, vol. 7, 127.

16. Jordan and Walsh, *King's Revenge*, 308.

17. Malcolm Gaskill, *Between Two Worlds: How the English Became Americans* (Oxford, 2014), 232.

18. Charles M. Andrews, *The Colonial Period of American History: England's Commercial and Colonial Policy* (New Haven, CT, 1938), 54–6.

19. Douglas C. Wilson, 'Web of Secrecy: Goffe, Whalley, and the Legend of Hadley', *New England Quarterly*, vol. 60 (1987), 532–3; Paul R. Lucas, 'Colony or Commonwealth: Massachusetts Bay, 1661–1666', *William and Mary Quarterly*, third ser., vol. 24, no. 1 (1967), 105; Pagliuco, *Great Escape*, 83–4; Herbert L. Osgood, *The American Colonies in the Seventeenth Century* (New York and London, 1907), 172–3.

20. Osgood, *American Colonies*, 174, 177.

21. Ibid., 172.

22. Ibid., 181–2, 185.

23. Wilson, 'Web of Secrecy', 534.

24. *CNYHS*, vol. 2 (1869), 85–6.

25. Welles, *Tercentenary*, 20–1.

26. Wilson, 'Web of Secrecy', 533.

27. A 1663 map of Hadley is available in Pagliuco, *Great Escape*, 88.

28. N.H. Keeble, *The Restoration: England in the 1660s* (Malden, MA, 2002), 160.

29. *CMHS*, fourth series, vol. 8, 127.

30. Samuel Pepys, *The Diary of Samuel Pepys*, ed. Robert Latham and William Matthews (Berkeley and Los Angeles, CA, 2000), I [1660], 199.

31. Nathaniel Hardy, *Lamentation, Mourning and Woe Sighed Forth in a Sermon* (London, 1666), 21, 28.

32. Wesley Frank Craven, *The Colonies in Transition, 1660–1713* (New York, Evanston, IL, and London, 1968), 49. Osgood, *American Colonies*, 152.

33. *CMHS*, fourth series, vol. 8, 128.

34. Ibid., 133.

35. Ibid., 133.

36. *CMHS*, third series, vol. 1 (Boston, MA, 1825), 60–1.

37. *CMHS*, fourth series, vol. 8, 135. Saltonstall had met Whalley and Goffe in Edinburgh in 1651.

38. Ibid., 136.

39. Ibid., 155.

40. Gaskill, *Between Two Worlds*, 277–93.

41. Thomas Hutchinson, *The History of Massachusetts, from the First Settlement thereof in 1628, until the year 1750* (Salem, MA, 1764), 201. A similar account appeared in *A Chronological Table of the most Remarkable Events in ... Massachusetts* (Boston, MA, 1764), 3: 'In 1675, the Indians attacked the town of Hadley, in time of public worship, when suddenly a grave and elderly person appeared in the midst of them, in his mien and dress he differed from the rest of the people, he not only encouraged them, but put himself at their head, rallied, instructed, and led them on to encounter the enemy, who by this means were repulsed. The deliverer of Hadley disappeared instantly, and the people remained in great consternation. This was General Goffe'.

42. 'Goffe and Whalley. Their Life in Hadley, Mass. – The "Angel of Hadley" Story Disproved', *New York Times* (19 August 1905). Cf. George Sheldon, 'The Traditionary Story of the Attack upon Hadley and the Appearance of Gen. Goffe, Sept 1 1675: Has it any foundation in fact?', *New England Historical and Genealogical Register*, 28 (Oct., 1874), 379–91.

43. The following account is a summary of Wilson, 'Web of Secrecy', 515–48.

44. Increase Mather, *A Brief History of the Warr with the Indians in New-England* (Boston, MA, 1676), 53–4, available online (ed. Paul Royster) at http://digitalcommons.unl.edu/cgi/viewcontent.cgi?article=1034&context=libraryscience.

45. Pagliuco, *Great Escape*, 96.

46. *Cal. S.P. Col.*, vol. 9, 1675–6 (October 1676), no. 1067; Franklin B. Dexter, 'Memoranda Respecting Edward Whalley and William Goffe', *PNHCHS*, vol. 2 (New Haven, CT, 1877), 141.

47. *Cal. S.P. Col.*, vol. 9, 1675–6 (June 1676), no. 953.

48. J.M. Sosin, *English America and the Restoration Monarchy of Charles II: Transatlantic Politics, Commerce and Kinship* (Lincoln, NE and London, 1980), 280.

49. *Cal. S.P. Col.*, vol. 11, 1681–5 (June 1683), no. 1121. Robert Noxon Toppan, *Edward Randolph ... 1676–1703*, vol. 1 (Boston, MA, 1898), 84, 100, 111, 173, 196; vol. 2, 207, 233, 276; vol. 3, 175, 234.

50. Ibid., vol. 4, 338.

51. Timothy Dwight, *Travels in New-England and New-York*, vol. 2 (New Haven, CT, 1821), 52.

52. Michael G. Hall, *Edward Randolph and the American Colonies, 1676–1703* (Chapel Hill, NC, 1960), 24, 34.

53. Jill Lepore, *The Name of War: King Philip's War and the Origins of American Identity* (New York, 1998), 59.

54. *CMHS*, fourth series, vol. 8, 156.

55. Ibid., 159.

56. Ibid., 224.

57. *Plan for Seizing and Carrying to New-York Coll. Wm. Goffe the Regicide* (Albany, NY, 1855), 4–5.

58. Dexter, 'Memoranda', 144–5.

59. *Plan for Seizing*, 10.

60. Dexter, 'Memoranda', 142.

61. *CMHS*, fourth series, vol. 8, 224.

62. Welles, *Tercentenary*, 26.

63. *CMHS*, fourth series, vol. 8, 159.

64. *Plan for Seizing*, 15–16.

65. For which see Carla Gardina Pestana, *The English Atlantic in an Age of Revolution, 1640–1661* (Cambridge, MA and London, 2004), 213–26.

66. Wesley Frank Craven, *The Colonies in Transition, 1660–1713* (New York, Evanston, IL, and London, 1968), 44.

67. Gaskill, *Between Two Worlds*, 218, 382.

68. Jordan and Walsh, *King's Revenge*, 2.

CHAPTER 4

1. Philagathos [Ezra Stiles], *A Poem, Commemorative of Goffe, Whaley, & Dixwell* (Boston, MA, 1793), 15–16.

2. John Adams diary entry 17 August 1774, available online at http://www.masshist.org/digitaladams/aea/cfm/doc.cfm?id=D21.

3. Abiel Holmes, *The Life of Ezra Stiles* (Boston, MA, 1798), 322–3.

4. Ibid.

5. [Thomas Hutchinson], *A Collection of Original Papers Relative to the History of the Colony of Massachusetts-Bay* (Boston, MA, 1769), 334–45.

6. *A Chronological Table of the Most Remarkable Events in the Province of the Massachusetts-Bay, from the Year 1602, when it was first discovered, to the Year 1770* (Boston, MA, 1771), 3.

7. Thomas Hutchinson, *History of the Colony of Massachusetts-Bay* (Boston, MA, 1764), 213–19.

8. Mark L. Sargent, 'Thomas Hutchinson, Ezra Stiles, and the Legend of the Regicides', *William and Mary Quarterly*, vol. 49, no. 3 (1992), 435.

9. Bernard Bailyn, *The Ordeal of Thomas Hutchinson* (Cambridge, MA, 1974), 56.

10. Ibid.

11. Sargent, 'Thomas Hutchinson', 436, 438.

12. Thomas Hutchinson's family politicized the way Hutchinson gained access to Goffe's diary. Thomas Hutchinson's great-grandson, Peter Orlando Hutchinson, like his great-grandfather, focused on Goffe 'skulking for his life in caves...suffering much privation and not a few hair-breadth escapes'—a picture intended to detract from any potential heroism and to suggest that the regicides' enemies were more tantalizingly close to their quarry than they really were. Peter Orlando suggested that Goffe's diary made its way into his great-grandfather's hands through Thomas Kellond, who had married the governor's aunt, Abigail. This explanation would suggest two things consistent with Thomas Hutchinson's rendering of the regicides. Firstly, that there were genuine and competent attempts to capture Whalley and Goffe: Kellond had got so close to Goffe that he was able to take a prized personal possession. Secondly, that Goffe's diary had not reached Hutchinson through the Russells and Mathers, two families active in the network of colonists who protected Whalley and Goffe, thereby downplaying that network's role in keeping the regicides safe. Peter Orlando Hutchinson (ed.), *The Diary and Letters of His Excellency Thomas Hutchinson* (Boston, MA, 1884), 32.

13. HL HM 550. Peter Oliver, 'The Origin and Progress of the American Revolution to the Year 1776, in a Letter to a Friend. London, March 1 1781', fols 23r, 29r.

14. Carla Gardina Pestana, *The English Atlantic in an Age of Revolution, 1640–1661* (Cambridge, MA and London, 2004), 214.

15. William Pencak, *America's Burke: The Mind of Thomas Hutchinson* (Lanham, MD, 1982), 73.

16. Hutchinson, *History of the Colony of Massachusetts-Bay*, 213–19.

17. Ibid.

18. Cf. the copy annotated by the merchant and Son of Liberty, Harbottle Dorr, in the Massachusetts Historical Society. *Boston Gazette and Country Journal* (20 November 1769), available online at http://www.masshist.org/dorr/volume/2/sequence/794. Gordon S. Wood, *The Americanization of Benjamin Franklin* (New York, 2004), 110. Cf. Andrew S. Walmsley, *Thomas Hutchinson and the Origins of the American Revolution* (New York and London, 1999), xiii–xiv.

19. Andrew Lacey, *The Cult of King Charles the Martyr* (Woodbridge, 2003); Howard Weinbrot, 'The Thirtieth of January Sermon: Swift, Johnson, Sterne, and the Evolution of Culture', *Eighteenth Century Life*, vol. 34, no. 1 (2010), 29–55.

20. William Waller Hening, *Statutes at Large, Being a Collection of all the Laws of Virginia* (New York, 1823), vol. 2, 19.

21. Franklin B. Dexter (ed.), *Literary Diary of Ezra Stiles*, vol. 1 (New York, 1901), 34–5.

22. A copy of Moss's sermon, held by the Historical Society of Pennsylvania, has marginalia showing that a William Frazer of Philadelphia owned it in October 1769; but another individual ('J.W.W.') directs readers to these words on page 19 of the sermon. Charles Moss, *A Sermon Preached before the House of Lords...January 30 1769* (Philadelphia, PA, 1769), 19; cf. James C. Spalding, 'Loyalist as Royalist, Patriot as Puritan: The American Revolution as a Repetition of the English Civil Wars', *Church History*, vol. 45, no. 3 (1976), 329–40 and Weinbrot, 'Thirtieth of January Sermon', 42.

23. Carl Bridenbaugh, *Mitre and Sceptre: Transatlantic Faiths, Ideas, Personalities and Politics, 1689–1775* (New York, 1962), 101–2.

24. Jeremy Gregory, 'Refashioning Puritan New England', *Transactions of the Royal Historical Society*, vol. 20 (2010), 99.

25. Francis J. Bremer, 'In Praise of Regicide: John Cotton on the Execution of Charles I', *William and Mary Quarterly*, vol. 37, no. 1 (1980), 103–24; Francis J. Bremer, *Congregational Communion: Clerical Friendship in the Anglo-American Puritan Community, 1610–1692* (Boston, MA, 1994), 175–9.

26. *CMHS*, third series, vol. 1 (Boston, MA, 1825), 83–4; W. DeLoss Love, *The Fast and Thanksgiving Days of New England* (Boston, MA and New York, 1895), 234–5; John Frederick Woolverton, *Colonial Anglicanism in North America* (Detroit, MI, 1984), 113.

27. *The Diary of Samuel Sewall*, ed. M. Halsey Thomas, vol. 1 (New York, 1973), 599.

28. James Peirce, *The Curse Causeless. A Sermon Preach'd at Exon, Jan. 30th 1716/17* (Boston, MA, 1728).

29. Ibid., iii.

30. Ibid., 10.

31. Ibid., 12.

32. Ibid., 11–12.

33. Ibid., 17.

34. Ibid., iv.

35. Jonathan Mayhew, *A Discourse Concerning Unlimited Submission* (Boston, MA, 1750), preface.

36. Ibid., 10–12.

37. Ibid., 21–2.

38. Ibid., 35.

39. Ibid., 40.

40. Ibid., 40.

41. Ibid., 41–3.

42. Ibid., 47.

43. Adams, *Works*, vol. 10, p. 284, cited in C.H. Van Tyne, 'Influence of the Clergy and Religious and Sectarian Forces on the American Revolution', *American Historical Review*, vol. 9, no. 1 (1913), 48.

44. Van Tyne, 'Influence of the Clergy', 50.

45. Ibid., 55.

46. George Coade, *A Letter to a Clergyman, Relating to His Sermon on the 30th of January* (New York, 1773).

47. Ibid., 10–11, 13, 16, 19.

48. Ibid., 27.

49. Ibid., 28.

50. John Allen, *An Oration Upon the Beauties of Liberty* (New London, 1773) [Ellis Sandoz (ed.), *Political Sermons of the American Founding Era*, vol. 1 (Indianapolis, IN, 1998), 307, 317, 320].

51. Abraham Keteltas, *God Arising and Pleading His People's Cause* (Newbury-Port, MA, 1777) [Sandoz, *Political Sermons*, 596].

52. Anon., *A Dialogue Between the Devil, and George III, Tyrant of Britain* (Boston, MA, 1782; Maryland, 1787; Maine, 1797) [Sandoz, *Political Sermons*, 691–2, 704].

53. Charles Inglis, *The Duty of Honouring the King, Explained and Recommended in a Sermon Preached in St George's and St Paul's Chapels, New York, on Sunday, January 30, 1780* (New York, 1780).

54. Ibid., 12.

55. Ibid., 12.

56. Ibid., 23.

57. Weinbrot, 'Thirtieth of January Sermon', 39, 46.

58. For a similar concern in Restoration sermons see Matthew Jenkinson, *Culture and Politics at the Court of Charles II* (Woodbridge, 2010), ch. 7.

59. Inglis, *Duty of Honouring the King*, 6.

60. Dexter (ed.), *Literary Diary of Ezra Stiles*, vol. 1, 45.

61. Ibid., 34–5.

CHAPTER 5

1. *Collections of the Connecticut Historical Society*, vol. 3 (Hartford, CT, 1895), 91.

2. Mark L. Sargent, 'Thomas Hutchinson, Ezra Stiles, and the Legend of the Regicides', *William and Mary Quarterly*, vol. 49, no. 3 (1992), 433.

3. Ibid.

4. Edmund S. Morgan, *The Gentle Puritan: A Life of Ezra Stiles, 1727–1795* (New Haven, CT and London, 1962), 458.

5. Franklin B. Dexter (ed.), *Literary Diary of Ezra Stiles*, vol. 1 (New York, 1901), 168–70.

6. Stiles, *History*, 30. Some still treat these stories as historical fact. Spencer, *Killers*, 273.

7. Nineteenth-century authors were also keen to exploit this dramatic episode in their historical fiction: Frederick Hull Cogswell had Whalley and Goffe standing 'in the water to their armpits, while the horses' hoofs clattered overhead and disappeared in the distance'. Frederick Hull Cogswell, *The Regicides: A Tale of Early Colonial Times* (New York, 1896), 202.

8. Stiles, *History*, 32.

9. Delia Salter Bacon, *Tales of the Puritans: The Regicides* (New Haven, CT, 1831), 285.

10. Stiles, *History*, 31.

11. Ibid.

12. Ibid., 33–4.

13. Benjamin Trumbull, *A Complete History of Connecticut*, vol. 1 (Hartford, CT, 1797), 254.

14. Bacon, *Tales of the Puritans*, 284.

15. John Gorham Palfrey, *History of New England During the Stuart Dynasty*, vol. 2 (Boston, MA, 1860), 504, n. 2.

16. Margaret Sidney, *The Judges' Cave* (Boston, MA, 1900), 315; W.H. Gocher, *Wadsworth, or The Charter Oak* (Hartford, CT, 1904), 83–4.

17. Sargent, 'Thomas Hutchinson', 441–2.

18. Stiles, *History*, 20.

19. Gordon S. Wood, *The Idea of America: Reflections on the Birth of the United States* (New York, 2011), 231–49. Cf. Morgan, *Gentle Puritan*, 458.

20. Eric Nelson, *The Royalist Revolution: Monarchy and the American Founding* (Cambridge, MA and London, 2014), esp. chs. 1–2.

21. Ibid., 56.

22. Alfred F. Young, 'English Plebeian Culture and Eighteenth-Century American Radicalism', in Margaret Jacob and James Jacob (eds.), *The Origins of Anglo-American Radicalism* (London, 1984), 195.

23. Ibid., 196; Alan Heimert, *Religion and the American Mind from the Great Awakening to the Revolution* (Cambridge, MA, 1966), 357.

24. Brendan McConville, *The King's Three Faces: The Rise and Fall of Royal America, 1688–1776* (Chapel Hill, NC, 2006), 92–100, 166–74, 270–2; James C. Spalding, 'Loyalist as Royalist, Patriot as Puritan: The American

Revolution as a Repetition of the English Civil Wars', *Church History*, vol. 45, no. 3 (1976), 329–40. For loyalist comparisons between the American Revolution and the English civil wars see J.C.D. Clark, *The Language of Liberty 1660–1832: Political Discourse and Social Dynamics in the Anglo-American World* (Cambridge, 1994), 357–8.

25. Nelson, *Royalist Revolution*, 37.

26. Rhys Isaac, *Landon Carter's Uneasy Kingdom: Revolution and Rebellion on a Virginia Plantation* (Oxford, 2004), 171–2. Carter did then moderate his language to suggest that George III's ministers, not the king himself, were acting tyrannically.

27. Young, 'English Plebeian Culture', 186, 195–9.

28. Bernard Bailyn, *The Ideological Origins of the American Revolution* (Cambridge, MA, 1992), 34–5, 145, and *passim*; cf. Blair Worden, *Roundhead Reputations: The English Civil Wars and the Passions of Posterity* (London, 2001), 32, 121, 127, 174, 210, 227, 334–6, 350–1, 353.

29. Winthrop D. Jordan, 'Familial Politics: Thomas Paine and the Killing of the King, 1776', *Journal of American History*, vol. 60 (1973), 302; Kevin J. Hayes, *George Washington: A Life in Books* (Oxford, 2017), 111–12.

30. Benjamin Trumbull, *A Complete History of Connecticut*, vol. 1 (Hartford, CT, 1797), 251.

31. Ibid., 251–4.

32. Gershom Bulkeley, *Bulkeley's Will and Doom, or the Miseries of Connecticut by and under an Usurped and Arbitrary Power* (1692) in *Collections of the Connecticut Historical Society*, vol. 3, 91–2.

33. Jonathan Boucher, *A View of the Causes and Consequences of the American Revolution* (London, 1797), 532.

34. Ibid., 448.

35. Ibid., 'Dedication', 353–4.

36. *Observations on American Independency* (1779), 6; *The True Interest of America Impartially Stated* (Philadelphia, PA, 1776), 52; Arthur Lee, *A Speech Intended to Have Been Delivered in the House of Commons, in Support of the Petition from the General Congress at Philadelphia* (London, 1775), 4; Dror Wahrman, 'The English Problem of Identity in the American Revolution', *American Historical Review*, vol. 106, no. 4 (2001), 1239–41.

37. Wahrman, 'English Problem of Identity', 1241.

38. Hannah Adams, *Summary History of New-England, From the First Settlement at Plymouth* (Dedham, 1799), 110.

39. Ibid., 113.

40. Ibid., 113.

41. Ibid., 114.

42. Jedidiah Morse, *The American Universal Geography... Third Edition* (Boston, MA, 1796), 457.

CHAPTER 6

1. Cora E. Lutz, 'Ezra Stiles and the Monument for Colonel John Dixwell', *Yale University Gazette*, vol. 55, no. 3 (1981), 116.

2. Henry T. Blake, 'Cut Ninety Years Ago', *New Haven Register* (September 1893), cited in Colin M. Caplan, *Westville: Tales from a Connecticut Hamlet* (Charleston, SC, 2009), 15–17.

3. Ebenezer Elliott, *Kerhonah, The Vernal Walk, Win Hill, and Other Poems* (London, 1835), 13, 21.

4. Edward Vallance, '"The Insane Enthusiasm of the Time": Remembering the Regicides in Eighteenth- and Nineteenth-Century Britain and North America', in Laurent Curelly and Nigel Smith (eds.), *Radical Voices, Radical Ways: Articulating and Disseminating Radicalism in Seventeenth- and Eighteenth-Century Britain* (Manchester, 2016), 241–2.

5. Ibid., 229–50.

6. Southey was inspired by Abiel Holmes's *Annals of America*, the first edition of which had been published in 1805 (which itself had used Stiles's (Holmes's father-in-law) *History* to describe Goffe's appearance in King Philip's War), and outlined a visit Holmes had made to the Judges Cave in New Haven. Abiel Holmes, *The Annals of America*, vol. 1 (Cambridge, MA, 1805), 369–72, esp. 372 n. 2.

7. Robert Southey, *Oliver Newman: A New-England Tale (Unfinished)* (London, 1845), 83–90. Cf. 'Southey's Oliver Newman', *The Spectator* (December 1845), 17. Robert Southey's outline for *Oliver Newman* was explained in a letter from the poet to Charles Watkin Williams Wynn (15 December 1814). See letter no. 2516 of the collection available online at Ian Packer and Lynda Pratt (eds.), 'The Collected Works of Robert Southey, Part Four: 1810–1815', in Neil Fraistat and Steven E. Jones (eds.), *Romantic Circles*: http://www.rc.umd.edu/editions/southey_letters/Part_Four/HTML.letterEEd.26.2516.html.

8. Walter Scott, *Peveril of the Peak*, ed. Alison Lumsden (Edinburgh, 2007), 144–8.

9. Cf. Mark L. Sargent, 'Thomas Hutchinson, Ezra Stiles, and the Legend of the Regicides', *William and Mary Quarterly*, vol. 49, no. 3 (1992), 443–4.

10. Vallance, 'The Insane Enthusiasm of the Time', 242.

11. 'The Cave of the Regicides', *Blackwood's Edinburgh Magazine*, vol. 90 (1847), 333.

12. 'Recent American Novels', *The North American Review* (July 1825), 98.

13. Ray Raphael, *Founding Myths that Hide our Patriotic Past* (New York, 2004), 1–6, 257. Cf. Gil Klein, 'The Use of Myth in History', *Colonial Williamsburg Journal* (Summer 2012).

14. Raphael, *Founding Myths*, 257.

15. Michael Kammen, *Mystic Chords of Memory: The Transformation of Tradition in American Culture* (New York, 1991), 63–5.

16. Douglas C. Wilson, 'Web of Secrecy: Goffe, Whalley, and the Legend of Hadley', *New England Quarterly*, vol. 60 (1987), 516.

17. Alexander B. Meek, 'Americanism in Literature', in W.G. Simms, *Views and Reviews in American Literature, History and Fiction* (New York, 1845), 2.

18. 'The Epochs and Events of American History as Suited to the Purposes of Art in Fiction', in W.G. Simms, *Views and Reviews in American Literature, History and Fiction* (New York, 1845), 23, 26, 27, 64.

19. Robert Clark, *History, Ideology and Myth in American Fiction, 1823–52* (London, 1984), 23.

20. Wilson, 'Web of Secrecy', 517.

21. James McHenry, *The Spectre of the Forest* (New York, 1823), 28, 102, 135, 139, 180, 188–9.

22. J.N. Barker, *The Tragedy of Superstition* (Philadelphia, PA, 1826), 17, 39.

23. James Fenimore Cooper, *The Wept of Wish-ton-Wish* (Philadelphia, PA, 1829), 162, 164, 192, 194, 248, 347.

24. Jill Lepore, *The Name of War: King Philip's War and the Origins of American Identity* (New York, 1998), 195.

25. Delia Salter Bacon, *Tales of the Puritans: The Regicides* (New Haven, CT, 1831), 29, 35, 46, 69, 73, 77, 79, 81, 118, 125.

26. These quotations are from William Leete Stone, *Mercy Disborough* (New York, 1844), 20–4, 32, 97–8. The story had appeared in Stone's *Tales and Sketches, Such as They Are* (New York, 1834).

27. Leonard Bacon, *Thirteen Historical Discourses, on the Completion of Two Hundred Years, from the Beginning of the First Church in New Haven* (New Haven, CT, 1839), 133.

28. Israel Perkins Warren, *The Three Judges* (New York, 1873), 4.

29. W.A. Caruthers, *The Cavaliers of Virginia*, vol. 1 (New York, 1834), 33–4, 38, 47.

30. Ibid., vol. 2 (New York, 1835), 218–19.

31. Ibid., 51.

32. The following account is based on W.E. Washburn's *The Governor and the Rebel: A History of Bacon's Rebellion in Virginia* (New York and London, 1972).

33. George Bancroft, *History of the United States of America, From the Discovery of the Continent*, vol. 1 (New York, 1886), 347.

34. Sacvan Bercovitch, 'How the Puritans Won the American Revolution', *The Massachusetts Review*, vol. 17, no. 4 (1976), 604–5, 613.

35. Sargent, 'Thomas Hutchinson', 445–6.

36. Gordon M. Sayre, *The Indian Chief as Tragic Hero* (Chapel Hill, NC, 2005), 119; Tice L. Miller, *Entertaining the Nation: American Drama in the Eighteenth and Nineteenth Centuries* (Carbondale, IL, 2007), 61; Lepore, *The Name of War*, 197; Sargent, 'Thomas Hutchinson', 446.

37. Lepore, *Name of War*, 191–2.

38. Nathaniel Hawthorne, 'The Gray Champion', *New England Magazine*, vol. 8 (January 1835), 20–6.

39. *The Salem Belle* (Boston, MA, 1842), 32, 73–5.

40. Henry William Herbert, *Ruth Whalley; Or, The Fair Puritan. A Romance of the Bay Province* (Boston, MA, 1845), 4, 20–1, 32–45.

41. James Kirke Paulding, *The Puritan and His Daughter* (New York, 1849), 1–8, 52–6, 73, 90–1, 115–16, 156–62.

42. Bercovitch, 'How the Puritans Won the American Revolution', 601–2.

43. G.H. Hollister, *Mount Hope* (New York, 1851), 82, 218.

44. Ibid., 84–5, 269–75.

45. J.R. Musick, *A Century Too Soon* (New York, 1893), 286.

46. 'Dixwell the Regicide', *Notes and Queries*, fifth series, vol. 9 (June 1878), 466.

47. John Warner Barber and Elizabeth G. Barber, *Historical, Poetical and Pictorial American Scenes: Principally Moral and Religious* (New Haven, CT, 1850), 26–7.

48. Henry David Thoreau, *Walden; Or, Life in the Woods* (Boston, MA, 1854), 149.

49. Walt Whitman, *Leaves of Grass: A Textual Variorum of the Printed Poems, vol. II: Poems 1860–1867*, ed. Sculley Bradley, Harold W. Blodgett, Arthur Golden, and William White (New York, 1980), 415.

50. Clarence Gohdes, 'Whitman and the "Good Old Cause"', *American Literature*, vol. 34, no. 3 (1962), 400–3.

51. 'Proceedings of the Annual Meeting, 1847', *Transactions of the American Art-Union* (1847), 14–15, 70.

52. Thomas Prichard Rossiter and Rossiter family papers, 1840–1961. Archives of American Art, Smithsonian Institution. Box 1, Folder 7: Checklist of Paintings by Thomas Prichard Rossiter (1957), 12. Available online at http://www.aaa.si.edu/collections/thomas-prichard-rossiter-and-rossiter-family-papers-8395#/CollectionsOnline/rossthom/Box_0001/Folder_007/+-ref14-ref21.

53. Ibid., 12–13.

54. *The Phrenological Journal*, vols 92–3 (May 1891), 219–20.

CHAPTER 7

1. Mark L. Sargent, 'Thomas Hutchinson, Ezra Stiles, and the Legend of the Regicides', *William and Mary Quarterly*, vol. 49, no. 3 (1992), 447–8.

2. *PMHS*, vol. 7 (1863–4), 280. John Gorham Palfrey, *History of New England*, vol. 3 (Boston, MA, 1864), preface and 164. Elisa Tamarkin, *Anglophilia: Deference, Devotion and Antebellum America* (Chicago, IL and London, 2008), 76.

3. Colin M. Caplan, *Westville: Tales from a Connecticut Hamlet* (Charleston, SC, 2009), 14.

4. Henry W. Box, *In Memoriam Abraham Lincoln* (Buffalo, NY, 1865), 28.

5. *Papers Relating to Foreign Affairs, Accompanying the Annual Message of the President to the First Session Thirty-Ninth Congress*, Part 3 (Washington, DC, 1866), 125.

6. Caroline A. Hayden, *Our Country's Martyr: A Tribute to Abraham Lincoln* (Boston, MA, 1865), 5.

7. Warren Hathaway, *A Discourse Occasioned by the Death of Abraham Lincoln* (Albany, NY, 1865), 10.

8. James Bayard Taylor, 'The Strange Friend', *Atlantic Monthly*, vol. 19, no. 111 (January 1867), 54–65. Cf. http://www.librarycompany.org/gothic/regicides.htm.

9. Robert Patterson Robins, 'Edward Whalley, the Regicide', *The Pennsylvania Magazine of History and Biography*, vol. 1, no. 1 (1877), 322. In 1868 another observer noted that the letters were 'in every respect...of surpassing interest' (even if, they said, 'Mrs Goffe['s]...Calvinistic theology is at times stiff enough to make one's hair stand on end'). *The Christian Examiner*, vol. 85 (Richmond, VA, 1868), 167–70.

10. Douglas C. Wilson, 'Web of Secrecy: Goffe, Whalley, and the Legend of Hadley', *New England Quarterly*, vol. 60 (1987), 517–18.

11. Michael Kammen, *Mystic Chords of Memory: The Transformation of American Culture* (New York, 1991), 88.

12. William B. Rhoads, *The Colonial Revival*, vol. 1 (New York and London, 1977), 395, 408, 551; Richard Guy Wilson, 'What Is the Colonial Revival?', in Richard Guy Wilson, Shaun Eyring, and Kenny Marotta (eds.), *Re-creating the American Past: Essays on the Colonial Revival* (Charlottesville, VA and London, 2006), 1–10; Kenneth L. Ames, 'Introduction', in Alan Axelrod (ed.), *The Colonial Revival in America* (New York and London, 1985), 1–14.

13. Henry Howe, *Outline History of New Haven* (1884), in Colin M. Caplan, *Westville: Tales from a Connecticut Hamlet* (Charleston, SC, 2009), 11.

14. George Bancroft, *History of the United States of America, From the Discovery of the Continent*, vol. 1 (New York, 1886), 347.

15. Henry T. Blake, 'Cut Ninety Years Ago', *New Haven Register* (September 1893), cited in Caplan, *Westville*, 15.

16. Charles Knowles Bolton, *On the Wooing of Martha Pitkin: Being a Versified Narrative of the Time of the Regicides in Colonial New England* (1895).

17. Charles Knowles Bolton, *The Founders: Portraits of Persons Born Abroad Who Came to the Colonies in North America Before the Year 1701*, vol. 2 (Boston, MA, 1919), 393–5.

18. Palfrey, *History of New England*, vol. 3, 8.

19. John R. Musick, *A Century Too Soon: A Story of Bacon's Rebellion* (London and Toronto, 1893), 5.

20. John Leete, *The Family of Leete* (London, 1906), 170.

21. Bacon, *Thirteen Historical Discourses*, 133.

22. Edward Grimm, *The King's Judges: An Original Comedy* (San Francisco, CA, 1892), 6, 21.

23. Ibid., 'History', 9, 21, 43.

24. Ibid., 14.

25. Ibid., 6.

26. Ibid., 40, 45.

27. Musick, *A Century Too Soon*, 200. Cf. Bancroft, *History of the United States*, vol. 1, 347.

28. Musick, *A Century Too Soon*, 162–80, 204.

29. Ibid., 366.

30. Frederick Hull Cogswell, *The Regicides: A Tale of Early Colonial Times* (New York, 1896), 7.

31. Ibid., 8.

32. Ibid., 212.

33. Ibid., 21.

34. Ibid., 56, 188, 253.

35. Ibid., 192.

36. Ibid., 134.
37. Ibid., 137.
38. Margaret Sidney, *The Judges' Cave* (Boston, MA, 1900), 7–8.
39. W.H. Gocher, *Wadsworth: or The Charter Oak* (Hartford, CT, 1904), 13.
40. Pagliuco, *Great Escape*, 92.
41. Franklin B. Dexter, 'Memoranda Respecting Edward Whalley and William Goffe', *PNHCHS*, vol. 2 (New Haven, CT, 1877), 140.
42. Pagliuco, *Great Escape*, 92.
43. Robert Patterson Robins, 'Edward Whalley, the Regicide', *The Pennsylvania Magazine of History and Biography*, vol. 1, no. 1 (1877), 59.
44. See, for example, *The Atlantic Monthly*, vol. 6, no. 23 (July 1860), 89–93. John Wingate Thornton wrote from Boston to John C. McCabe on 29 December 1851, asking for information concerning Daniel Gookin's family. HL MS BR Box 117 (24).
45. Robins, 'Edward Whalley', 55.
46. Ibid., 61–2.
47. Ibid., 62.
48. Ibid., 62–3.
49. *The Pennsylvania Magazine of History and Biography*, vol. 1, no. 1 (1877), 230–1.
50. Robins, 'Edward Whalley', 63.
51. Ibid., 359.
52. Franklin B. Dexter (ed.), *Extracts from the Itineraries and Other Miscellanies of Ezra Stiles* (New Haven, CT, 1916), 520.
53. Sargent, 'Thomas Hutchinson', 439. Cf. Ezra Stiles, *Literary Diary*, ed. Franklin B. Dexter, vol. 3 (New York, 1901), 168–70.
54. Timothy Dwight, *Travels in New-England and New-York*, vol. 1 (New Haven, CT, 1821), 353.
55. 'Goffe and Whalley', *The New York Times* (19 August 1905).
56. Delia Salter Bacon, *Tales of the Puritans: The Regicides* (New Haven, CT, 1831), 295.
57. Dexter, 'Memoranda', 146.
58. Ibid., 144.
59. John Warner Barber and Elizabeth G. Barber, *Historical, Poetical and Pictorial American Scenes: Principally Moral and Religious* (New Haven, CT, 1850), 26.
60. *Memoir of Jonathan Leavitt by a Sister* (New Haven, CT, 1822), 66.
61. 'Grave of Goff the Regicide Judge', *The New York Times* (15 July 1894).
62. *The History of Middlesex County, 1635–1885* (New York, 1884), 198.

63. http://www.colebrookhistoricalsociety.org/PDF%20Images/Regicides, %20Conclusion.pdf.

64. 'Historic Judges' Cave, Near New Haven, Is a Good Goal for Motorists', *The New York Times* (16 August 1914).

65. P. Henry Woodward, 'True Story of the Regicides', *Saturday Chronicle* (April 1918), cited in Colin M. Caplan, *Westville: Tales from a Connecticut Hamlet* (Charleston, SC, 2009), 12–15.

66. C. Newton, 'Letters of a New England Exile', *Americana*, vol. 14 (1920), 208–26.

67. Aline Havard, *The Regicide's Children* (New York, 1927); *Boys' Life* (December 1927), 82.

68. Lemuel Aiken Welles, 'A Glance at New England Character', *Yale Literary Magazine*, vol. 57 (1892), 19–21.

69. Welles, *History*, 34, 123.

70. Ibid., 34.

71. Ibid., 43.

72. Ibid., 63.

73. Everett Whitlock, 'America's Sperrys Sprang from Old Westville Home', in Colin M. Caplan, *Westville: Tales from a Connecticut Hamlet* (Charleston, SC, 2009), 10.

74. Lewis Sprague Mills, *The Story of Connecticut* (West Rindge, NH, 1932, 1935, 1943, 1953, 1958), 154–8.

75. G. Harrison Orlans, 'The Angel of Hadley in Fiction: A Study of the Sources of Hawthorne's "Gray Champion"', *American Literature*, vol. 4 (1932), 256–69.

76. Alexander Winston, 'The Hunt for the Regicides', *American Heritage Magazine*, vol. 16, no. 1 (December 1964).

77. Louis B. Wright, *The British Tradition in America* (Birmingham, AL, 1954), 2, 7, 31.

78. Leo Sauvage, 'The Oswald Affair', *Commentary*, vol. 37, no. 3 (March 1964).

CHAPTER 8

1. Jill Lepore, *The Story of America: Essays on Origins* (Princeton, NJ and Oxford, 2012), 3.

2. Delia Salter Bacon, *Tales of the Puritans* (New Haven, CT, 1831), 275.

3. Peter M. LeTourneau and Robert Pagini, *The Traprock Landscapes of New England: Landscape, History and Culture* (Middleton, CT, 2017), 25.

4. A.A. Gill, 'Restoration London's Burning! Alack!', *The Times* (6 April 2014).

5. Kathleen Kent, *The Wolves of Andover: A Novel* (London, 2010).

6. Whitlock, Everett, 'America's Sperrys Sprang from Old Westville Home', in Colin M. Caplan, *Westville: Tales from a Connecticut Hamlet* (Charleston, SC, 2009), 10.

APPENDIX IV

1. *An Exact and Most Impartial Accompt of the Indictment, Trial, and Judgment (according to Law) of Nine and Twenty Regicides* (London, 1660), 49.

2. If the year of printing (1660) is Old Style, then the *Accompt* could have been printed any time up to 24 March 1661 (New Style).

3. Franklin B. Dexter (ed.), 'Dixwell Papers', *PNHCHS*, vol. 6 (New Haven, CT, 1900), 344, 347–9.

4. Ibid., 351.

5. *CMHS*, fourth series, vol. 8, 224.

6. Mark Goldie, 'The Hilton Gang and the Purge of London in the 1680s', in Howard Nenner (ed.), *Politics and the Political Imagination in Later Stuart Britain* (Woodbridge, 1998), 43–73; Grant Tapsell, *The Personal Rule of Charles II, 1681–85* (Woodbridge, 2007).

7. Dexter (ed.), 'Dixwell Papers', 351–2.

8. Ibid., 373.

9. Welles, *Tercentenary*, 27.

10. Some detractors claimed that the baby was not actually Mary's, but had been smuggled into her chamber in a warming pan.

11. Dexter (ed.), 'Dixwell Papers', 356–7.

Bibliography

MANUSCRIPTS

British Library, London

BL Lansdowne MS 822

Huntington Library, San Marino, California

HL Goodspeed Coll. Folder 2, 'Charles II to John Endecott, signed Edward Nicholas'

HL HM 175, 'Anonymous memorandum book and journal of a voyage from London to Boston [1768–1773]'

HL HM 550, 'Origin and Progress of the American Rebellion in the year 1776, in a letter to a friend'

HL MS BR Box 117 (24), John Wingate Thornton to John C. McCabe (29 December 1851)

Houghton Library, Harvard, Massachusetts

Harvard MS Sparks 10, N.E. Pap. IV, 'Walley & Goffe. Account of their Reception at Boston'

Massachusetts Historical Society, Boston, Massachusetts

John Adams diary entry 17 August 1774, available online at http://www. masshist.org/digitaladams/aea/cfm/doc.cfm?id=D21

Smithsonian Institution, Washington, DC

Thomas Prichard Rossiter and Rossiter family papers, 1840–1961. Archives of American Art, Smithsonian Institution. Box 1, Folder 7: 1840–1961. Archives of American Art, SmithsRossiter (1957), available online at http://www.aaa.si.edu/collections/thomas-prichard-rossiter-and-rossiter-family-papers-8395#/CollectionsOnline/rossthom/Box_0001/Folder_007/+-ref14-ref21

PRINTED PRIMARY, PRE-1800

Adams, Hannah, *Summary History of New-England, From the First Settlement at Plymouth* (Dedham, 1799)

Allen, John, *An Oration Upon the Beauties of Liberty* (New London, 1773)

Allen, William, *A Faithful Memorial of that Remarkable Meeting of Many Officers of the Army in England, at Windsor Castle, in the Year 1648* (London, 1659)

Bate, George, *The Lives, Actions and Execution of the Prime Actors, and Principall Contrivers of that Horrid Murder of . . . King Charles the First* (London, 1661)

Baxter, Richard, *Apology Against the Modest Exceptions of Mr T. Blake* (London, 1654)

Boston Gazette and Country Journal (20 November 1769), available online at http://www.masshist.org/dorr/volume/2/sequence/794

Boucher, Jonathan, *A View of the Causes and Consequences of the American Revolution* (London, 1797)

A Chronological Table of the Most Remarkable Events in the Province of the Massachusetts-Bay, from the Year 1602, when it was first discovered, to the Year 1770 (Boston, MA, 1771)

Coade, George, *A Letter to a Clergyman, Relating to his Sermon on the 30th of January* (New York, 1773)

Davenport, John, *The Saints Anchor-hold* (London, 1661)

A Dialogue Between the Devil, and George III, Tyrant of Britain (Boston, MA, 1782; Maryland, 1787; Maine, 1797)

An Exact and Most Impartial Accompt of the Indictment, Trial, and Judgment (according to Law) of Nine and Twenty Regicides (London, 1660)

Gordon, William, *The History of the Rise, Progress, and Establishment of the Independence of the United States of America*, vol. 1 (London, 1788)

Hardy, Nathaniel, *Lamentation, Mourning and Woe Sighed Forth in a Sermon* (London, 1666)

Holmes, Abiel, *The Life of Ezra Stiles* (Boston, MA, 1798)

[Hutchinson, Thomas], *The History of Massachusetts, from the First Settlement thereof in 1628, until the year 1750* (Boston, MA, 1764 and 1767)

[Hutchinson, Thomas], *A Collection of Original Papers Relative to the History of the Colony of Massachusetts-Bay* (Boston, MA, 1769)

Inglis, Charles, *The Duty of Honouring the King, Explained and Recommended in a Sermon Preached in St George's and St Paul's Chapels, New York, on Sunday, January 30, 1780* (New York, 1780)

Keteltas, Abraham, *God Arising and Pleading His People's Cause* (Newbury-Port, MA, 1777)

A Looking Glass for Traytors (London, 1660)

Mather, Increase, *A Brief History of the Warr with the Indians in New-England* (Boston, MA, 1676), available online (ed. Paul Royster) at http://digital-commons.unl.edu/cgi/viewcontent.cgi?article=1034&context=libraryscience

Mayhew, Jonathan, *A Discourse Concerning Unlimited Submission* (Boston, MA, 1750)

Morse, Jedidiah, *The American Universal Geography . . . Third Edition* (Boston, MA, 1796)

Moss, Charles, *A Sermon Preached before the House of Lords . . . January 30 1769* (Philadelphia, PA, 1769)

Peck, Francis, *Desiderata Curiosa*, vol. 2 (London, 1779)

Peirce, James, *The Curse Causeless. A Sermon Preach'd at Exon, Jan. 30th 1716/17* (Boston, MA, 1728)

Philagathos [Ezra Stiles], *A Poem, Commemorative of Goffe, Whaley, & Dixwell* (Boston, MA, 1793)

Rushworth, John, *Historical Collections of Private Passages of State*, vol. 7: 1647–8 (London, 1721)

The Speeches and Prayers of Some of the Late King's Judges (London, 1660)

Stiles, Ezra, *A History of Three of the Judges of Charles I* (Hartford, CT, 1794)

'S., W.' [Sanderson, William?], *A Compleat Collection of the Lives, Speeches, Private Passages, Letters and Prayers of those Persons Lately Executed* (London, 1661)

'S., W.' [Sanderson, William?], *Rebels No Saints: Or, a Collection of the Speeches, Private Passages, Letters and Prayers of those Persons Lately Executed* (London, 1661)

Trumbull, Benjamin, *A Complete History of Connecticut*, vol. 1 (Hartford, CT, 1797)

Wharton, Sir George (?), *A second narrative of the late parliament (so called) . . . by a friend to the good old cause of justice, righteousnesse, the freedom and liberties of the people, which hath cost so much bloud and treasury to be carried on in the late wars, and are not yet settled* (London, 1658)

PRINTED PRIMARY, POST-1800

Bacon, Delia Salter, *Tales of the Puritans: The Regicides* (New Haven, CT, 1831)

Bacon, Leonard, *Thirteen Historical Discourses on the Completion of Two Hundred Years from the Beginning of the First Church in New Haven* (New Haven, CT, 1839)

Bancroft, George, *History of the United States of America, From the Discovery of the Continent* (New York, 1886)

Barber, John Warner, *Interesting Events in the History of the United States* (New Haven, CT, 1829)

Barber, John Warner and Elizabeth G. Barber, *Historical, Poetical and Pictorial American Scenes: Principally Moral and Religious* (New Haven, CT, 1850)

Barker, James Nelson, *The Tragedy of Superstition* (Philadelphia, PA, 1826)

Blake, Henry T., 'Cut Ninety Years Ago', *New Haven Register* (September 1893)

Bolton, Charles Knowles, *On the Wooing of Martha Pitkin: Being a Versified Narrative of the Time of the Regicides in Colonial New England* (Boston, MA, 1894)

Bolton, Charles Knowles, *The Founders: Portraits of Persons Born Abroad Who Came to the Colonies in North America Before the Year 1701*, vol. 2 (Boston, MA, 1919)

Box, Henry W., *In Memoriam Abraham Lincoln* (Buffalo, NY, 1865)

Boys' Life (December 1927)

Bryant, Arthur (ed.), *The Letters, Speeches and Declarations of King Charles II* (London, 1935)

Bulkeley, Gershom, *Bulkeley's Will and Doom, or the Miseries of Connecticut by and under an Usurped and Arbitrary Power* (1692) in *Connecticut Historical Society Collections*, vol. 3 (Hartford, CT, 1895)

Calendar of State Papers Colonial, America and West Indies available online at http://www.british-history.ac.uk/cal-state-papers/colonial/america-west-indies

Calendar of State Papers Domestic available online at http://www.british-history.ac.uk/cal-state-papers/domestic

Caruthers, William Alexander, *The Cavaliers of Virginia, Or the Recluse of Jamestown. An Historical Romance of the Old Dominion*, 2 vols (New York, 1834–5)

'The Cave of the Regicides', *Blackwood's Edinburgh Magazine*, vol. 90 (1847), 333–49

The Christian Examiner, vol. 85 (Richmond, VA, 1868)

Cogswell, Frederick Hull, 'The Regicides in New England', *New England Magazine* (1893), 187–99

Cogswell, Frederick Hull, *The Regicides: A Tale of Early Colonial Times* (New York, 1896)

Collections of the Massachusetts Historical Society, third series, vol. 1 (Boston, MA, 1825)

Collections of the Massachusetts Historical Society, third series, vol. 7 (Boston, MA, 1838)

Collections of the Massachusetts Historical Society, third series, vol. 10 (Boston, MA, 1849)

Collections of the Massachusetts Historical Society, fourth series, vol. 8 (Boston, MA, 1868)

Collections of the New York Historical Society, vol. 2 (New York, 1869)

Cooper, James Fenimore, *The Wept of Wish-ton-Wish: A Tale* (Philadelphia, PA, 1829)

Coster, George, *A Sermon, preached at Pembroke Parish Church, in Bermuda, on Tuesday, January 30, 1821, the Day of the Martyrdom of Charles I* (Halifax, VA, 1821)

Crandell, Myra C., *Molly and the Regicides* (New York, 1968)

Cromwell, Oliver, *The Writings and Speeches of Oliver Cromwell*, ed. W.C. Abbott and C.D. Crane, vol. 2 (Cambridge, MA, 1939; repr. Oxford, 1988)

Dexter, Franklin B., 'Memoranda Respecting Edward Whalley and William Goffe', *Papers of the New Haven Colony Historical Society*, vol. 2 (New Haven, CT, 1877)

Dexter, Franklin B. (ed.), 'Dixwell Papers', *Papers of the New Haven Colony Historical Society*, vol. 6 (New Haven, CT, 1900)

Dexter, Franklin B. (ed.), *The Literary Diary of Ezra Stiles* (New York, 1901)

Dexter, Franklin B. (ed.), *Extracts from the Itineraries and Other Miscellanies of Ezra Stiles* (New Haven, CT, 1916)

'Dixwell the Regicide', *Notes and Queries*, fifth series, vol. 9 (June 1878), 466.

Documents Relative to the Colonial History of New York, vol. 3 (Albany, NY, 1853)

Dunn, Jack, *The Diary of General William Goffe* (South Hadley, MA, 2007)

Dwight, Timothy, *Travels in New-England and New-York*, vol. 1 (New Haven, CT, 1821)

Elliott, Ebenezer, *Kerhonah, The Vernal Walk, Win Hill, and Other Poems* (London, 1835)

Evelyn, John, *Diary*, ed. Guy de la Bedoyere (Woodbridge, 1995)

Gocher, William Henry, *Wadsworth: or The Charter Oak* (Hartford, CT, 1904)

'Goffe and Whalley. Their Life in Hadley, Mass.—The "Angel of Hadley" Story Disproved', *New York Times* (19 August 1905)

'Grave of Goff the Regicide Judge', *New York Times* (15 July 1894)

Grimm, Edward, *The King's Judges: An Original Comedy* (San Francisco, CA, 1892)

Hathaway, Warren, *A Discourse Occasioned by the Death of Abraham Lincoln* (Albany, NY, 1865)

Havard, Aline, *The Regicide's Children* (New York, 1927)

Hawthorne, Nathaniel, 'The Gray Champion', in *The New England Magazine* (Boston, MA, 1835)

Hayden, Caroline A., *Our Country's Martyr. A Tribute to Abraham Lincoln* (Boston, MA, 1865)

Hening, William Waller, *Statutes at Large, Being a Collection of All the Laws of Virginia* (New York, 1823)

Herbert, Henry William, *Ruth Whalley, or The Fair Puritan: An Historical Romance in the Days of Witchcraft* (Boston, MA, 1845)

'Historic Judges' Cave, Near New Haven, is a Good Goal for Motorists', *The New York Times* (16 August 1914)

The History of Middlesex County, 1635–1885 (New York, 1884)

Hoadly, Charles J., *Records of the Colony or Jurisdiction of New Haven, 1653–1665* (Hartford, CT, 1858)

Hollister, G.H., *Mount Hope . . . An Historical Romance* (New York, 1851)

Holmes, Abiel, *The Annals of America*, vol. 1 (Cambridge, MA, 1805)

Hooban, Ric, *Off With His Head: The Story of the Fighting Whalley* (Pittsburgh, PA, 2009)

Howe, Henry, *An Outline History of New Haven* (New Haven, CT, 1884)

Hull, John, 'Diary', in *Archaeologia Americana*, vol. 3 (Cambridge, 1857)

Hutchinson, Thomas, *The Diary and Letters of His Excellency Thomas Hutchinson*, ed. Peter Orlando Hutchinson (Boston, MA, 1884)

Kent, Kathleen, *The Wolves of Andover* (London, 2010)

Knapp, Samuel L., *The Library of American History* (New York, 1835)

Leavitt, 'Miss', *Memoir of Jonathan Leavitt* (New Haven, CT, 1822)

Lee, Arthur, *A Speech Intended to Have Been Delivered in the House of Commons, in Support of the Petition from the General Congress at Philadelphia* (London, 1775)

Leete, Edward L., *The Family of William Leete* (New Haven, CT, 1884)

Ludlow, Edmund, *A Voyce from the Watch Tower, Part Five: 1660–1662*, ed. A.B. Worden, *Camden Fourth Series*, vol. 21 (London, 1978)

Mason, Augustus L., *The Romance and Tragedy of the Pioneer Life* (Cincinnati, OH, 1883)

McCall, John C., *Witch of New England* (Philadelphia, PA, 1824)

McHenry, James, *The Spectre of the Forest, or, Annals of the Housatonic* (New York, 1823)

Meek, Alexander B., 'Americanism in Literature' (1844), in W.G. Simms, *Views and Reviews in American Literature, History and Fiction* (New York, 1845)

Mills, Lewis Sprague, *The Story of Connecticut* (West Rindge, 1932, 1935, 1943, 1953, 1958)

Murray, W.H.H., *Daylight Land* (Boston, MA, 1888)

Musick, J.R., *A Century Too Soon* (New York, 1893)

New England Historical and Genealogical Register, vol. 22 (Boston, MA, 1868)

Observations on American Independency (1779)

Packer, Ian and Lynda Pratt (eds.), 'The Collected Works of Robert Southey, Part Four: 1810–1815', in Neil Fraistat and Steven E. Jones (eds.), *Romantic Circles*: http://www.rc.umd.edu/editions/southey_letters/Part_Four/HTML.letterEEd.26.2516.html

Papers Relating to Foreign Affairs, Accompanying the Annual Message of the President to the First Session Thirty-Ninth Congress, part 3 (Washington, DC, 1866)

Paulding, James Kirke, *The Puritan and His Daughter* (New York, 1849)

Pepys, Samuel, *The Diary of Samuel Pepys*, ed. Robert Latham and William Matthews (Berkeley and Los Angeles, CA, 2000)

The Phrenological Journal, vols. 92–3 (May 1891)

Plan for Seizing and Carrying to New-York Coll. Wm. Goffe the Regicide (Albany, NY, 1855)

'Proceedings of the Annual Meeting, 1847', *Transactions of the American Art-Union* (1847)

Proceedings of the Massachusetts Historical Society, vol. 7 (Boston, MA, 1863–4)

The Putney Debates (1647) online: http://oll.libertyfund.org/pages/1647-the-putney-debates

'Recent American Novels', *The North American Review* (July 1825)

'A Representation of the state of affaires in New England as Collected out of Severall Letters & by reporte of Severall persons wch Lately came from thence as followeth', *Collections of the New York Historical Society*, vol. 2 (New York, 1869)

The Salem Belle (Boston, MA, 1842)

Sandoz, Ellis (ed.), *Political Sermons of the American Founding Era* (Indianapolis, IN, 1998)

Sauvage, Leo, 'The Oswald Affair', *Commentary*, vol. 37, no. 3 (March 1964)

Scott, Walter, *Peveril of the Peak*, ed. Alison Lumsden (Edinburgh, 2007)

Sewall, Samuel, *The Diary of Samuel Sewall*, ed. M. Halsey Thomas, vol. 1 (New York, 1973)

Sidney, Margaret, *The Judges' Cave; Being a Romance of the New Haven Colony in the Days of the Regicides, 1661* (Boston, MA, 1900)

Simms, W.G., 'The Epochs and Events of American History as Suited to the Purposes of Art in Fiction', in *Views and Reviews in American Literature, History and Fiction* (New York, 1845), 20–102

Southey, Robert, *Oliver Newman: A New-England Tale (Unfinished)* (London, 1845)

'Southey's *Oliver Newman*', *The Spectator* (December 1845)

Stiles, Ezra, *Literary Diary of Ezra Stiles*, ed. Franklin B. Dexter, vol. 1 (New York, 1901)

Stone, John Augusta, *Metamora* (1829)

Stone, William Leete, *Tales and Sketches, Such as They Are* (New York, 1834)

Stone, William Leete, *Mercy Disborough* (New York, 1844)

Taylor, James Bayard, 'The Strange Friend', *Atlantic Monthly*, vol. 19, no. 111 (Boston, MA, 1867)

Thoreau, Henry David, *Walden; Or, Life in the Woods* (Boston, MA, 1854)

Thurloe, John, *A Collection of the State Papers of John Thurloe*, ed. Thomas Birch, 7 vols (London, 1742)

Toppan, Robert Noxon, *Edward Randolph . . . 1676–1703*, 5 vols (Boston, MA, 1898)

The True Interest of America Impartially Stated (Philadelphia, PA, 1776)

Warren, Israel Perkins, *The Three Judges: Story of the Men who Beheaded Their King* (New York, 1873)

Whitman, Walt, *Leaves of Grass: A Textual Variorum of the Printed Poems, vol. II: Poems 1860–1867*, ed. Sculley Bradley, Harold W. Blodgett, Arthur Golden, and William White (New York, 1980)

Woodward, P. Henry, 'True Story of the Regicides', *Saturday Chronicle* (April 1918), cited in Colin M. Caplan, *Westville: Tales from a Connecticut Hamlet* (Charleston, SC, 2009)

Yonge, Charlotte M., *A Pictorial History of the World's Great Nations, from the Earliest Dates to the Present Time* (New York, 1882)

SECONDARY

Ames, Kenneth L., 'Introduction', in Alan Axelrod (ed.), *The Colonial Revival in America* (New York and London, 1985)

Anderson, Virginia DeJohn, 'New England in the Seventeenth Century', in Nicholas Canny (ed.), *The Origins of Empire: British Overseas Enterprise to the Close of the Seventeenth Century* (Oxford and New York, 1998), 193–217

Andrews, Charles M., *Colonial Self-Government, 1652–1689* (New York and London, 1904)

Andrews, Charles M., *The Colonial Period of American History: England's Commercial and Colonial Policy* (New Haven, CT, 1938)

Andrews, Charles M., *The Colonial Period of American History* (New Haven, CT, 1939)

Ashley, Maurice, *Cromwell's Generals* (London, 1954)

Axelrod, A. (ed.), *The Colonial Revival in America* (New York, 1985)

Bailyn, Bernard, *The Ordeal of Thomas Hutchinson* (Cambridge, MA, 1974)

Bell, Michael Davitt, *Hawthorne and the Historical Romance of New England* (Princeton, NJ, 1971)

Bercovitch, Sacvan, 'How the Puritans Won the American Revolution', *The Massachusetts Review*, vol. 17, no. 4 (1976), 597–630

Bliss, Robert M., *Revolution and Empire: English Politics and the American Colonies in the Seventeenth Century* (New York, 1990)

Breen, T.H., *Character of the Good Ruler: A Study of Puritan Political Ideas in New England, 1630–1730* (New Haven, CT, 1974)

Bremer, Francis J., 'In Praise of Regicide: John Cotton on the Execution of Charles I', *William and Mary Quarterly*, vol. 37, no. 1 (1980), 103–24

Bremer, Francis J., 'Increase Mather's Friends: The Transatlantic Congregational Network of the Seventeenth Century', *Proceedings of the American Antiquarian Society*, vol. 94, no. 1 (1984), 59–95

Bremer, Francis J., *Congregational Communion: Clerical Friendship in the Anglo-American Puritan Community, 1610–1692* (Boston, MA, 1994)

Bremer, Francis J., *The Puritan Experiment* (Lebanon, NH, 1995)

Bridenbaugh, Carl, *Mitre and Sceptre: Transatlantic Faiths, Ideas, Personalities and Politics, 1689–1775* (New York, 1962)

Brown, David, *Walter Scott and the Historical Imagination* (London, 1979)

Calder, Isabel M., *The New Haven Colony* (New Haven, CT, 1934)

Caplan, Colin M., *Westville: Tales from a Connecticut Hamlet* (Charleston, SC, 2009)

Catterall, Ralph C.H., 'Sir George Downing and the Regicides', *The American Historical Review*, vol. 17, no. 2 (1912), 268–89, http://www.colebrookhistoricalsociety.org/PDF%20Images/Regicides,%20Conclusion.pdf

Clark, J.C.D., *The Language of Liberty 1660–1832: Political Discourse and Social Dynamics in the Anglo-American World* (Cambridge, 1994)

Clark, Robert, *History, Ideology and Myth in American Fiction, 1823–52* (London, 1984)

Craven, Wesley Frank, *The Colonies in Transition, 1660–1713* (New York, Evanston, IL, and London, 1968)

Crawford, Patricia, 'Charles Stuart, That Man of Blood', *Journal of British Studies*, vol. 16, no. 2 (1977), 41–61

Cressy, David, *Coming Over: Migrations and Communication between England and New England in the Seventeenth Century* (Cambridge, 1987)

Crotty, William S., 'Presidential Assassinations', *Society*, vol. 9, no. 7 (May 1972), 18–29

Dekker, George, 'Sir Walter Scott, the Angel of Hadley, and American Historical Fiction', *Journal of American Studies*, vol. 17 (1983), 211–27

Durston, Christopher, *Cromwell's Major-Generals* (Manchester, 2001)

'English Heritage Battlefield Report: Naseby [14 June] 1645' (1995)

Firth, C.H., *The Last Years of the Protectorate, 1656–1658*, 2 vols (London, 1909)

Fiske, John, *The Beginnings of New England* (Boston, MA, 1898)

Fitzgibbons, Jonathan, '"Not in Any Doubtfull Dispute"? Reassessing the Nomination of Richard Cromwell', *Historical Research*, vol. 83 (2010), 281–300

Fletcher, Anthony, 'The Religious Motivation of Cromwell's Major Generals', in Derek Baker (ed.), *Religious Motivation: Biographical and Sociological Problems for the Church Historian* (Oxford, 1978), 259–66

Gaskill, Malcolm, *Between Two Worlds: How the English Became Americans* (Oxford, 2014)

Gill, A.A., 'Restoration London's Burning! Alack!', *The Times* (6 April 2014)

Gohdes, Clarence, 'Whitman and the "Good Old Cause"', *American Literature*, vol. 34, no. 3 (1962), 400–3

Goldie, Mark, 'The Hilton Gang and the Purge of London in the 1680s', in Howard Nenner (ed.), *Politics and the Political Imagination in Later Stuart Britain* (Woodbridge, 1998), 43–73

Gould, Philip, *Covenant and Republic: Historical Romance and the Politics of Puritanism* (Cambridge, 2009)

Gregory, Jeremy, 'Refashioning Puritan New England', *Transactions of the Royal Historical Society*, vol. 20 (2010), 85–112

Hall, David D., *Reforming People: Puritanism and the Transformation of Public Life in New England* (New York, 2011)

Hall, Michael G., *Edward Randolph and the American Colonies, 1676–1703* (Chapel Hill, NC, 1960)

Hayes, Kevin J., *George Washington: A Life in Books* (Oxford, 2017)

Heimert, Alan, *Religion and the American Mind from the Great Awakening to the Revolution* (Cambridge, MA, 1966)

Hopper, Andrew, *Turncoats and Renegadoes: Changing Sides during the English Civil Wars* (Oxford, 2012)

Isaac, Rhys, *Landon Carter's Uneasy Kingdom: Rebellion and Revolution on a Virginia Plantation* (Oxford, 2004)

Jenkinson, Matthew, 'A New Author for the "Observations" in *Rebels No Saints* (1661)?', *Notes and Queries*, vol. 52, no. 3 (2005), 311–14

Jenkinson, Matthew, *Culture and Politics at the Court of Charles II* (Woodbridge, 2010)

Jenkinson, Matthew, 'John Crowne, the Restoration Court, and the "Understanding" of *Calisto*', *The Court Historian*, vol. 15, no. 2 (2010), 145–55

Jenkinson, Matthew, 'Regicides on the Run', *Huntington Library Quarterly*, vol. 76, no. 2 (2013), 293–8

Jenkinson, Matthew, 'Remembering Regicides in America, 1660–1800', in George Southcombe and Grant Tapsell (eds.), *Revolutionary England, c.1630–c.1660: Essays in Honour of Clive Holmes* (Abingdon and New York, 2017), 235–50

Jordan, Don and Michael Walsh, *The King's Revenge: Charles II and the Greatest Manhunt in British History* (London, 2012)

Jordan, Ethan (ed.), 'Thomas Hutchinson and Ezra Stiles on the Regicides (1764, 1795)', *The Akron Heron*, no. 5 (May 2006)

Jordan, Winthrop D., 'Familial Politics: Thomas Paine and the Killing of the King, 1776', *Journal of American History*, vol. 60 (1973), 294–308

Kammen, Michael, *Mystic Chords of Memory: The Transformation of Tradition in American Culture* (New York, 1991)

Keeble, N.H., *The Restoration: England in the 1660s* (Malden, MA, 2002)

Klein, Gil, 'The Use of Myth in History', *Colonial Williamsburg Journal* (Summer 2012)

Lacey, Andrew, *The Cult of King Charles the Martyr* (Woodbridge, 2003)

Le Claire, Lesley, 'The Survival of the Manuscript', in Michael Mendle (ed.), *The Putney Debates of 1647: The Army, Levellers and the English State* (Cambridge, 2001), 19–35

Leete, John, *The Family of Leete* (London, 1906)

Lepore, Jill, *The Name of War: King Philip's War and the Origins of American Identity* (New York, 1998)

Lepore, Jill, *The Story of America: Essays on Origins* (Princeton, NJ and Oxford, 2012)

LeTourneau, Peter M. and Robert Pagini, *The Traprock Landscapes of New England: Landscape, History and Culture* (Middleton, CT, 2017)

Love, W. DeLoss, *The Fast and Thanksgiving Days of New England* (Boston, MA and New York, 1895)

Lucas, Paul R., 'Colony or Commonwealth: Massachusetts Bay, 1661–1666', *William and Mary Quarterly*, third ser., vol. 24, no. 1 (1967), 88–107

Lutz, Cora E., 'Ezra Stiles and the Monument for Colonel John Dixwell', *Yale University Library Gazette*, vol. 55, no. 3 (1981), 116–20

Lutz, Cora E., 'Ezra Stiles and the Legend of Hadley', *Yale University Library Gazette*, vol. 73 (April 1998), 115–23

Madison, Robert D., 'Submission and Restoration in *The Wept of Wish-ton-Wish*', *James Fenimore Cooper Society Miscellaneous Papers*, no. 11 (1999)

Mahlberg, Gaby, '*Les Juges Jugez, se Justifiants* (1663) and Edmund Ludlow's Protestant Network in Seventeenth-Century Switzerland', *Historical Journal*, vol. 57, no. 2 (2014), 369–96

Major, Philip (ed.), *Literatures of Exile in the English Revolution and its Aftermath, 1649–90* (Farnham, 2010)

Major, Philip, *Writings of Exile in the English Revolution and Restoration* (Farnham, 2013)

McConville, Brendan, *The King's Three Faces: The Rise and Fall of Royal America, 1688–1776* (Chapel Hill, NC, 2006)

McWilliams, John, *New England's Crises and Cultural Memory* (Cambridge, 2009)

Mendle, Michael (ed.), *The Putney Debates of 1647: The Army, the Levellers and the English State* (Cambridge, 2001)

Miller, Tice L., *Entertaining the Nation: American Drama in the Eighteenth and Nineteenth Centuries* (Carbondale, IL, 2007)

Morgan, Edmund S., *The Gentle Puritan: A Life of Ezra Stiles, 1727–1795* (New Haven, CT and London, 1962)

Nelson, Eric, *The Royalist Revolution: Monarchy and the American Founding* (Cambridge, MA and London, 2014)

Nenner, Howard, 'Trial of the Regicides: Retribution and Treason in 1660', in Howard Nenner (ed.), *Politics and the Political Imagination in Late Stuart Britain* (Woodbridge, 1998), 21–42

Newton, C., 'Letters of a New England Exile', *Americana*, vol. 14 (1920), 208–26

Orlans, G. Harrison, 'The Angel of Hadley in Fiction: A Study of the Sources of Hawthorne's "Gray Champion"', *American Literature*, vol. 4 (1932), 256–69

Osgood, Herbert L., *The American Colonies in the Seventeenth Century* (New York and London, 1907)

Pagliuco, Christopher, *The Great Escape of Edward Whalley and William Goffe* (Charleston, SC, 2012)

Palfrey, John Gorham, *History of New England During the Stuart Dynasty* (Boston, MA, 1860)

Palfrey, John Gorham, 'The Regicide Colonels in New England', *Atlantic Monthly*, vol. 6 (July 1860), 89–93

Pencak, William, *America's Burke: The Mind of Thomas Hutchinson* (Lanham, MD, 1982)

Pestana, Carla Gardina, *The English Atlantic in an Age of Revolution, 1640–1661* (Cambridge, MA and London, 2004)

Phillips, J., 'William Goffe the Regicide', *English Historical Review*, vol. 7 (1892), 717–20

Rannie, D. W., 'Cromwell's Major Generals', *English Historical Review*, vol. 10 (1895), 471–506

Raphael, Ray, *Founding Myths: Stories that Hide our Patriotic Past* (New York, 2004)

Reid, Margaret K., *Cultural Secrets as Narrative Form: Storytelling in Nineteenth-Century America* (Columbus, OH, 2004)

Rhoads, William B., *The Colonial Revival*, 2 vols (New York and London, 1977)

Robins, Robert Patterson, 'Edward Whalley, the Regicide', *The Pennsylvania Magazine of History and Biography*, vol. 1, no. 1 (1877), 55

Rowse, A. L., *The Regicides and the Puritan Revolution* (London, 1994)

Sargent, Mark L., 'Thomas Hutchinson, Ezra Stiles, and the Legend of the Regicides', *William and Mary Quarterly*, vol. 49, no. 3 (1992), 431–48

Sargent, Mark L., 'The Witches of Salem, the Angel of Hadley, and the Friends of Philadelphia', *American Studies*, vol. 34, no. 1 (1993), 108–20

Sayre, Gordon M., *The Indian Chief as Tragic Hero* (Chapel Hill, NC, 2005)

Schofield, Mary-Peale, 'The Three Judges of New Haven', *History Today*, vol. 12 (1962), 346–53

Sheldon, George, 'The Traditionary Story of the Attack upon Hadley and the Appearance of Gen. Goffe, Sept 1 1675: Has it any foundation in fact?', *New England Historical and Genealogical Register*, vol. 28 (October 1874), 379–91

Sosin, J.M., *English America and the Restoration Monarchy of Charles II: Transatlantic Politics, Commerce, and Kinship* (Lincoln, NE and London, 1980)

Spalding, James C., 'Loyalist as Royalist, Patriot as Puritan: The American Revolution as a Repetition of the English Civil Wars', *Church History*, vol. 45, no. 3 (1976), 329–40

Spencer, Charles, *Killers of the King: The Men Who Dared to Execute Charles I* (London, 2014)

Tamarkin, Elisa, *Anglophilia: Deference, Devotion and Antebellum America* (Chicago, IL and London, 2008)

Tapsell, Grant, *The Personal Rule of Charles II, 1681–85* (Woodbridge, 2007)

Vallance, Edward, ' "The Insane Enthusiasm of the Time": Remembering the Regicides in Eighteenth- and Nineteenth-Century Britain and North America', in Laurent Curelly and Nigel Smith (eds.), *Radical Voices, Radical Ways: Articulating and Disseminating Radicalism in Seventeenth- and Eighteenth-Century Britain* (Manchester, 2016), 229–50

Van Tyne, C.H., 'Influence of the Clergy and Religious and Sectarian Forces on the American Revolution', *American Historical Review*, vol. 9, no. 1 (1913), 44–64

Wahrman, Dror, 'The English Problem of Identity in the American Revolution', *American Historical Review*, vol. 106, no. 4 (2001), 1236–62

Walmsley, Andrew S., *Thomas Hutchinson and the Origins of the American Revolution* (New York and London, 1999)

Washburn, W.E., *The Governor and the Rebel: A History of Bacon's Rebellion in Virginia* (New York and London, 1972)

Wedgwood, C.V., *The Trial of Charles I* (London, 1964)

Weinbrot, Howard, 'The Thirtieth of January Sermon: Swift, Johnson, Sterne, and the Evolution of Culture', *Eighteenth Century Life*, vol. 34, no. 1 (2010), 29–55

Welles, Lemuel Aiken, 'A Glance at New England Character', *Yale Literary Magazine*, vol. 57 (1892), 19–21

Welles, Lemuel Aiken, *The History of the Regicides in New England* (New York, 1927)

Welles, Lemuel Aiken, 'The Regicides in Connecticut', *Tercentenary Commission of the State of Connecticut* (New Haven, CT, 1935)

Whitlock, Everett, 'America's Sperrys Sprang from Old Westville Home', in Colin M. Caplan, *Westville: Tales from a Connecticut Hamlet* (Charleston, SC, 2009)

Wilson, Douglas C., 'Web of Secrecy: Goffe, Whalley, and the Legend of Hadley', *New England Quarterly*, vol. 60 (1987), 515–48

Wilson, Richard Guy, 'Introduction: What Is the Colonial Revival?', in Richard Guy Wilson, Shaun Eyring, and Kenny Marotta (eds.), *Re-creating the American Past: Essays on the Colonial Revival* (Charlottesville, VA and London, 2006), 1–10

Winship, Michael P., *Godly Republicanism: Puritans, Pilgrims, and a City on a Hill* (Cambridge, MA, 2012)

Winston, Alexander, 'The Hunt for the Regicides', *American Heritage Magazine*, vol. 16, no. 1 (December 1964), 26–9

Wood, Gordon S., *The Americanization of Benjamin Franklin* (New York, 2004)

Wood, Gordon S., *The Idea of America: Reflections on the Birth of the United States* (New York, 2011)

Woolverton, John Frederick, *Colonial Anglicanism in North America* (Detroit, MI, 1984)

Worden, Blair, *Roundhead Reputations: The English Civil Wars and the Passions of Posterity* (London, 2001)

Wright, Louis B., *The British Tradition in America* (Birmingham, AL, 1954)

Young, Alfred F., 'English Plebeian Culture and Eighteenth-Century American Radicalism', in Margaret Jacob and James Jacob (eds.), *The Origins of Anglo-American Radicalism* (London, 1984), 185–212

Zook, Melinda S., *Protestantism, Politics and Women in Britain, 1660–1714* (Basingstoke, 2013)

Picture acknowledgements

Figure 1. Courtesy of Cory T. Way

Figure 2. Courtesy of Matthew Jenkinson and Jemma Kilkenny

Figure 3. © National Portrait Gallery, London, D28978. Courtesy of the National Portrait Gallery, London

Figure 4. Parliamentary Archives, HL/PO/JO/10/1/297A. Courtesy of Parliamentary Archives

Figure 5. © The British Library Board. BL 669 f. 26. (25). Courtesy of the British Library

Figure 6. Courtesy of Matthew Jenkinson

Figure 7. Courtesy of the New Haven Museum

Figure 8. Private collection

Figure 9. Private collection

Figure 10. Courtesy of the New Haven Museum

Figure 11. Courtesy of the New Haven Museum

Figure 12. Courtesy of Colin M. Caplan

Figure 13. Courtesy of the Huntington Library, San Marino, California

Figure 14. Private collection

Figure 15. Private collection

Figure 16. Courtesy of the New Haven Museum

Index